From Start to Finish

WordPerfect 6.1

for Windows

Sue Orrell and Carol Elston

PITMAN
PUBLISHING

PITMAN PUBLISHING
128 Long Acre, London, WC2E 9AN

A Division of Longman Group UK Limited

© Sue Orrell and Carol Elston 1993

First published in Great Britain 1993

British Library Cataloguing-in-Publication Data
A catalogue record for this book is available from the British Library

ISBN 0 273 03815 X

Printed in England by Clays Ltd, St Ives plc

Contents

Introduction vi
Working through this book vi
Icons used throughout the book vi
Using the accompanying diskettes vii
The scenario vii

Microsoft Windows viii
Windows applications viii
The mouse viii
Mouse techniques viii
Using the keyboard ix
The desktop x

Getting started xi
Hardware requirements xi
Installing WordPerfect for Windows xi
Loading WordPerfect for Windows xv
Creating a data directory xvi

Part 1 Elementary level

1   Finding your way around 2
1.1   The WordPerfect screen 2
1.2   Using the WordPerfect menu system 6
1.3   Dialog boxes 8
1.4   Using the ruler 10
1.5   Using the button bar 11
1.6   Getting help 11

2   Document basics 15
2.1   Creating a document 15
2.2   Saving a document 16
2.3   Printing a document 18
2.4   Leaving WordPerfect for Windows 19
2.5   Consolidation exercise 20

3   Making simple changes 21
3.1   Preparing for this chapter 21
3.2   Opening a document window 21
3.3   The Open dialog box options 23
3.4   Moving around a document 26

3.5   Deleting and inserting text 27
3.6   Consolidation exercise 29

4   Working with blocks of text 30
4.1   Preparing for this chapter 30
4.2   Selecting blocks using the mouse 30
4.3   Selecting blocks using the keyboard 31
4.4   Deleting blocks 31
4.5   Restoring text 32
4.6   Copying text 32
4.7   Moving text 32
4.8   Consolidation exercise 34

5   Print preview 35
5.1   Preparing for this chapter 35
5.2   Using Print preview 35
5.3   Print preview options 36

6   Working with multiple documents 39
6.1   Preparing for this chapter 39
6.2   Creating a new document window 39
6.3   Moving between document windows 40
6.4   Closing a document window 40

7   Changing text appearance 41
7.1   Preparing for this chapter 41
7.2   Fonts 42
7.3   Point sizes 43
7.4   Text appearance 44
7.5   Text size 44
7.6   Initial fonts 46
7.7   WordPerfect codes 46
7.8   Removing attributes 47
7.9   Auto code placement 49
7.10   Document initial codes 49
7.11   Default initial codes 49

8   Document appearance 51
8.1   Text justification 51
8.2   Centring one line 51
8.3   Right justifying one line 52

8.4   Line spacing 53
8.5   Using tabs 54
8.6   Changing tabs 55
8.7   Using tabs with bullet points 56
8.8   Indenting text 58
8.9   Inserting dates 59
8.10   Page breaks 60

9   Advanced editing 62
9.1   Preparing for this chapter 62
9.2   Spell checking a document 62
9.3   Using the thesaurus 65
9.4   Searching a document 66
9.5   Using Search and replace 68

10   Simple mail merge 70
10.1   Preparing for this chapter 70
10.2   Creating a primary merge file 70
10.3   Producing a secondary merge file 72
10.4   Merging the primary and secondary files 74

11   Consolidation 75

Part 2 Intermediate level

---

12   Working with large documents 80
12.1   Setting paper size 80
12.2   Setting margins 80
12.3   Page numbering 83
12.4   Headers and footers 85
12.5   Footnotes and endnotes 87

13   Hints and tips for printing 91
13.1   Preparing for this chapter 91
13.2   Printer drivers 91
13.3   Creating paper sizes 92
13.4   Editing paper sizes 94
13.5   Using the advance feature 94
13.6   Printing labels 96
13.7   Print options 98
13.8   Print Manager 101

14   Further mail merge features 104
14.1   Preparing for this chapter 104
14.2   Mail merge overview 104
14.3   Using merge with envelopes 106
14.4   Using merge with mailing labels 107
14.5   Adding records 109
14.6   Sorting a secondary merge file 110

14.7   Adding and deleting fields 111
14.8   Eliminating blank lines and fields 113
14.9   Eliminating blank fields 113
14.10 Selecting records for a mail merge 115

15   Tables 118
15.1   Using the ruler 118
15.2   Using the menu 119
15.3   Moving around a table 120
15.4   Entering information into a table 121
15.5   Formatting text in a table 122

16   Editing tables 126
16.1   Preparing for this chapter 126
16.2   Changing table layout 126
16.3   Changing column widths using the menu 128
16.4   Changing column widths using the ruler 129
16.5   Joining and splitting cells 130
16.6   Changing table lines 131
16.7   Inserting rows and columns 132
16.8   Deleting rows and columns 133
16.9   Deleting tables 134
16.10 Consolidation exercise 134
16.11 Copying and moving table information 136
16.12 Table options 138
16.13 Drawing lines and boxes 139
16.14 Graphic lines 142

17   Using the maths facilities 144
17.1   Preparing for this chapter 144
17.2   Creating formulae 144
17.3   Calculating totals 147
17.4   Re-calculating formulae 148
17.5   Deleting formulae 148
17.6   Copying formulae 148

18   Importing spreadsheet information 152

19   Graphics 155
19.1   Preparing for this chapter 155
19.2   Using graphic images 155
19.3   Creating a graphics box 156
19.4   Incorporating text 156
19.5   Incorporating graphics 159
19.6   Changing box appearance 161
19.7   Placing tables in boxes 162
19.8   Adding captions 163
19.9   Numbering graphic boxes 164
19.10 Positioning captions 165
19.11 Re-numbering boxes 165

19.12 Editing graphics 165
19.13 Working with borders 168
19.14 Text wrapping 169
19.15 Deleting graphic boxes 169
19.16 Creating a template document 169

20 Macros 172
20.1 Preparing for this chapter 172
20.2 Creating macros 172
20.3 Running macros 173
20.4 Attaching and removing macros from menu 174
20.5 Assigning macros to the button bar 175
20.6 Customising the button bar 175
20.7 Using a button bar 176
20.8 Editing a button bar 176
20.9 Button bar options 176

21 Consolidation 177
21.1 Preparing for this chapter 177
21.2 Exercises 177

Part 3 Advanced level

22 Working with columns 184
22.1 Preparing for this chapter 184
22.2 Creating newspaper style columns 185
22.3 Column codes 186
22.4 Using a combination of column layouts 187
22.5 Moving between columns 188
22.6 Changing column widths 188
22.7 Creating parallel columns 188

23 Defining styles 190
23.1 Preparing for this chapter 190
23.2 Types of styles 191
23.3 Creating styles 191
23.4 Applying styles 194
23.5 Creating a style library 194
23.6 Using a style library 195

24 Paragraph numbering 197
24.1 Numbering overview 197
24.2 Defining a numbering style 199
24.3 Using the outline feature 201
24.4 Copying, moving and deleting an outline family 203

25 Generating an index 206
25.1 Preparing for this chapter 206
25.2 Creating index entries 206
25.3 Marking index entries 208
25.4 Defining an index 209
25.5 Generating an index 210

26 Table of contents 212
26.1 Preparing for this chapter 212
26.2 Marking table of contents entries 212
26.3 Defining a table of contents 213
26.4 Generating lists 215

27 Creating a master document 216
27.1 Preparing for this chapter 216
27.2 Creating a master document 216
27.3 Expanding a master document 218
27.4 Condensing a master document 219
27.5 Generating lists 219
27.6 Printing 219

28 File management 220
28.1 Preparing for this chapter 220
28.2 Accessing the File Manager 220
28.3 The navigator window 222
28.4 The file list window 222
28.5 Quick list window 223
28.6 Using the File Manager 223

29 Consolidation 226
29.1 Preparing for this chapter 226
29.2 Exercise 226

Appendix A - Menus 228

Appendix B - Keyboard shortcuts 229
Moving around a document 229
Deleting text 230
Function keys 230
Useful keys 231

Index 233

Introduction

WordPerfect for Windows has become one of the leading wordprocessing packages on the market. In addition to offering standard wordprocessing options it boasts a wide range of very sophisticated features which enable the user to produce first class documents.

This book is designed to take a novice user of WordPerfect for Windows through all the steps necessary to make them an accomplished user. It is divided into three parts, Elementary, Intermediate and Advanced.

Working through this book

Each part of the book is designed to build upon the skills developed in the previous part. Exercises are used throughout to enable each topic to be put into practice. As some exercises require the use of documents (or *files*) created in earlier chapters, it is recommended that all the exercises of a particular part be worked through in a logical order. However, should users wish to skip sections of the book, they will find a list of documents which need to be created before they can progress through the current part. The name of the document will be accompanied by a reference to the chapter number where the document should have been created.

Icons used throughout the book

 The *diskette* icon is used to indicate exercises which may require you to copy new files from disk. It is also used to indicate information that is important to disk users.

 The icon of the *person seated at the computer* is used to indicate exercises or information that is of importance to readers who have not purchased the diskettes.

 The *bomb* icon is used as a warning. Wherever you see the icon take special care and read the information carefully.

 The *arrow* icon indicates an exercise or activity.

Using the accompanying diskettes

 A set of three diskettes to accompany each part of the book can be purchased from Pitman Publishing (*see* order form at the end of the book). Each diskette will contain the documents or files required to complete each chapter in each particular part. The documents will be stored in a *sub-directory* bearing the name of the relevant chapter. Purchasing the diskettes will enable you to copy the files onto your machine and practise the sections which are relevant to you without having to build each file from scratch.

If you are working through Part 1, place the diskette labelled Part 1 in floppy diskette drive A: or B:. Select the **File manager** option from the **File** menu. Double click on [-a-] or [-b-] in the **Drives column** of the **Navigator** window, depending on whether you are using floppy diskette drive A: or B:. A pointing hand should appear to the right of the selected drive. If it does not, try double clicking the drive letter a second time.

Each diskette has been divided into sub-directories containing the files for each chapter. A list of sub-directories should appear in the next column to the right. Double click the appropriate chapter number. For example double click **[CH3]** if you want to load the files for Chapter 3. The files in Chapter 3 sub-directory should appear in the third column.

Select the **Copy** option from the **File** menu or click the **Copy** button on the button bar. The **Copy file(s)** dialog box will appear with the appropriate drive and chapter number set as the current directory. For example, if you have selected [-a-] as the floppy diskette drive and [CH3] as the chapter number, the **Current dir:** should be set to **a:\CH3**.

Type ***.*** in the **File(s) to be copied:** box. Click in the **To:** box and type **C:\WPWIN\DATA*.***. Check the **Replace files with same name** option if you want the files you are copying to overwrite any existing files. Check the **Confirm replace** option if you want WordPerfect to prompt you before replacing existing files. Click the **Copy** button. The **Copy directory/file(s)** dialog box will appear. Select the **Files in directory only** option and click the **OK** button. Choose the **Exit** option from the **File** menu to close the File Manager.

All existing documents referred to in the chapter and any new documents requiring a substancial amount of typing will be copied to your hard disk.

The scenario

Throughout this book, material will be produced which can be used in setting up your own business. You will begin by creating an initial "start up" letter, informing potential clients of your business aims, and gradually develop the skills to produce desktop published material.

Microsoft Windows

Microsoft Windows makes the learning of software applications an easy and enjoyable process. Windows has replaced the need to give keyboard instructions to the computer, with choices presented in the form of pull-down *menus* and pictures, known as *icons*. It presents information in a graphical format rather than as a list of commands.

Windows applications

Some software applications, such as WordPerfect for Windows, are especially designed to run with Windows. They are known as *Windows applications*. Windows applications share a common menu system and screen display, so making it easy both to transfer information from one application to another and to learn how to use other Windows applications.

The mouse

Although many of the features of an application can be accessed using the keyboard, some cannot. Windows applications are designed to be used with the *mouse*, a pointing device used to select menu items and icons.

As you move the mouse along a flat surface, a small icon representing the current *cursor* position will move around the screen. The shape of the icon will change depending upon its position on the screen. If you point the mouse into the menu bar, it will appear as an arrow (known as the mouse *pointer*). If you move into the typing area, it will appear as a tall, thin I shape (known as the *I-Beam*).

Mouse techniques

Click   To select a menu item or type text, you will need to point the mouse into the menu item or typing area and press the left hand mouse button. This technique is known as *clicking*. Sometimes you will be required to press the left hand mouse button two or three times in rapid succession. This is known as double clicking or triple clicking the left mouse button. The right mouse button is rarely used. Throughout this book, the term *click* will be used to mean depress the left mouse button.

Drag   On occasion you will also be asked to *drag* the mouse. This requires you to position the mouse at a starting point, press and hold down the left mouse button and *move* the mouse to a new position on the screen. This technique is most commonly used to select blocks of text.

Highlight   Some mouse operations will cause the area around text or menu items to become black. This is known as *reverse video* or *highlighting*. It indicates that a menu item has been selected or that text has been selected ready for some operation to be performed.

Using the keyboard

Initially you may prefer to select menu items and buttons using the mouse. However, as you become increasingly familiar with WordPerfect operations, you may prefer to use keyboard shortcuts for many of the features. Keys on the keyboard will be represented throughout the text in boxes. For example, you might be asked to press the Enter key to continue with an operation. This will be represented in the text as the Enter key.

There are several keys on the keyboard which generally need to be pressed in conjunction with other keys before a function will be carried out. These are the Alternate key, more commonly known as the Alt key, the Control key, Ctrl , and the Shift key, Shift . Each of these keys needs to be pressed and held down whilst pressing a second key at the same time. For example, to move the cursor to the top of the document you would press and hold down the Ctrl key and then press Home . You would then release both keys before continuing with the next operation.

Where there is more than one key in a sequence of steps these will be displayed within the same box. For instance, to save a file using the keyboard you would need to press and hold down the Alt key, press the letter F and then the letter S . This sequence would be shown as Alt F S .

Keys only need to be pressed or held for a very short time to perform an action. For example, the Backspace key can be pressed to delete characters before the cursor position. Each time the Backspace key is pressed, one character will be deleted.

 If you hold the Backspace key down, its action will be quickly repeated and many characters will be deleted in one go.

A summary of keystrokes can be found in Appendix B.

Throughout this book, you will be given instructions on how to select menu items and icons using the mouse and, wherever possible, a keyboard alternative will also be given.

The desktop

In all Windows applications, the computer screen represents a desktop. When you want to work with an application you will give instructions for it to be copied into the computer's memory. This is referred to as *loading* the application. It will then be displayed in a frame or *window* on the desktop. As you create documents or files, they too will be displayed in their own window. Each window may be moved or re-sized on the screen much as you might move things around on your desk.

Getting started

Before launching into this book it is important to consider the topics covered in this chapter. They are relevant to all readers whether they intend to work through the book from start to finish or just complete certain chapters. This chapter considers the hardware required to run WordPerfect, looks at the procedure for installing and loading WordPerfect and gives instructions on how to create a directory to store the documents created throughout the book. It is suggested that you consider the hardware requirements at this stage and, if necessary, install WordPerfect onto your computer. If you intend to work through Part 1 you can load WordPerfect and create the data sub-directory when instructed in Chapter 2. If launching into Parts 2 or 3, complete the instructions in this chapter before continuing.

Hardware requirements

Before purchasing WordPerfect for Windows, check that you have the necessary hardware to run the program efficiently. You will need:

- a personal computer with a 286, 386 or higher processor;

- a minimum of 2 MB of memory running in Windows standard or enhanced mode;

- Microsoft Windows Version 3.0 or higher;

- an EGA, VGA, 8514/A graphics adaptor or a Hercules graphics card;

- a minimum of 6 MB of free hard disk space and a 3 1/2" disk drive (1.44 MB) or a 5 1/4" disk drive (1.2 MB).

A mouse is also recommended.

Installing WordPerfect for Windows

Before installing WordPerfect for Windows you must make sure that Windows Version 3.0 or higher is installed on your machine. If you have not already done so, install Windows before continuing (refer to the Microsoft Windows manual for help).

During the installation, WordPerfect will make an evaluation of the hardware with which you are working and offer you the chance to confirm that it is correct and to change it if it is not. Make sure that you know the correct screen and printer types before beginning the installation.

During the installation process you will be presented with several installation screens. At the first screen you will be prompted to choose the type of installation you require. At subsequent screens you will be prompted to indicate the equipment with which you are working.

Two types of keyboard can be activated with WordPerfect for Windows. You will be asked whether you wish to use the CUA (Common User Access) keyboard which takes the Windows standard format or the WordPerfect 5.1 for DOS keyboard. If you are unsure as to which keyboard to use, it is recommended that you choose the default (standard) option, **CUA**.

With the CUA keyboard, keys which are common to other Windows applications are available in WordPerfect for Windows. For example, the $\boxed{\textbf{Alt}}$ key can be used to access the menu bar, the $\boxed{\textbf{Esc}}$ key can be used to leave a menu. $\boxed{\textbf{Alt F4}}$ will exit the application. If you choose to use the WordPerfect 5.1 for DOS keyboard, keys will have the same function as in the DOS version of WordPerfect. For example, $\boxed{\textbf{Alt F4}}$ will turn the *block* feature on.

It is worth noting for future reference that, once in WordPerfect, the keyboard can be changed. This is achieved by selecting the **Preferences** option from the **File** menu followed by the **Keyboard** option. From within the **Keyboard** dialog box, choose **Select**. A list of available keyboard files will appear. Choose **WordPerfect for DOS 5.1**. If at a later stage you wish to return to using the CUA keyboard, select the **Default** button in the **Keyboard** dialog box.

To install WordPerfect for Windows, work through the following procedure:

1   Place the Installation/Program 1 diskette into the *floppy disk drive* (*see* your computer manual for location).

2   At the DOS prompt (normally **C:**), type **A:INSTALL** and press the $\boxed{\textbf{Enter}}$ key.

3   The following screen will appear asking whether you would like to continue with the installation. Press $\boxed{\textbf{Enter}}$ to continue.

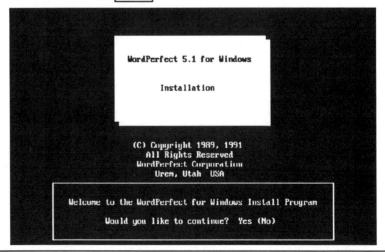

4 You will be presented with a set of WordPerfect installation options. Type the number corresponding to the type of installation required (*see* below). If you are unsure which option to choose, press 1 to perform a basic installation. WordPerfect will then install all standard files into appropriate sub-directories.

```
┌──────────────────────────────────────────────────────────────────────────┐
│ WordPerfect Installation Options              Installation Problems?       │
│                                                  Contact WordPerfect       │
│                                                                            │
│  ▶ 1 - Basic      Install standard files into default directories, for example │
│                   c:\wpwin\, c:\wpwin\graphics\, and c:\wpwin\macros\.      │
│                                                                            │
│    2 - Custom     Install standard files to directories you specify.       │
│                                                                            │
│    3 - Network    Install standard files to a network drive.  Only a network │
│                   supervisor should use this option.                       │
│                                                                            │
│    4 - Printer    Install additional or updated WordPerfect Printer Files. │
│                                                                            │
│    5 - Interim    Install Interim Release program files.  Use this option only if │
│                   you are replacing existing WordPerfect for Windows files. │
│                                                                            │
│    6 - Copy       Install every file on a diskette into a directory you specify │
│                   (useful for installing all the Printer .ALL files).      │
│                                                                            │
│    7 - Language   Install additional WordPerfect language modules.         │
│                                                                            │
│    8 - README     View WordPerfect for Windows README files.               │
│                                                                            │
│                                                                            │
│  Selection: 1                                 (F1 for Help; Esc to exit)   │
└──────────────────────────────────────────────────────────────────────────┘
```

5 A message will appear at the bottom of the screen prompting you to enter the drive where the WordPerfect files can be located. Accept the drive offered by WordPerfect if it is correct or type in the correct drive. Press Enter to continue.

6 A screen similar to the following illustration will appear, indicating the amount of space required to install WordPerfect and the amount of space available on the hard disk. The amount of space required depends upon the type of installation selected earlier. If there is not enough space to install WordPerfect, press N to indicate that you do not wish to continue with the installation. You will be returned to the **Installation options** screen from which you can choose a different type of installation or press Esc to exit from the installation. Follow the instructions in your DOS manual to create more space on your hard disk. If there is enough space, press Y to continue with the installation.

```
┌─────────────────────────────────────────────────────────┐
│              Available Disk Space                         │
│                                                           │
│                       Drive:         C:                   │
│         Total Bytes on drive:     42,366,976              │
│                  Bytes used:      31,744,000              │
│                  Bytes free:      10,622,976              │
│ Bytes required for all of WPWIN:   9,750,000              │
│   Bytes free after full install:     872,976             │
│                                                           │
│  Do you wish to continue?   Yes (No)                      │
│                                                           │
└─────────────────────────────────────────────────────────┘
```

7 WordPerfect will then decompress and copy files appropriate to the type of installation selected. When the files have been copied from the current disk, there will be a beep and a prompt to enter the next disk. Insert each disk in the drive as prompted. Respond appropriately to any prompts which appear.

8   You will be asked to select the preferred keyboard. Unless you have previously
    used the DOS version of WordPerfect, it is recommended that you choose the
    default, CUA, keyboard (*see* page xii for further details on keyboard types). To
    choose the CUA keyboard, press the Enter key.

9   It will be recommended that you choose a WordPerfect printer driver for each of
    your printers. Select **Yes** as the response to the prompt "would you like to
    install WordPerfect printer driver(s)?" and insert the Printers 1 diskette when
    prompted. Several printers may be installed.

10 Press the cursor arrow keys and the Page Dn key until the triangle points to
    the first printer to be installed and then press the Enter key. In the following
    illustration the Page Dn key has been pressed several times until the **HP
    Laserjet III PostScript** printer is in view, followed by the ↓ key until the
    triangle is pointing towards this printer.

Printer selector

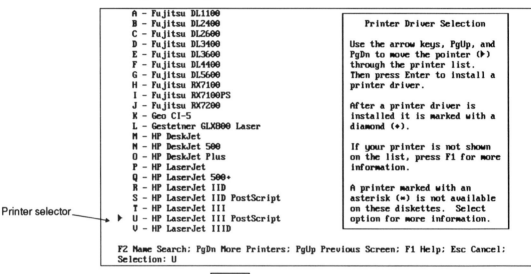

```
      A - Fujitsu DL1100
      B - Fujitsu DL2400                         Printer Driver Selection
      C - Fujitsu DL2600
      D - Fujitsu DL3400               Use the arrow keys, PgUp, and
      E - Fujitsu DL3600               PgDn to move the pointer (▶)
      F - Fujitsu DL4400               through the printer list.
      G - Fujitsu DL5600               Then press Enter to install a
      H - Fujitsu RX7100               printer driver.
      I - Fujitsu RX7100PS
      J - Fujitsu RX7200               After a printer driver is
      K - Geo CI-5                     installed it is marked with a
      L - Gestetner GLX800 Laser       diamond (♦).
      M - HP DeskJet
      N - HP DeskJet 500               If your printer is not shown
      O - HP DeskJet Plus              on the list, press F1 for more
      P - HP LaserJet                  information.
      Q - HP LaserJet 500+
      R - HP LaserJet IID              A printer marked with an
      S - HP LaserJet IID PostScript   asterisk (*) is not available
      T - HP LaserJet III              on these diskettes.  Select
   ▶  U - HP LaserJet III PostScript   option for more information.
      V - HP LaserJet IIID

 F2 Name Search; PgDn More Printers; PgUp Previous Screen; F1 Help; Esc Cancel;
 Selection: U
```

11 After pressing the Enter key, you will then be prompted to confirm that you
    wish to select or install the current printer. If you select **Yes**, a diamond shape
    will indicate that the printer has been selected. You will then be prompted to
    install another printer. Continue until all the required printers have been
    selected.

12 You may now be given the opportunity to read about recent updates to the
    WordPerfect program. It is worth taking the time to do this.

13 When the installation is complete, a message will appear. If necessary, press
    any key to exit from the installation procedure, remove the last disk from the
    drive and press Ctrl Alt Del (press all three keys at the same time) to *reboot*
    the computer.

Loading WordPerfect for Windows

The steps to follow for loading WordPerfect depend upon the way your machine has been set up. WordPerfect can only be started from within Windows so the first step is to load Windows. Having switched on your computer, you may find that your system has been set up to go straight into a menu from which Windows can be selected or straight into Windows itself. If this is not the case, you must return to the DOS prompt and type the appropriate commands to load Windows.

1 If your computer displays a menu or the DOS shell, select **Windows**. Skip to step 6.

2 If Windows is not available from the menu or DOS shell select the option to exit from the menu and return to the DOS prompt.

3 The current DOS prompt will probably read **C:** If Windows cannot be found on drive C, change to the appropriate drive by typing the drive letter followed by a colon and then pressing the | **Enter** | key. If Windows is on drive D, for example, type **D:** and press | **Enter** |.

4 Type **CD\WINDOWS** and press the | **Enter** | key to change to the sub-directory where Windows has been installed.

5 Type **WIN** and press | **Enter** | to load Windows.

6 The Program Manager is generally the first window you will see on entering Windows. "Program Manager" will appear at the top of the window in the *title bar*. If the Program Manager is not already open, locate the icon labelled "Program Manager", point the mouse into the icon and double click the left mouse button to open it. You should see a screen similar to the following.

"Program Manager" displayed in the title bar

Program icons - the icons available on your machine will be dependent on the software packages loaded

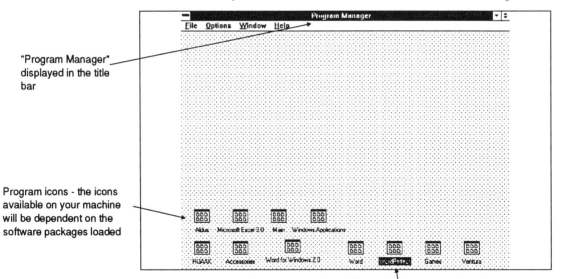

7 Within the Program Manager there should be an icon representing the WordPerfect program group. Point the mouse to the icon and double click the

left mouse button to open the group. The open program group will be displayed as below.

Double click on the WordPerfect icon to load the program

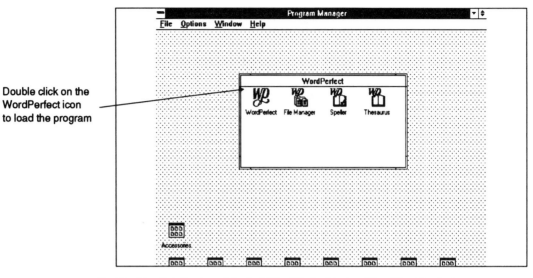

8 Double click the icon labelled WordPerfect to load the WordPerfect program. When prompted, type your licence number and press the Enter key.

Creating a data directory

Before creating your first document, it is a good idea to create a sub-directory on the hard disk into which documents can be saved. A disk can be divided into separate areas and files stored in an appropriate area on the disk in much the same way that files are stored in a filing cabinet. The top storage area of a disk is known as the *root* and each area of the disk below the root is known as a sub-directory.

The installation program creates a sub-directory called **WPWIN** as the standard or default sub-directory into which files will be saved. You will create a sub-directory below the WPWIN sub-directory called **DATA** and set this as the default sub-directory so that all files will be saved into it. If you are new to WordPerfect and are working through from start to finish, you will be instructed to follow the instructions below at the beginning of Chapter 2. If you intend to progress straight on to Parts 2 or 3, you will need to complete the following instructions at this stage.

1 Load WordPerfect for Windows, using the steps outlined in the previous section.

2 Select the **File manager** option from the **File** menu. The File Manager gives you control over file handling procedures and will be covered in detail in Chapter 28. The File Manager screen will appear as shown in the following illustration:

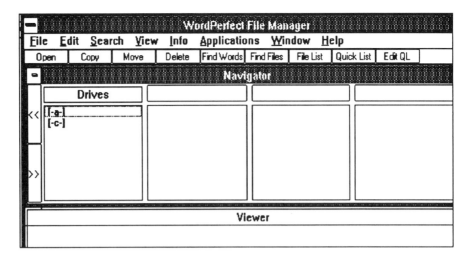

3 The **Navigator** window displays a list of available drives in the first column. Select the drive where WordPerfect is installed by double clicking in the drive letter. A pointing hand will appear to indicate the current drive.

4 The column to the right of the drives column lists all sub-directories and files below the root (top) of the current drive. Sub-directories are displayed within square brackets. If the sub-directory you require is not displayed, click in the *scroll bars* to display the full list (*see* The scroll bar, page 5). Locate the WordPerfect for Windows sub-directory **[WPWIN]** and double click the mouse on this sub-directory name. A pointing hand will indicate when it has been selected.

5 The third column will now display a list of sub-directories and files within **[WPWIN]**. At this point, access the **File** menu at the top of the screen.

6 Select the **Create directory** option or press [**Ctrl T**]. A *dialog box* should appear with the current sub-directory set to **C:\WPWIN**.

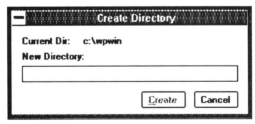

7 With the *insertion point* in the **New directory** box, type **data** as the name for the new sub-directory and click the **Create** button to create this directory. **[data]** should now appear as a sub-directory in the column labelled **WPWIN**.

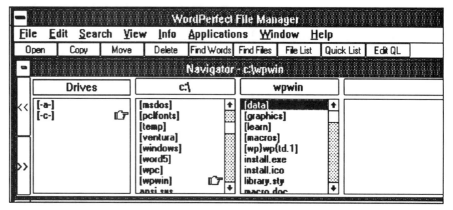

8   The next step is to exit from the File Manager and establish this new sub-directory as the default sub-directory into which all documents are to be saved. Select the **Exit** option from the **File** menu or press | **Alt F4** |.

9   Access the **File** menu and select the **Preferences** option followed by **Location of files**. The **Location of files** dialog box contains information relating to the storage of different types of WordPerfect files.

10 Click in the **Documents:** text box and type in the full *path* where the data files are to be stored, **C:\WPWIN\DATA** (*see* above example).

11 Alternatively, click the disk icon to the right of the **Documents:** text box. The **Select directory** dialog box will appear.

12 The current sub-directory will be displayed in the **Directory name** box. If this is incorrect, type in a new path or select a sub-directory from the list of available directories. **C:\WPWIN** usually appears as the current sub-directory. If this is the case, select **[data]** from the list of directories and click the **OK** button. The path in the **Documents:** box should now read **C:\WPWIN\DATA**.

13 Click the **OK** button. **C:\WPWIN\DATA** will now be set as the current sub-directory each time you save a document.

Part 1

Elementary level

1   Finding your way around

This chapter is designed to provide a complete overview of the components that make up the WordPerfect environment. It is suggested that you read through the information now and then refer back to the relevant sections as you progress through the book.

1.1   The WordPerfect screen

When loading WordPerfect for the first time, the WordPerfect screen should resemble the example below.

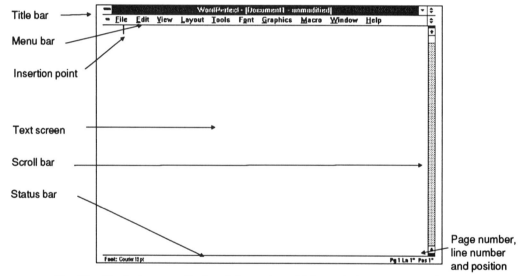

The WordPerfect screen displays information which can help you to control the appearance of your documents. For example, from the *menu bar* across the top of the screen you will be able to choose from a list of text styles and sizes and from the *status bar* at the bottom of the screen you will be able to tell which page of the document you are working on.

Underneath the menu bar there is a large area reserved for typing your document. This is referred to as the *text screen* or *typing screen*.

The title bar

Across the top of the screen you will see a bar known as the title bar. This will display the name of the current WordPerfect document. WordPerfect will give each document created a consecutive number until you save the document with an appropriate name.

WordPerfect - [Document1 - unmodified]

The menu bar

Many WordPerfect features can be selected from the menu bar, displayed beneath the title bar. Menu options (or commands) are logically grouped under the headings File, Edit, View, Layout and so on. For information on how to use the menu system, *see* 1.2, Using the WordPerfect menu system, on page 6.

| File | Edit | View | Layout | Tools | Font | Graphics | Macro | Window | Help |

The text screen

The area underneath the menu bar is the typing or text screen. A flashing cursor (known as the insertion point) will appear near the top left-hand corner of the screen. This is where text will appear as you type.

Using the mouse

The mouse changes shape depending upon its position on the screen. Whilst in the area of the menu bar or title bar, it appears as an arrow (known as the mouse pointer). Whilst in the typing area, it appears as a tall, thin I shape (known as an I-Beam). The I-Beam can be used to reposition the cursor or insertion point in the document simply by moving the I-Beam to a new location and pressing or clicking the left mouse button.

Windows

WordPerfect for Windows is a program or application and, when loaded, it runs in its own frame or window. Within the application window another window is opened to contain the first document. Providing you have enough memory, up to nine document windows can be opened at any one time.

Each window contains its own control menu which can be used, amongst other things, to move, re-size and close the window. There are two types of control menu, the *document control menu* which displays menu items relevant to the current document window and the *application control menu* which displays menu items relevant to the application (in this case, WordPerfect for Windows).

The document control menu

The document control menu is represented by a small hyphen to the left of the menu bar. You can either point and click the left mouse button in this hyphen or press ⌐Alt⌐ plus the hyphen key to access the document control menu. Press the ⌐Esc⌐ key to leave a menu.

```
Restore
Move
Size
Minimize
Maximize

Close Ctrl+F4

Next
```

The application control menu

The application control menu is represented by a slightly larger hyphen to the left of the title bar. Click in the hyphen to the left of the title bar or press **Alt Spacebar** to see this menu.

The minimise button

To the right of the title bar and menu bar there are a set of arrows. These are known as the *minimise, maximise* and *restore buttons*.

A down-pointing arrow represents the minimise button. If you click the minimise button to the right of the title bar, this will reduce the WordPerfect application to an icon. If you click the minimise button to the right of the menu bar, this will minimise the current document window to an icon. It is important to note that if the window is already maximised there may only be a restore button displayed.

1   Load WordPerfect as outlined in Getting started, page xv.

2   Click the minimise button to the right of the title bar.

3   The application will now be represented by an icon, known as the WordPerfect program group. This is usually displayed at the bottom of the screen. Depending on how your system is set up, this may be difficult to find. You may need to minimise each window until the program group icon is visible.

4   To restore WordPerfect to its previous size, locate the icon and either point the mouse into the icon and double click the left button or click once and select the **Restore** option from the pop-up menu.

The maximise button

The maximise button is represented by an up-pointing arrow. A maximise button may be available for the document window, application window or both. It will enlarge the window to fill the maximum amount of workspace available.

1   Click the maximise button for both the document and application window if there is one visible on your screen.

The restore button

Two restore buttons will be displayed; one to the right of the application window and one to the right of the document window. The *application restore button* reduces the application window to medium size in the program manager. The *document restore button* reduces the document window to medium size within WordPerfect. This is shown in the following examples.

The document window is now medium size within WordPerfect

The maximise button has been selected to restore the document window to full size

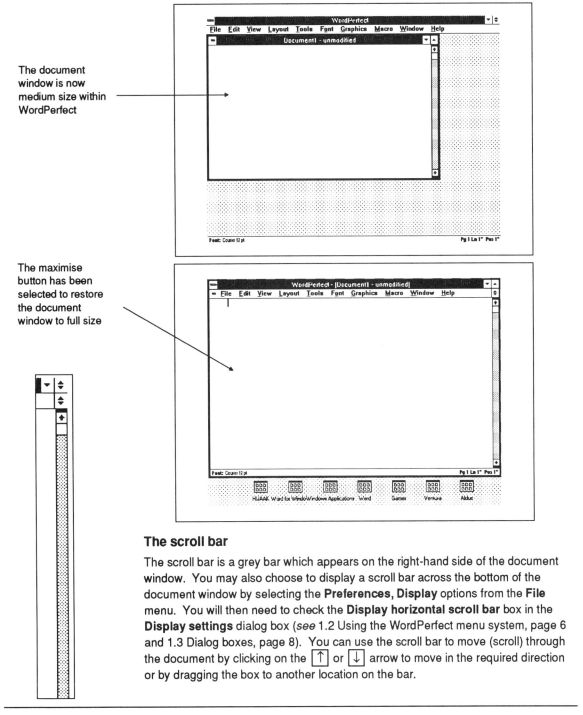

The scroll bar

The scroll bar is a grey bar which appears on the right-hand side of the document window. You may also choose to display a scroll bar across the bottom of the document window by selecting the **Preferences, Display** options from the **File** menu. You will then need to check the **Display horizontal scroll bar** box in the **Display settings** dialog box (*see* 1.2 Using the WordPerfect menu system, page 6 and 1.3 Dialog boxes, page 8). You can use the scroll bar to move (scroll) through the document by clicking on the ↑ or ↓ arrow to move in the required direction or by dragging the box to another location on the bar.

For instance, to move a short distance, click on the scroll arrow which represents the direction in which you wish to move. To move to the middle of the document, click on the scroll box, hold the mouse button down and drag until it is positioned half way down the bar.

The status bar

The status bar is a bar across the bottom of the screen which displays the current font and the position of the insertion point. The status bar in the following example displays three codes:

- Pg 1 indicates that the insertion point is on page 1 of the document.

- Ln 1" indicates that the first typing line will appear 1" down the page when the document is printed.

- Pos 1" indicates that the text will appear 1" in from the left edge of the paper. Although the insertion point and subsequent text typed appears in the top left-hand corner of the screen, margins may have been set up which affect the position of printed text.

Font: Courier 12 pt   Pg 1 Ln 1" Pos 1"

1.2   Using the WordPerfect menu system

To select a menu using the mouse, point to the menu item required and click the left mouse button. A pull-down menu will appear. For example, pointing and clicking in the **Tools** menu item on the menu bar will produce the following pull-down menu.

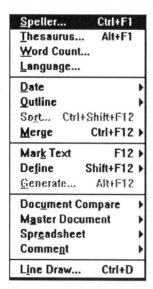

To pull down a menu using the keyboard, hold down the Alt key and press the underlined letter of the menu item (press Alt T to pull down the **Tools** menu, for example). Alternatively, press the Alt key to move into the menu bar and then use cursor arrow keys to point to the required menu item. When a menu item becomes highlighted, press the Enter key to pull down the corresponding menu. For example, pressing the Alt key to move into the menu bar, the right cursor arrow five times to highlight the **Tools** menu item and then Enter will pull down the menu. Working through the exercises in this book there will be many occasions when you will be required to pull down or access a menu.

For a full range of pull-down menus, see Appendix A.

Having pulled down a menu, make a further selection by pointing the mouse into the desired option and clicking the left mouse button or by pressing the underlined letter of the option on the keyboard. Alternatively, you can also use the cursor movement keys to highlight an option and then press the Enter key.

Cancelling a menu

To cancel a menu using the mouse, click anywhere outside of the menu area. Using the keyboard, press the Esc key as many times as necessary.

Pull-down menus

Some pull-down menus include the following features:

- A triangle represents a cascading menu. Selecting an option with a triangle displayed next to it will reveal a further pull-down menu.

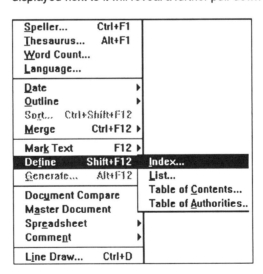

- Dimmed menu items indicate options which cannot be selected at this stage.

- Menu items followed by ellipses (three dots) produce an associated dialog box.

- Menu items with a tick beside them are currently selected.

- Some menu items can be selected directly by using a keyboard shortcut. Where relevant, the keystroke(s) required are displayed.

1.3   Dialog boxes

Dialog boxes appear when WordPerfect requires further information before carrying out a selected option. They can also provide useful information as to which options are currently set. The different types of options available within dialog boxes are illustrated below.

Text boxes

Text boxes are used in dialog boxes that require user input. Text can be entered directly into the text box at the point of the flashing cursor.

Text in reverse video

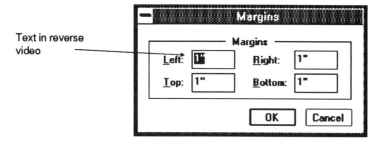

In this example, measurements relevant to each margin can be typed into the text boxes. To type text into a text box click the mouse at the beginning of a box. A flashing cursor will appear. Press the | Delete | key until the current characters are deleted. Type in the new text.

Alternatively:

- Click the mouse before the first character in a text box.

- Drag the mouse across the text. It should change to reverse video.

- Type in the new text. This will replace the existing text.

If you prefer to select options using the keyboard, hold down the | Alt | key and press the underlined letter of the dialog box option.

List boxes

A list box displays a list of available choices. If there are more choices than can be displayed, a set of scroll bars will appear which can be used to scroll through all the available options. Select from the list by pointing and clicking on the required option.

Check boxes

Check boxes are small squares. An option may be selected by clicking in the square. A check mark will appear [X] to indicate that the option has been selected. To de-select an option, click in the square a second time and the check mark will be removed.

The following dialog box is displayed when the **Font** option is selected from the **Font** menu. Two lists appear, one offering a choice of fonts and the other a choice of font sizes. A set of check boxes appear which determine the appearance and size of the font. In this example, the following choices have been made: Helvetica, 18 point size, Bold, Double Underline, Shadow and Very Large.

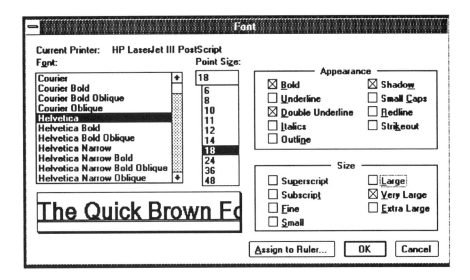

Option buttons

Option buttons are small circles which turn black when selected. Usually, only one option is relevant at any one time. Click in the circle to select.

Scroll arrow lists

Instead of displaying a full list of options, small scroll arrows may be displayed. These are generally used with boxes displaying measurements. Click on the up arrow to increase the measurement one increment at a time and on the down arrow to decrease the measurement one increment at a time.

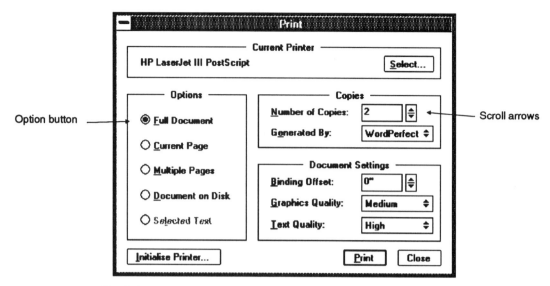

Option button

Scroll arrows

The **Print** dialog box contains option buttons so that you may choose whether to print the entire document, just the current page or one of the other options. Scroll arrows appear to enable you to select to print more than one copy.

1.4   Using the ruler

A ruler may be displayed at the top of a document by selecting the **Ruler** option from the **View** menu. Selecting the **Ruler** option a second time will hide the ruler from view.

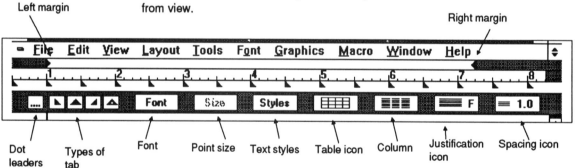

Left margin

Right margin

Dot leaders

Types of tab

Font

Point size

Text styles

Table icon

Column

Justification icon

Spacing icon

The ruler consists of a set of icons which provide easy access to the following features:

- margins

- tabs

- fonts

- sizes

- styles

- tables

- columns

- alignment

- spacing

Each of these features can also be accessed through the menu. Selecting the appropriate menu options will sometimes offer a greater degree of control than selecting the equivalent option from the ruler. For example, changing the position of a tab on the ruler requires pointing the mouse into the tab icon and dragging the tab to a new position. However, when changing a tab position through the menu, you can type in the exact position for the tab. Tabs will be dealt with in detail in Chapter 8.

1.5 Using the button bar

A *button bar* may also be displayed at the top of the document to provide easy access to frequently used menu commands. To display the button bar, select **Button bar** from the **View** menu. To remove the button bar, select the **Button bar** option a second time.

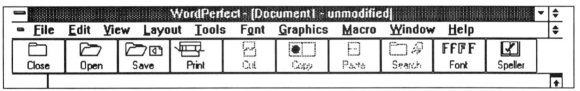

To select a button from the button bar, simply point into the icon with the mouse and click the left button. As with the ruler, there may be times when you will need to select commands from the menu rather than using the button bar because menu commands may offer a greater degree of flexibility. For instance, selecting the **Save** button will save the current document to disk. If you need to save the document under a new name, you will have to select **Save as** from the **File** menu. However, button bars can be customised by adding and deleting new buttons. You can also create as many new button bars as you have need for. This will be dealt with in Chapter 20.

1.6 Getting help

Help can be obtained at any time by pressing F1 . Pressing F1 with an empty screen will produce the *help index*, a list of help topics in alphabetical order. Move up and down the list using the scroll bars to the side of the screen.

As you point the mouse into the list of topics, it will change shape into a pointing hand. The idea is to point the hand at the topic for which you require help and then click the left-hand mouse button.

In the following example, bold has been selected from the list of help index topics.

Bold

Bold is an appearance attribute that lets you add various enhancements to printed text.

To type emboldened text

1   Choose Bold from the Font menu.

2   Type the text.

3   Choose Bold from the Font menu again to turn the Bold attribute off.

To embolden existing text

1   Select the text to be emboldened.

2   Choose Bold from the Font menu.

Some words are displayed with a solid underline and some, such as "attribute" (*see* above), have a dashed underline. By pointing to a term with a solid underline and clicking the mouse, you will be taken to a further screen of help on this topic. By pointing to a term with a dashed underline, clicking on it and holding the mouse button down, a definition of the term will appear. Click away from the term when you have read the definition. In the following example, a definition of "attribute" is displayed.

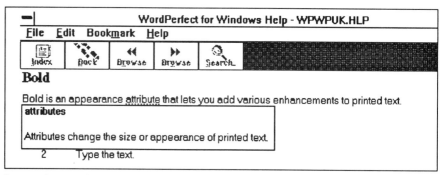

Across the top of the screen is a help button bar. A button bar is the name given to a set of icons or buttons. To select a button from the button bar, point and click the mouse into the required button. Alternatively, press Alt plus the underlined letter displayed on the button. Each button is described below.

- **Index** - displays the help index.

- **Back** - takes you back one screen at a time to the previous help screen, until you finally reach the help index.

- **Browse >>** - displays the next topic in a set of related topics. Eventually, if you select Browse >> enough times, you will reach the last topic and the button will become dimmed.

- **Browse <<** - displays the previous topic in a set of related topics.

- **Search** - produces a list of help *keywords*. Select a help keyword from the list. The keyword will then appear in the **Search for:** box. In the following example, the **Add printer** option has been selected from the list.

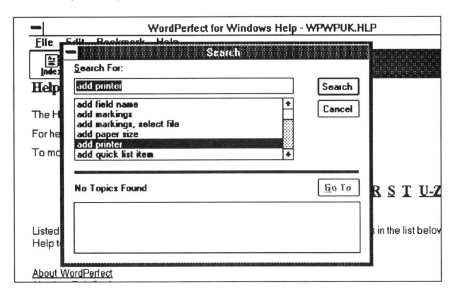

Clicking on the **Search** button will produce a list of topics related to the keyword. For example, when the **Add printer** option is searched for, five related topics are listed.

To get help on one of those topics, select the topic and click on the **Go to** button.

Context-sensitive help may be achieved by selecting a menu or dialog box item and then pressing F1 . The help given will be relevant to the menu or dialog box item selected.

In the following example, the **Preferences** option has been selected, using the cursor arrow keys, from the **File** menu and then F1 has been pressed.

Preferences

When Preferences is chosen from the File menu, the Preferences menu is displayed. Using the items on this menu, you can customise WordPerfect to suit your needs. These items are: Location of Files, Backup, Environment, Display, Print, Keyboard, Initial Codes, Document Summary, Date Format, Merge, Table of Authorities, and Equations.

To accommodate most users, many Preferences options are preset in WordPerfect. A list of these preset options can be found in in Appendix D: Initial Settings in the WordPerfect for Windows Reference Manual. If you are happy with the way WordPerfect is set up, you need not use Preferences.

If you change a Preferences option, WordPerfect records that change either in a WP{WP}.SET file, or in a file with an .INI extension. The change takes effect immediately and remains in effect until you change that option again. Some WordPerfect features allow you to temporarily override the options you have set in Preferences.

Alternatively, you can press Shift F1 and a thought bubble will appear with a question mark icon (?) inside. Point the question mark icon into a menu item and hold the mouse button down. Select the menu command for which you require help and click the left mouse button.

To exit the help screen, select the **Exit** option from the **File** menu in the help screen.

2   Document basics

Now that you know how to move around the WordPerfect screen and make use of the menu system, it is time to create a document and save it to disk. Immediately underneath the menu bar you will find a large empty area, known as the text screen or the *document window*. A flashing cursor, known as the insertion point, should appear near the top left-hand corner of the screen. The document window is the equivalent of a piece of paper in a typewriter and the flashing cursor indicates where text will appear as you begin to type.

As you type, text will be inserted into the document window and the flashing cursor will be pushed to the right. There is a limit to how much text can fit across the page which is determined by the size of the paper with which you are working and the amount of space to be left at either side of the paper, known as the left or right *margin*. For example, A4 paper is approximately 8.5 inches wide but with 1" of space left at both sides of the paper, text could only be printed in the remaining 6.5". Setting paper size and margins will be dealt with in Chapter 12.

As text reaches the right-hand margin, it will automatically *wrap* onto the next line. This is known as *wordwrap*. If you need to begin a new line or paragraph independently of wordwrap, press the ⏎ Enter key, represented in the following screen as the ⏎ symbol.

In the following exercise, you will create a business letter for a new company.

1   If not already loaded, load WordPerfect as outlined in Loading WordPerfect for Windows, page xv.

2   Follow the instructions on page xvi to create a sub-directory on the hard disk. This will be used to store the documents created throughout this book.

3   Type 16th March, 1992 as the date at the top of the letter.

4   Press the Enter key three times - this will end the line containing the date and move your cursor two lines down the screen.

5   Type **Dear Ms Shaw,** as the opening to the letter.

6   Press the Enter key twice to create a line of space between the salutation and the rest of the letter.

7   Type the following text, only pressing the Enter key where you see the ⏎ symbol.

```
╔══════════════════════════════════════════════════════════╗
║                 WordPerfect - [Document1]                  ║
╠══════════════════════════════════════════════════════════╣
   File   Edit   View   Layout   Tools   Font   Graphics   Macro   Window   Help
```

16th March, 1992 ↵
 ↵
 ↵
Dear Ms Shaw, ↵
 ↵
Further to our telephone conversation, I would like to take this
opportunity to introduce you to a new Leeds based company,
Efficient Office. As a local company, we have a unique service
to offer your business - expert secretarial and desktop
publishing skills at very competitive prices. ↵
 ↵
Our aim is to provide a complete office related service. Our
range of services include: ↵
 ↵
Typing ↵
Word processing ↵
Desktop publishing ↵
Photocopying ↵
 ↵
You can be assured that with Efficient Office, you will receive
our best attention at all times. We would appreciate the
opportunity of meeting with you to discuss our services and will
telephone you in a few weeks time. ↵
 ↵

2.2   Saving a document

Text typed into the WordPerfect document screen is temporarily held in the
computer's memory until such time as the document is saved. Saving the
document places a permanent copy of the document onto a hard or floppy disk
(unless you perform an operation to remove the information from the disk). The
document can then be edited and re-saved as many times as necessary.

To save a document for the first time, select the **Save as** option from the **File** menu
or press ⌷ Alt F A ⌷ or ⌷ F3 ⌷. The **Save as** dialog box will appear.

16 Elementary level

The first thing to check is that the **Current dir:** (current directory) option is set to the sub-directory into which you want to save your documents.

The flashing cursor (insertion point) should appear in the **Save as:** box. This is where the *filename* will appear as you type. If the insertion point does not appear in the **Save as:** box, point and click the mouse into the box or press $\boxed{\textbf{Alt A}}$.

There are certain conventions which must be adhered to when naming files. They are as follows:

- A filename can consist of a combination of letters and numbers up to a maximum of eight characters.

- A filename can be followed by a period (full stop) and a three-character extension. The extension can be used to identify the type of file that has been created. For example, WordPerfect graphics files contain the extension .WPG. Initially the files created in this book will be given the extension .WP to indicate that they are documents created in WordPerfect. With some of the later files the extension is omitted.

- A filename cannot contain spaces or punctuation marks with the exception of the hyphen or underscore.

- Filenames usually appear in lower case (in fact, WordPerfect will not allow you to type them in upper case). However, filenames throughout this book are shown in upper case, for purposes of clarity.

For example, it would be acceptable to name a document LETTER1.WP but not LETTER 1.WP, because spaces are not allowed in filenames.

1   Select the **Save as** option from the **File** menu.

2   The first thing to check is that the current sub-directory reads **C:\WPWIN\DATA**. If the current sub-directory is set to **C:\WPWIN**, point the mouse into the list of **Directories** in the right-hand panel and double click on the **[data]** sub-directory. The **Current dir:** should now read **C:\WPWIN\DATA**.

3   Type **NEWLETT.WP** in the **Save as:** box and click on the **Save** button.

The name of the file and the sub-directory in which it has been saved will now appear at the top of the screen as **[C:\WPWIN\DATA\NEWLETT.WP - UNMODIFIED]**. The word "unmodified" indicates that the document has not been changed since last saved. As you make changes to the document, the word "unmodified" will disappear, only to reappear again as the document is saved.

From now on, each time the document is changed you can save the changes simply by selecting the **Save** option from the **File** menu or by pressing $\boxed{\textbf{Alt F S}}$ or $\boxed{\textbf{Shift F3}}$. A message will appear in the status bar to the effect that the document is being saved.

It is important to note that if text is selected (highlighted) when you choose the **File Save** option, the **Save selected text** dialog box will be displayed. If this was not intended, click away from the text and select the **Save** option again.

If you want to keep a copy of the document in its present state and have another version of the file on disk to edit, select the **Save as** option from the **File** menu and type in a new filename. If a document has already been saved with this name, the following dialog box will appear:

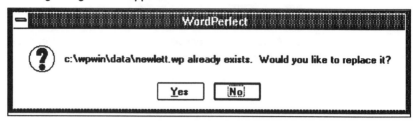

This box displays a warning that a file by that name already exists. You can choose to replace the existing file on disk with the current file by clicking the **Yes** button, or choose to leave the existing file intact by clicking the **No** button and then saving the current file with an original name.

2.3   Printing a document

To print a document select the **Print** option from the **File** menu, press Alt F P or F5 . The **Print** dialog box will appear.

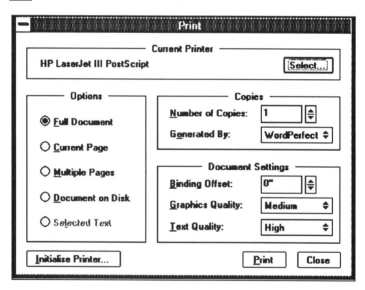

If you want to print with a printer other than that specified in the **Current printer** box, click the **Select** button. A list of available printers will appear. Use the ↓ or ↑ arrow keys until the required printer is highlighted or point and click the mouse into the required printer name. When the required printer is highlighted, click the **Select** button again.

From the available **Options**, select the portion of the document you want to print. For example, select the **Full document** option to print the entire document. Finally, click the **Print** button.

 In this exercise you will print the current file.

1 Select the **Print** option from the **File** menu.

2 Click the **Select** button if the current printer is not the one with which you wish to print. Choose another printer from the available list and click the **Select** button again.

3 Select the **Full document** option.

4 Click the **Print** button.

2.4   Leaving WordPerfect for Windows

There is a set procedure to follow for leaving the WordPerfect for Windows program. Pull down the **File** menu and select the **Exit** option or, as a shortcut, press ⌐ Alt F4 ⌐. WordPerfect will prompt you to save any documents which have been changed since last saving.

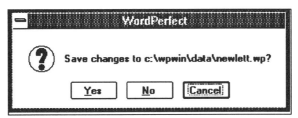

Click the **Yes** button when prompted to save each document in turn or the **No** button if you do not wish to save a document. Click the **Cancel** button if you change your mind and wish to stay in the program. If you do choose to exit the program, you will be taken back to the Windows Program Manager.

At this point you may decide to load another application by locating and double clicking on the relevant program group or you may decide to exit from Windows altogether. Again, you should follow the correct procedure and not simply switch the machine off. To exit from Windows either select the **Exit Windows** option from the Program Manager **File** menu or press ⌐ Alt F4 ⌐.

 Exiting from WordPerfect for Windows

1 Press ⌐ Alt F4 ⌐ to exit from WordPerfect for Windows.

2 Click the **Yes** button if prompted to save any files.

3 Select the **Exit Windows** option from the **File** menu of the Windows Program Manager.

4   Follow the procedure outlined in Loading WordPerfect for Windows on page xv, to re-access the WordPerfect for Windows program.

Consolidation exercise

1   Load WordPerfect for Windows if not already loaded.

2   Type the following letter remembering to only press the [Enter] key at the end of a paragraph or to force a new line.

```
WordPerfect - [c:\wpwin\data\printing.wp - unmodified]
File   Edit   View   Layout   Tools   Font   Graphics   Macro   Window   Help
Brian Simmons
Customer Service Department
Triam Stationery
Wolverhampton

11th December 1992

Dear Mr Simmons,

Further to our telephone conversation, I am writing to confirm
that there are two items missing from the delivery of stationery
which we received on 9th December.  We have also been sent
several items which were not part of our order.  The items and
their catalogue codes are as follows.

The missing items are:

10 reams of A4 copier paper (CP 941)
2 reels of sticky tape (CE 210)

The following items were not part of our order:

1000 A5 envelopes (EN 129)
12 A4 diaries (DI 120)
20 boxes paper clips (PC 364)

I would be grateful if you would give this matter your urgent
attention.

Yours Sincerely
Tim Price
```

3   Save the document as **PRINTING.WP**.

4   Print the document.

5   Exit from WordPerfect.

3   Making simple changes

In Chapter 2 you looked at creating, saving and printing a simple document. You also looked at how to exit from and return to the WordPerfect program. In this chapter you will concentrate on making changes to a document. Before making changes however, there are several important skills to be developed:

● opening a document;

● moving around a document;

● making simple changes such as deleting text, inserting text and using *typeover*.

3.1   Preparing for this chapter

In order to complete this chapter you need the following documents:

Filename	File type	Chapter
NEWLETT.WP	Document	2
PRINTING.WP	Document	2

 If you have not created these documents in the previous chapters you will need to refer back to the chapter numbers listed above and create the files.

 If you have purchased the disks that accompany this book you can copy the necessary files from the appropriate floppy disk. To do this complete the following instructions:

 1   Make sure you have created a sub-directory on the hard disk called **C:\WPWIN\DATA** (*see* Creating a data directory, page xvi).

2   Load WordPerfect for Windows (*see* Loading WordPerfect for Windows, page xv).

3   Follow the instructions for Using the diskettes on page vii.

3.2   Opening a document window

Once a document has been saved and closed, it may then be opened at any time. If you want to open a document which you have recently worked on, pull down the **File** menu. At the bottom of the **File** menu you should see the names of the last four opened files. Select the name of the file from the list and WordPerfect will automatically open it. If there is no list at the bottom of the **File** menu, pull down the **File** menu and select the **Preferences** option followed by the **Environment** option. In the **Environment settings** dialog box, select the option **Display last open filenames**.

If you have not recently worked on the file you wish to open, select the **Open** option from the **File** menu or press F4 . The **Open file** dialog box will appear as below.

The current sub-directory should be set to **C:\WPWIN\DATA**. If it is not, a list of sub-directories below the current sub-directory and a list of drives will be displayed on the right-hand side of the box. A different sub-directory or drive from the list displayed may then be selected.

To open a file stored within the sub-directory above the current sub-directory (known as the *parent directory*), double click the double dots in the directories list. In the following example, **C:\WPWIN\DATA** was set as the current sub-directory and the double dots were selected to change the current sub-directory to **C:\WPWIN**, the *parent* of **C:\WPWIN\DATA**.

The list of files on the left now reflects those stored in **C:\WPWIN** and the sub-directories displayed on the right are those below **C:\WPWIN**.

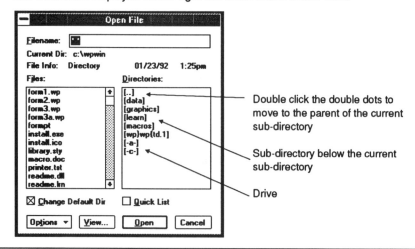

1   Select the **Open** option from the **File** menu.

2   Change the current sub-directory to **C:\WPWIN\DATA** if it does not already appear to be set to this.

3   Select **PRINTING.WP** from the list of files and click the **Open** button. Repeat the steps to open **NEWLETT.WP**.

4   Pull down the **Window** menu. Both **NEWLETT.WP** and **PRINTING.WP** should be listed.

5   Select the **Close** option from the **File** menu to close **NEWLETT.WP** and then select the **Close** option again to close **PRINTING.WP**. You should be left with a new document window into which you can type.

3.3	The Open dialog box options

The **Open** dialog box presents you with options which enable you to manipulate the chosen document. Some of the available options are discussed in this section.

Across the bottom of the **Open** dialog box several buttons are displayed. Select a filename from the list of files and then click the appropriate button as follows.

View

By clicking the **View** button, a window is produced displaying part of the selected document. This is illustrated in the following example.

Buttons which enable the manipulation of the document selected above.

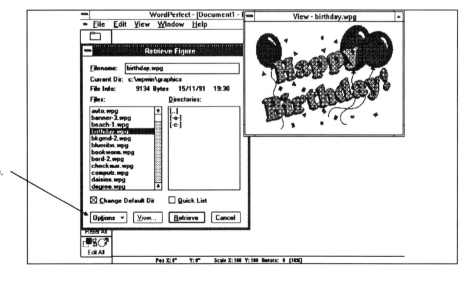

To display the document in a full window, click the **maximise** button (*see* page 4). The **maximise** button will now have changed to a **restore** button. Click the **restore** button to restore the window to its original size. Use the scroll bars to move across or up and down the document. To close the **View** window, click the **Document control** menu (the hyphen to the left of the window) and select the **Close** option.

Options

A list of available options within the **Open** dialog box can be viewed by positioning the mouse pointer on the **Options** button and holding the button down.

Delete

To delete the currently selected file from disk, select the **Delete** option . A **Delete file** dialog box will appear containing the full path and name of the document and prompting you to confirm that you really do want to delete it. Click the **Cancel** button if you do not.

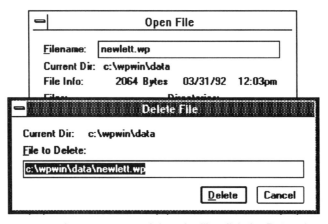

If you are sure that you want to delete the file, click the **Delete** button.

Copy

Select the **Copy** option to copy a file from one area (sub-directory) of the hard disk to another or from one drive to another. The **Copy file** dialog box will appear displaying the current sub-directory and a section labelled **From** and a section labelled **To**.

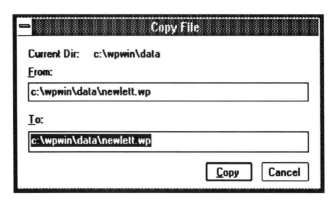

The **From** section contains the full path and filename of the currently selected file. The **To** section contains a highlighted copy of the path and filename. The idea is to type a new path to which the file can be copied and, if you wish, a new filename. As you begin to type, the current path and filename in the **To** section will be overwritten.

Move/rename

Select the **Move/rename** option to move a file from one destination on a disk to another. The **Move/rename** dialog box which appears is similar in layout to that of the **Copy file** dialog box. The difference is that by selecting **Copy**, the original file will be left in place and a *copy* will be placed elsewhere whereas with **Move**, the original file will be *moved* to a new destination.

Find

Imagine that you have forgotten the name of the file that you were working on last week but you can remember the file extension or some of the file content. You can use the **Find** dialog box to search for the file. Select the **Find** option to search for filenames containing a particular set of characters or files containing specific words. The following dialog box will appear.

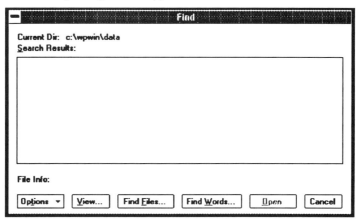

Click the **Find files** button to search for filenames containing a particular pattern of characters. Remember that a filename can consist of up to eight characters followed by a full stop (period) and up to three characters as an extension to the filename. A group of special characters known as *wildcards* may be used to search for files. The * can be used to represent any number of characters and the ? can be used to represent a single character. If the file pattern contains *.*, WordPerfect will search for all files because the * before the full stop represents any number or combination of characters in the filename and the * after the full stop represents filenames with any extension. For example, to search for all files with a .WP extension you would type *.WP in the **File pattern** box.

Once you have established which file pattern you are searching for, the next step is to inform WordPerfect where to search. In most cases, you will either wish to search the entire drive or the current directory.

Click the **Find** button to perform the search. WordPerfect will then produce a list of files matching the file pattern specified from the area of the disk specified. This is known as the **Search results** list.

1 Select the **Open** option from the **File** menu.

2 Click the **Options** button and select the **Find** option.

3 Click the **Find files** button.

4 Type ***.WP** as the **File pattern** and select **Directory** as the area to search. Click the **Find** button. **NEWLETT.WP** and **PRINTING.WP** will appear in the **Search results** list.

5 Select **Find words**. Type **stationery** in the **Word pattern** box.

6 Click the **Find** button. **PRINTING.WP** will appear in the **Search results** list.

7 Select the file by clicking on it and then click the **Open** button to open this file.

8 Close **PRINTING.WP**.

3.4   Moving around a document

Making changes to an existing document is known as *editing*. However, before you begin editing it is a good idea to save the existing document to disk. If you make any mistakes whilst editing you then have the opportunity to close the document without saving the changes, and your original document will be saved intact.

If you look at your screen you will see a flashing cursor or insertion point. This marks the current cursor position and the idea is to move the insertion point to the part of the document to be changed. Once the insertion point is in the correct position, there are a number of special keys which can be used to make changes to the text.

The easiest way to position the insertion point in the relevant piece of text is to move the mouse I-Beam into the text and click the left mouse button. Alternatively, there are many keys available on the keyboard to enable you to move the insertion point quickly around the document. They are outlined below.

Ctrl Home	top of document
Ctrl End	bottom of document
Page Dn	bottom of current screen
Page Up	top of current screen
Home	beginning of current line
End	end of current line

↓	one line down
↑	one line up
→	one character to the right
←	one character to the left
Ctrl →	one word to the right
Ctrl ←	one word to the left
Ctrl ↓	one paragraph down
Ctrl ↑	one paragraph up
Alt Page Dn	top of next page
Alt Page Up	top of previous page

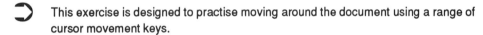

This exercise is designed to practise moving around the document using a range of cursor movement keys.

1   Open **NEWLETT.WP** if not already open and press Ctrl Home to make sure that the insertion point is at the top of the letter.

2   Press Ctrl ↓ twice to move to the first character of the paragraph beginning "Further to our telephone conversation".

3   Press Ctrl → several times to position the insertion point before "I would like".

4   Press Page Dn . The insertion point should now be below the paragraph "telephone you in a few weeks time".

5   Press Ctrl Home to move to the top of the document and then press Home to move to the beginning of the line. Press End to move to the end of the line.

3.5   Deleting and inserting text

On a simple level, the term editing refers to correcting typing mistakes by inserting, deleting and over-typing characters.

Deleting

With the insertion point in the correct position, the following keys can be used to delete text. The Backspace key deletes characters to the left of the insertion point. The Delete key deletes characters at the insertion point. If you want to use the backspace key to delete then you must place the insertion point *after* the character to be deleted.

Inserting

WordPerfect is automatically in *insert mode* which means that any text typed at the insertion point will be inserted into the document.

Typeover

To type over existing text, position the insertion point before the characters to be replaced and press the Insert key. This acts as a toggle switch and WordPerfect will now be in *typeover mode*. The word "typeover" will appear in the status bar at the bottom of the screen to indicate that characters typed from this point on will overwrite those at the insertion point. Press the Insert key again to switch back to insert mode.

This exercise will make use of a variety of editing keys.

1　Press Ctrl Home to move to the top of **NEWLETT.WP**.

2　Press the → cursor arrow until the insertion point is after the number "6". Press the Backspace key once to remove the "6" and type in **7** instead.

3　Press Ctrl → to move the insertion point to the "M" of "March". Press Insert. Typeover should now appear in the status bar. Type **April** and press Insert again to return to insert mode. Delete the comma after "April".

4　Press Ctrl ↓ once and then Ctrl → twice. The insertion point should now be before the "S" of "Shaw". Press Delete four times to delete "Shaw" and type **Croft**.

5　Use the cursor movement and editing keys described above to change the word "Leeds" to "Yorkshire".

6　Move to the end of the document by pressing Ctrl End and, if necessary, move up to the last line of the last paragraph. Move to the end of the line by pressing End. Press Ctrl ← twice and Backspace until the words "a few" have been deleted. Type in **two**, and if necessary, press the Spacebar to place a space before "weeks".

7　Move the insertion point before the words "Word processing" and press Enter to create an extra line of space above these words. Move the insertion point before "Desktop publishing" and press Enter to insert a line of space above. Insert a line of space above "Photocopying".

8　With the insertion point before "Photocopying", press the Backspace key to delete the previous character, which in this case is the symbol placed there by pressing the Enter key. This will have the effect of removing the blank line.

9　Move to the blank line between "Word processing" and "Desktop publishing" and press Delete to delete the blank line. Delete the blank line between "Typing" and "Word processing".

10　Select the **Save** option from the **File** menu to update the version of the document on disk to include these changes.

The document should resemble the following example:

```
17th April 1992


Dear Ms Croft,

Further to our telephone conversation,I would like to take this
opportunity to introduce you to a new Yorkshire based company,
Efficient Office.  As a local company, we have a unique service
to  offer  your  business  -  expert  secretarial  and  desktop
publishing skills at very competitive prices.

Our aim is to provide a complete office related service.  Our
range of services include:

Typing
Word processing
Desktop publishing
Photocopying

You can be assured that with Efficient Office, you will receive
our  best  attention  at  all  times.   We  would  appreciate  the
opportunity of meeting with you to discuss our services and will
telephone you in two weeks time.
```

3.6   Consolidation exercise

1   Open the document window containing **PRINTING.WP**.

2   Make the following changes to the document.

Ms Helen Trent	~~Brian Simmons~~ Customer Service Department Trian Stationery Wolverhampton
January 1993	11th ~~December 1992~~
Ms Trent	Dear Mr Simmons,
three	Further to our telephone conversation, I am writing to confirm that there are ~~two~~ items missing from the delivery of stationery
4th January	which we received on ~~9th December~~. We have also been sent several items which were not part of our order. The items and their catalogue codes are as follows.
	The missing items are:
2 year planners (CE 56)	~~10 reams of A4 copier paper (CP 941)~~ 2 reels of sticky tape (CE 210)
	The following items were not part of our order:
12 boxes of floppy disks	1000 A5 envelopes (EN 129) 12 A4 diaries (DI 120) 20 boxes paper clips (PC 364)
	I would be grateful if you would give this matter your urgent attention.
	Yours Sincerely Tim Price

3   Save and print the document.

4 Working with blocks of text

The operations performed so far have been carried out on single characters. Operations such as deleting, copying and moving can also be applied to large groups of text, known as *blocks*. A block of text can consist of one or more characters and once the block has been selected, the operation can be applied.

4.1 Preparing for this chapter

In order to complete this chapter you need the following documents:

Filename	File type	Chapter
NEWLETT.WP	Document	2 & 3
PRINTING.WP	Document	2 & 3

 If you have not created these documents in the previous chapters you will need to refer back to the chapter numbers listed above and create the files.

 If you have purchased the disks that accompany this book you can copy the necessary files from the appropriate floppy disk. To do this complete the following instructions:

1 Make sure you have created a sub-directory on the hard disk called **C:\WPWIN\DATA** (*see* Creating a data directory, page xvi).

2 Load WordPerfect for Windows (*see* Loading WordPerfect for Windows, page xv).

3 Follow the instructions for Using the diskettes on page vii.

4.2 Selecting blocks using the mouse

To select a block of text with the mouse, move the I-Beam to the first character to be selected, hold the mouse button down and drag in any direction. This area of text will be displayed in reverse video, sometimes referred to as *highlighted* text or *selected* text. Release the mouse when all of the text with which you wish to work is displayed in reverse video.

A quick method of selecting a block of text is to position the insertion point at the first character, move the I-Beam to the last character, hold down the Shift key and press the left mouse button.

There are several quick ways of selecting groups of text with the mouse.

- Point the I-Beam into a word and double click the left mouse button in rapid succession to select the word.

- Triple click to select the current sentence.

- Click the mouse button four times to select the current paragraph.

- To remove the selection, click anywhere in the text screen.

The following screen shows a sentence which has been selected by positioning the I-Beam in the sentence and then clicking the left mouse button three times.

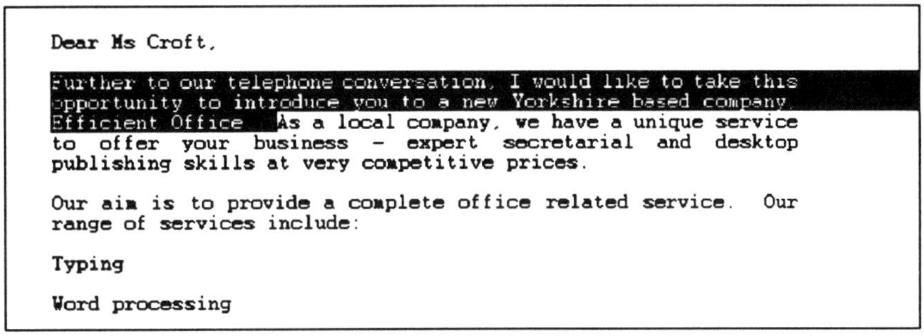

```
Dear Ms Croft,

Further to our telephone conversation, I would like to take this
opportunity to introduce you to a new Yorkshire based company.
Efficient Office. As a local company, we have a unique service
to  offer  your  business  -  expert  secretarial  and  desktop
publishing skills at very competitive prices.

Our aim is to provide a complete office related service.  Our
range of services include:

Typing

Word processing
```

4.3   Selecting blocks using the keyboard

The keyboard can also be used to select text. Press $\boxed{\text{F8}}$ to switch to *select mode*. A select mode indicator will appear in the status bar. Press any cursor movement key covered in the previous section to extend the highlighted area in the desired direction. For example, press $\boxed{\text{F8}}$ followed by $\boxed{\text{End}}$ to extend the selection from the current insertion point to the end of the line.

You can also press any character to extend the selection to the next character of that type. For example, pressing a full stop will extend the selection to the end of the sentence and pressing $\boxed{\text{Enter}}$ will extend the selection to the end of the paragraph. To remove the selection, press $\boxed{\text{F8}}$ and move the insertion point in any direction.

4.4   Deleting blocks

Once text has been selected, press the $\boxed{\text{Delete}}$ or $\boxed{\text{Backspace}}$ key to remove the text or select the **Cut** option from the **Edit** menu.

There are some useful shortcuts for deleting. For example, to delete a word, place the insertion point in the word and press $\boxed{\text{Ctrl Backspace}}$. To delete text from the insertion point to the end of a line, press $\boxed{\text{Ctrl Delete}}$.

4.5   Restoring text

If you have deleted the wrong block of text by mistake, select the **Undo** option from the **Edit** menu or press ⃞ Alt Backspace ⃞ before making any further changes to the document. This will bring back the last piece of text deleted.

WordPerfect remembers the last three pieces of text deleted. If you have already made changes to the document and want to restore text deleted previously, position the insertion point at the point where the text is to be restored and select the **Undelete** option from the **Edit** menu or press ⃞ Alt Shift Backspace ⃞. The last piece of text deleted will appear in reverse video at the insertion point accompanied by the following dialog box.

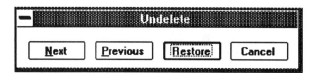

If this text is the one you want to restore, click the **Restore** button. If you want to restore a piece of text deleted earlier, click the **Previous** button. The previous piece of deleted text will appear at the insertion point. Click the **Restore** button if this is the piece of text to be restored. If not, click the **Previous** button again or the **Next** button to see either the previous piece of deleted text, or text deleted after that currently appearing in reverse video.

 1   Open **NEWLETT.WP** if not already open.

2   Select "telephone" in the first paragraph and delete it.

3   Make sure that the insertion point remains in the same position and select the **Undelete** option from the **Edit** menu. The word "telephone" will now appear in reverse video at the point of the insertion point.

4   Click the **Restore** button to restore "telephone" into its original position.

4.6   Copying text

A selected block of text can be duplicated by selecting the **Copy** option from the **Edit** menu or by pressing ⃞ Ctrl Insert ⃞. A copy of the text may then be placed elsewhere in the document by moving the insertion point and then selecting **Paste** from the **Edit** menu or by pressing ⃞ Shift Insert ⃞.

4.7   Moving text

A selected block of text may be moved by selecting **Cut** from the **Edit** menu or by pressing ⃞ Shift Delete ⃞. The selected text will be removed from the document.

Place the insertion point where you want the text to go and select **Paste** from the **Edit** menu or press Shift Insert .

⮑ Editing a document

1 Using **NEWLETT.WP**, position the insertion point before the first character of the date, hold down the left mouse button and drag across until the day and month appear in reverse video. Press the Delete key and type **21st May,**.

2 Select "Croft" by pointing the I-Beam into "Croft" and double click the left mouse button. Type **Fairbank**. Notice that "Fairbank" has now replaced "Croft" and that there was no need to delete "Croft".

3 Change the document until it resembles the example below.

```
▬  File   Edit   View   Layout   Tools   Font   Graphics   Macro   Window   Help
      21st May, 1992 ↵
      ↵
      ↵
      Dear Mr Fairbank, ↵
      ↵
      Further  to  our  recent  conversation,  I  would  like  to  take  this
      opportunity  to  introduce  you  to  a  new  Manchester  based  company,
      Future  Printing.   As  a  local  company,  we  have  a  unique  service
      to  offer  your  business  -  expert  printing  and  desktop  publishing
      services at very competitive prices. ↵
      ↵
      Our range of services include: ↵
      ↵
      Colour Printing ↵
      Stationery ↵
      Desktop publishing ↵
      ↵
      I  have  enclosed  a  brochure  for  your  attention.    Should  you  have
      any  queries  regarding  our  services,  please  do  not  hestitate  to
      contact me. ↵
      ↵
      Yours Sincerely ↵
      ↵
      T.M. Denning ↵
      Managing Director
```

4 Save the document as **INTRODUC.WP**.

⮑ Using the **Copy, Cut** and **Paste** options from the **Edit** menu

1 Select "Our" in "Our range of services" and delete it.

2 Select "Future Printing" in the first paragraph and then the **Copy** option from the **Edit** menu. Place the insertion point before "range of services" and select **Paste** from the **Edit** menu. Type **'s** and press the Spacebar to insert an extra character space.

3 Select the paragraph containing the word "Stationery" by clicking the mouse four times in the paragraph. Select the **Cut** option from the **Edit** menu. Place the insertion point before "Colour Printing" and select **Paste** from the **Edit** menu.

4 Save the document with the changes.

4.8   Consolidation exercise

1 Open the document **PRINTING.WP** and make the following changes using the commands introduced in this chapter.

```
Sylvia Trent
Customer Service Department
Triam Stationery
Wolverhampton

11th January 1993

Dear Ms Trent,

Further to our telephone conversation, I am writing to confirm
that there are three items missing from the delivery of
stationery which we received on 4th January.  We have also been
sent several items which were not part of our order.  The items
and their catalogue codes are as follows.

The following items were not part of our order:

1000 A5 envelopes (EN 129)
12 A4 diaries (DI 120)
20 boxes paper clips (PC 364)

The following items were missing from the delivery:

2 reels of sticky tape
12 boxes of floppy diskettes
2 year planners

I would be grateful if you would give this matter your urgent
attention.

Yours Sincerely
```

2 Save the changes.

5 Print preview

5.1 Preparing for this chapter

In order to complete this chapter you need the following document:

Filename	File type	Chapter
PRINTING.WP	Document	2

 If you have not created this document in the previous chapters you will need to refer back to the chapter number listed above and create the file. Please note, this file has been modified in subsequent chapters.

 If you have purchased the disks that accompany this book you can copy the necessary files from the appropriate floppy disk. To do this complete the following instructions:

 1   Make sure you have created a sub-directory on the hard disk called **C:\WPWIN\DATA** (*see* Creating a data directory, page xvi).

2   Load WordPerfect for Windows (*see* Loading WordPerfect for Windows, page xv).

3   Follow the instructions for Using the diskettes on page vii.

5.2 Using Print preview

Your printer may not be capable of reproducing some of the attributes available in the **Font** dialog box. To get some idea of how text will appear when printed, select the **Print preview** option from the **File** menu or press **Shift F5**. This option allows you to preview the document before printing, so saving time and paper. Make sure that you do not have any text highlighted when selecting the **Print preview** option otherwise the option will appear to be unavailable. It is important to note that the size of the preview page is dependent on the option chosen when **Print Preview** was last in use. For example, if you preview a document and select the **Full page** option, the next time you preview a document the **Full page** option will still be current.

 1   Open **PRINTING.WP** if it is not already open.

2   Select the **Print preview** option from the **File** menu. A screen similar to the following illustration should appear, (the size of the previewed document may differ):

Print preview
button bar

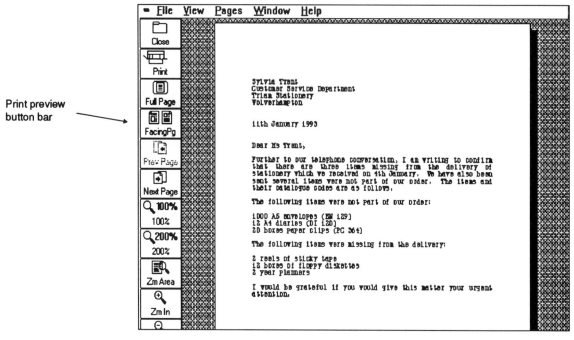

Across the top of the screen there is a menu bar displaying menu items which are relevant to Print preview. The first three menu items are detailed below. A button bar containing icons equivalent to many of the menu options will normally be displayed down the left-hand side of the screen.

5.3   Print preview options

File

From the **File** menu you can choose to **Print** or **Close** the preview screen. You can also press F5 to **Print** or Ctrl F4 to **Close**.

View

The **View** menu controls the size at which you can view the current document. There are several options available:

- **100%** - shows the document at approximately the size it will be when printed.

- **200%** - shows the document at twice the printed size.

- **Zoom in** - each time **Zoom in** is selected, WordPerfect will increase the document size in increments of 25% up to 400% of actual size.

- **Zoom out** - has the opposite effect to **Zoom in**. The document will decrease in size in increments of 25%, down to 44% of the actual size.

- **Zoom area** - allows you to magnify a portion of the document. A set of cross hairs will appear as in the following example. Position the cross hairs at the top left-hand corner of the area you want to magnify, click the left mouse button and drag the mouse around the area. A rectangle will appear as you drag. When you release the mouse button, the selected portion of the document will be magnified on the screen.

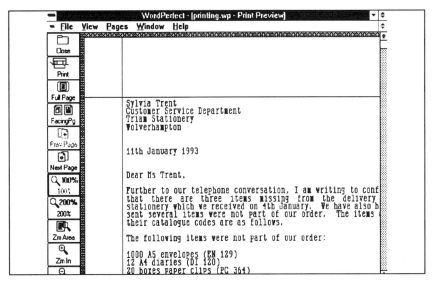

- **Zoom to full width** - displays the full width of the document.

- **Reset** - resets the view size to that displayed when the window was last closed.

 Using the **View** menu

1 Select **200%** from the **View** menu to see the document twice the size it would be when printed.

2 Change the view size to **100%** by selecting the appropriate button on the button bar.

3 Click on the **Zm in** button on the button bar to increase the size of the document by **25%**.

4 Select **100%** from the **View** menu.

5 Click on the **Zm area** button on the button bar and drag a box around the address.

6 Click on the **100%** button to return the document to actual size.

7 Select the **Zoom to full width** option from the **View** menu.

Pages

The **Pages** menu displays the document as a set of pages so giving a clear idea of the layout of entire pages as opposed to the appearance of specific sets of characters. The options are as follows:

- **Full page** - displays the current page as though it were a printed sheet of paper.

- **Facing pages** - displays two pages on the screen at a time. If you have set different headers and footers for even and odd pages you will be able to see how they appear when placed side by side.

- **Go to page** - allows you to specify the next page to preview.

- **Previous page** - previews the previous page.

- **Next page** - previews the following page.

1 Practise using each of the options from the **Page** menu.

2 Click the **100%** button on the button bar.

3 Click on the **Close** button to return to the normal editing screen.

6   Working with multiple documents

6.1   Preparing for this chapter

In order to complete this chapter you need the following document:

Filename	File type	Chapter
PRINTING.WP	Document	2

 If you have not created this document in the previous chapters you will need to refer back to the chapter number listed above and create the file. Please note, this file has been modified in subsequent chapters.

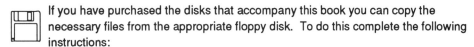 If you have purchased the disks that accompany this book you can copy the necessary files from the appropriate floppy disk. To do this complete the following instructions:

1   Make sure you have created a sub-directory on the hard disk called **C:\WPWIN\DATA** (*see* Creating a data directory, page xvi).

2   Load WordPerfect for Windows (*see* Loading WordPerfect for Windows, page xv).

3   Follow the instructions for Using the diskettes on page vii.

6.2   Creating a new document window

Having finished working on the current document for the time being, you may decide to begin working on a new document. To create a new document, select the **New** option from the **File** menu or press Shift F4 . A blank document window will appear on the screen into which you can begin to type.

If you do not close the current document before creating a new document, you will have two document windows open at the same time. However, only one document window can be *active*. That is, you can only work in one document window at a time. It is possible to have up to nine windows open at any one time although you may not have enough computer memory available to have this number open.

The new document window will be placed on top of the current document window and will appear with the following information in the title bar:

WordPerfect - [Document2 - unmodified]

6.3　Moving between document windows

You can move between document windows by pulling down the **Window** menu. Documents which are currently open will be listed at the bottom of the **Window** menu. The document which is currently active will have a tick placed before it in the list. The active document contains the insertion point in preparation for you to begin typing or editing. To move into another document window, simply select the name of the document from the **Window** menu.

1　With **PRINTING.WP** still open, select the **New** option from the **File** menu. A blank screen with **WordPerfect - [Document2 - unmodified]** will appear.

2　Pull down the **Window** menu. You should see the following list of open files:
　1 **C:\WPWIN\DATA\PRINTING.WP - UNMODIFIED**
　2 **DOCUMENT2 - UNMODIFIED**

3　Select document number **1** to make **PRINTING.WP** the active or current document.

4　Pull down the **Window** menu and then select document number **2** to make the new document current.

6.4　Closing a document window

Although you can have up to nine documents open at any one time, you may need to close documents when you have finished working with them in order to conserve computer memory. To close a document window, select the **Close** option from the **File** menu or press Ctrl F4 . If you have made changes to the document since last saving, you will be prompted to save the document.

1　Select the **Close** option from the **File** menu to close the current document. Only **PRINTING.WP** should now be open.

7　Changing text appearance

By now you should be familiar with the basic steps required to create, edit, save and print a document. WordPerfect is a very sophisticated package and there are many features available to help improve the appearance of your document. In this chapter you will master the following skills:

- applying fonts

- setting point sizes

- changing text appearance

- setting text size

- setting a standard font

- using WordPerfect codes

- removing attributes

7.1　Preparing for this chapter

In order to complete this chapter you need the following document:

Filename	File type	Chapter
INTRODUC.WP	Document	4

 If you have not created this document in the previous chapters you will need to refer back to the chapter number listed above and create the file.

 If you have purchased the disks that accompany this book you can copy the necessary files from the appropriate floppy disk. To do this complete the following instructions:

1　Make sure you have created a sub-directory on the hard disk called **C:\WPWIN\DATA** (*see* Creating a data directory, page xvi).

2　Load WordPerfect for Windows (*see* Loading WordPerfect for Windows, page xv).

3　Follow the instructions for Using the diskettes on page vii.

The appearance of text can be controlled and altered by selecting options directly from the **Font** menu. Pull down the **Font** menu.

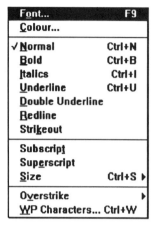

As you can see, there are a set of text *attributes* such as bold, italics, and underline available. You can also choose to change the font and size from the options listed. Options which have a tick beside them have already been selected. All of these choices and more are also available from within the **Font** dialog box which can be accessed by selecting the **Font** option from the **Font** menu.

The first step in changing the appearance of text is to select the text or position the insertion point at the beginning of the text to be changed. If you select a block of text, only the selected text will change. If you position the insertion point, all text from that point on will change.

To access the **Font** dialog box, select the **Font** option from the **Font** menu or click the **Font** button on the button bar. Alternatively, press F9 from the main screen.

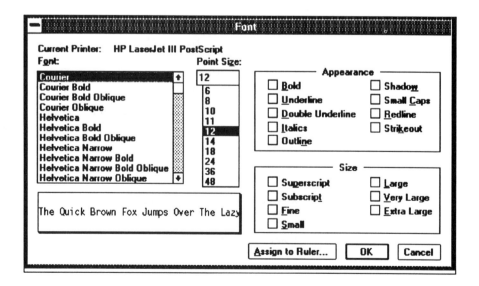

A variety of styles of text (*fonts*) will be listed underneath the **Font** option. The fonts or styles available depend very much on which printer is current. As you select from this list, sample text will appear in the box below. A shortcut method of selecting from the list is to press the letter of the required font. For example, if the highlight is currently on Courier, press the letter $\boxed{\text{t}}$ to move quickly to Times Roman.

Courier 12 point

Courier bold 14 point

Helvetica bold oblique 14 point

ITC Avant Garde Gothic Demi 14 point

ITC Bookman Light 14 point

ITC Zapf Chancery Medium italic 24 point

New Century Schoolbook bold 12 point

7.3   Point sizes

A list of *point sizes* appears to the right of the list of fonts. The point size refers to the height of the characters, taken from the lowest point in a group of characters (the *descender*) to the highest point in a group of characters (the *ascender*). 72 points are equal to one inch in height, 36 points to half an inch, 18 points to a quarter of an inch and so on. If you choose 72 points as the size, the word "type" would measure one inch in height from the top of the "t" to the bottom of the "y".

The range of point sizes listed as available depends upon the font chosen. However, some printers such as PostScript printers, have the capability to *scale* fonts to a required size. If your printer is capable of scaling fonts, you can type the point size straight into the **Point size** box.

Six points

Ten points

Twelve points

Fourteen points

Twenty four points

Thirty six points

Forty eight points

A set of attributes may be applied to text by selecting from the **Appearance** option. The range and effect of **Appearance** options is dependent upon the printer selected. For instance, only PostScript printers can reproduce **Outline**.

```
Bold text

Italic text

Underlined text

Double underlined text



Strikeout
|
```

Appearance attributes can be applied to selected text or may be put in place before text is typed. In the latter case, position the insertion point and select the required attributes. Type the text up to the point where you wish to begin typing normal text again and then select the **Normal** option from the **Font** menu.

There are a set of keyboard shortcuts available for the most commonly used attributes:

Ctrl B	bold
Ctrl I	italics
Ctrl U	underline
Ctrl N	normal text
End	resumes normal text

If you need to see how the text will appear on printing, select the **Print preview** option from the **File** menu. Alternatively, open the file called **PRINTER.TST** which can be found in the same sub-directory as the WordPerfect program files (usually **C:\WPWIN**) and print it. This will give you a good indication of the capabilities of your printer.

7.5   Text size

Both the width and height of a set of characters can be altered by selecting an appropriate **Size** from the **Font** dialog box. Each size is set to be a percentage of the current font. For example, **Small** may be 80% of the current font size whilst **Large** may be 120%.

Fine text

Small text

Large text

Very large text

Extra large text

To change the settings for each size, pull down the **File** menu and then select the **Preferences** option followed by the **Print** option. The **Print settings** dialog box will appear.

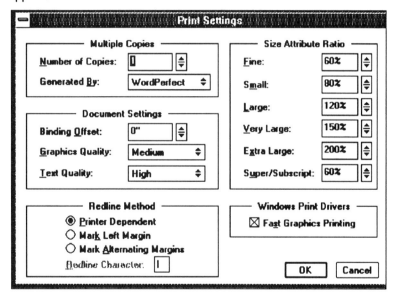

The **Size attribute ratio** information can be changed as required.

 Changing the appearance of text

1   Close any open files and open **INTRODUC.WP**.

2   Press Ctrl Home to move to the top of the document.

3   Pull down the **Font** menu.

4   Select the **Font** option.

5   Select **Times roman**, **12 points** and click on the **OK** button. The entire document should now change to this font.

6   Select "Future Printing" in the first paragraph.

7   Pull down the **Font** menu and select **Bold**.

8   Select the block where the three services are listed.

9   Select the **Font** option from the **Font** menu.

10 Select the **Outline** and **Shadow** options from the **Appearance** box and **Large** as the **Size**. Click on the **OK** button. Print preview the document.

7.6   Initial fonts

To use the same font throughout a document, select the **Document** option from the **Layout** menu followed by the **Initial font** option. Choose the font and point size and click on the **OK** button. This font will affect all text throughout the document until a new font code is found. If a font has already been selected for the document the initial font will be ignored.

7.7   WordPerfect codes

Whenever you change the position or attributes of text, WordPerfect inserts an instruction into the document in the form of a code. These codes are not usually visible but you can look at them by selecting the **Reveal codes** option from the **View** menu or by pressing Alt F3 . The document window will split horizontally in two parts, the top half containing the document and the bottom half the same document text with the formatting codes displayed. As you move the insertion point in the top window, the information displayed in the bottom half of the window will change correspondingly. The size of either window can be changed by dragging the line dividing the two windows.

Attribute codes will be inserted before and after a selected block of text or at the insertion point. For example, if bold has been applied to a block of text, there will be a [Bold On] code at the start of the text and a [Bold Off] code at the end. Any text typed in the middle of these codes will assume the bold attribute.

If you have requested several attributes to be applied to a block of text, such as bold and double underline, the codes will be listed in turn. For example, [Bold On] [Dbl Und On] text [Bold Off] [Dbl Und Off]. If you want to begin typing normal text, it is a good idea to reveal codes and press the → until the insertion point is past the last code and then resume typing.

If you have not selected a block of text but simply positioned the insertion point before selecting an attribute, there will be a code to switch on the attribute but no code to switch the attribute off. All text after the insertion point will be affected by this attribute until a counteracting code is inserted.

Revealing codes

1 Move to the top of **INTRODUC.WP**.

2 Pull down the **View** menu and select the **Reveal codes** option. The WordPerfect screen will divide into two, the document in the top half of the screen and the document plus any relevant codes in the bottom half of the screen.

a new Manchester based company, **Future Printing**. As a local company, we have a unique service to offer your business - expert printing and desktop publishing services at very competitive prices.

Future Printing's range of services include:

Stationery

[Font:Times Roman 12pt]21st May, 1992[HRt]
[HRt]
[HRt]
Dear Mr Fairbank,[HRt]
[HRt]
Further to our recent conversation, I would like to take this opportunity t
ntroduce you to[SRt]
a new Manchester based company, [Bold On]Future Printing[Bold Off]. As a l
l company, we have a unique[SRt]
service to offer your business [ ] expert printing and desktop publishing s
ices at very[SRt]
competitive prices.[HRt]
[HRt]
Future Printing's range of services include:[HRt]
[HRt]

---

3 As you have selected a new font, size and other attributes for the current document, you should be able to identify the codes which have been inserted. For example, at the top of the document you should see [Font:Times Roman 12pt], and [Bold On] and [Bold Off] will appear either side of "Future Printing". Notice also that at the end of each paragraph a [Hrt] code is displayed. This means that the | **Enter** | or | **Return** | key has been pressed and a hard return has been entered into the document.

4 Pull down the **View** menu and select the **Reveal codes** option to switch the codes off.

5 Save your document.

7.8	**Removing attributes**

Revealing codes serves a dual purpose. The codes enable you to see what attributes have been applied to the text and to remove them if necessary. To remove an attribute whilst revealing codes, position the cursor on the attribute code either side of the text and press the | **Delete** | key.

Alternatively, select the text, access the **Font** menu or the **Font** dialog box and select the attribute for a second time, so switching it off.

 1 Using **INTRODUC.WP**, reveal codes.

2 Remove code for [Bold On] or [Bold Off] so that "Future Printing" returns to normal text.

3   Save and close your document.

 1   Create the following document and save it as **REPLY.WP**.

Future Printing

for a professional and flexible service at a competitive price

Future Printing is a small Manchester based company, determined
to bring back the personal touch to the printing industry.   We
would like the opportunity to convince you that it is possible
to   receive   first   class,   reliable   service   from   a   small
independently run concern and save money into the bargain!

Listed below are just some of the services we can offer.   To find
out more, please return the pre-paid card and keep the list of
services for future reference.

Stationery
Colour Printing
Desktop Publishing
35mm Slides
Presentation Services
Brochures
Posters

---

2   Position the insertion point at the top of the document, select the **Button bar**
     option from the **View** menu and click the **Font** button.

3   Select **Times roman, 12 points** from the **Font** dialog box.

4   Position the mouse in the heading "Future Printing" and triple click the left button
     to select this paragraph.

5   Select **ITC Avant garde gothic book** as the font or, if this font is not available,
     select another font of your choice.

6   Still with the heading selected, select **Bold, Outline** and **Shadow** as
     appearance attributes and **Extra large** as the size.

7   Triple click the mouse in the paragraph beginning "for a professional...".

8   Select **ITC Avant garde gothic book oblique** as the font or another font of your
     choice.

9   Select **Bold** as the appearance attribute and **Large** as the size.

10   Select the list of services.

11   Select **ITC Avant garde gothic book** as the font and **Shadow** and **Bold** as the
     attributes.

12   Print preview the document and then select the **Save** option from the button bar
     to save the document.

7.9 Auto code placement

Those of you familiar with WordPerfect 5.1 for DOS may have come across the problem of conflicting codes. Codes will generally be placed in a document from the current insertion point onwards. For example, if the insertion point was at the beginning of a paragraph when you set a left margin of 2", the entire paragraph and all subsequent text would be indented 2". If you then placed the insertion point within the paragraph and changed the left margin to say 3", you may well have found that the first part of the paragraph was indented to 2" and the latter part plus all subsequent text was indented to 3".

WordPerfect for Windows automatically inserts specific codes at the beginning of a paragraph or page or other relevant location to overcome this problem and replaces existing or conflicting codes. This feature is known as *auto code placement*. With auto code placement selected, for example, the code to change a left margin would automatically be placed at the start of the current paragraph irrespective of the position of the insertion point within the paragraph. Auto code placement is selected by default when WordPerfect is installed but can be changed by pulling down the **File** menu and selecting the **Preferences** option followed by the **Environment** option.

7.10 Document initial codes

Formatting codes designed to affect the whole document can be inserted into a document by accessing the **Layout** menu and then selecting the **Document, Initial codes** options. A **Reveal codes** window will appear displaying any existing codes affecting the current document. Select those options from the **Layout** menu which you would like to apply to the entire document and then click the **Close** button. Although these codes will not appear in the document, they will affect all text until a new or competing code is found. To change the codes, repeat the above steps, highlight the code in the **Reveal codes** window and press the ⟨Delete⟩ key.

7.11 Default initial codes

WordPerfect uses standard settings for each document created. For example, each document will print with 1" margins to the top, bottom, left and right of the text. All documents are single spaced. To change these standard or default settings for all future documents you must alter the initial codes. Select the **Preferences** option from the **File** menu and choose **Initial codes**. The current standard settings will appear as codes in an otherwise empty document window. At the top of the window you will see:

WordPerfect - [Document name - Default Initial Codes]

Choose formatting options in the usual way to establish new default settings. For example, access the **Layout** menu and then select the **Page** option followed by **Paper size** and select a new paper size. Select **Close** when you have finished.

Changing document initial codes

1 Using **REPLY.WP** access the **Layout** menu and choose the **Document** option followed by **Initial codes**.

2 Press ⌐Ctrl F8⌐ to access the **Margins** dialog box and type **2"** for each margin. Click the **Close** button. The document margins have been set to two inches all round.

3 Repeat the above steps to return to the **Document initial codes** window and delete the following codes:

[T/B Mar: 2", 2"]
[L/R Mar: 2", 2"]

4 Click the **Close** button to return to the document. The document margins have been changed back to the defaults.

5 Select the **Preferences** option from the **File** menu and choose **Initial codes**. Set the margins to **1.5"** all round. Create a new document and notice that the margins for this document are set to 1.5". Change the default initial codes for the margins back to 1" all round.

8   Document appearance

The appearance of a document can be improved by altering text justification and spacing and with the use of indents, tabs and page breaks.

8.1   Text justification

There are four types of justification:

- Left justification - aligns text with the left margin. When a word is too large to fit onto a line it will wrap onto the next line so leaving a gap at the end of the line. Left justified text produces an even left margin and a "ragged" right margin.

- Right justification - produces an even right margin and a "ragged" left margin.

- Centre justification - aligns text evenly between the left and right margin.

- Full justification - aligns text evenly with both the left and right margin.

You can alter the justification of selected text or position the insertion point at the start of a block of text to change the justification from that point onwards. To change justification, either select the justification icon from the ruler and then the appropriate type of justification from the pop-up menu, or select the **Justification** option from the **Layout** menu and then **Left**, **Right**, **Centre** or **Full**.

Alternatively, use one of the following keyboard shortcuts:

Ctrl L	left justification
Ctrl R	right justification
Ctrl J	centre justification
Ctrl F	full justification

8.2   Centring one line

To centre one line at a time pull down the **Layout** menu and select the **Line** option followed by the **Centre** option or press Shift F7 . You may need to press End and ↓ to move past the centre code to type the next line as left justified. As with other formatting features, a code is inserted in the document when you choose to centre text.

To remove centring, press Alt F3 to reveal codes and look for [Just:Centre] if you have selected the centre justification icon on the button bar or [Centre] if you have followed one of the other methods. Position the insertion point in the centre code and press the Delete key.

8.3 Right justifying one line

There may be times when you want to right justify one line at a time - a line of an address, for instance. Position the insertion point at the beginning of the line and select the **Layout** menu and then the **Line, Flush right** options or press Alt F7

To move past the code for right justification and begin typing the next line, press End followed by ↓. To return the line to the default, left justification, remove the code [Flsh Rgt].

⤴ Fonts and alignment

1 Create the following document and save as **CONFER.WP**:

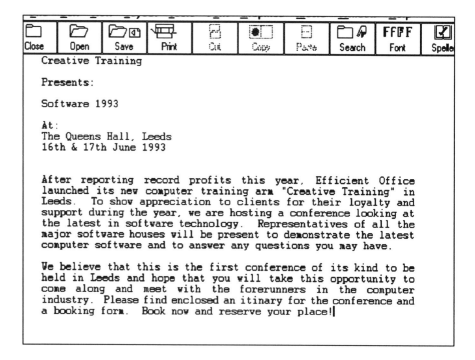

2 Select the **Ruler** option from the **View** menu.

3 Select all the text before the first paragraph.

4 Click and hold the alignment icon on the ruler and select **Centre** from the pull-down menu.

5 Change the document using the formatting options covered in the previous chapter so that it looks like the following example (choose alternative fonts if those specified are not available):

Helvetica, bold, 36 point

Helvetica, 18 point, outline and shadow

Helvetica, 14 point, bold

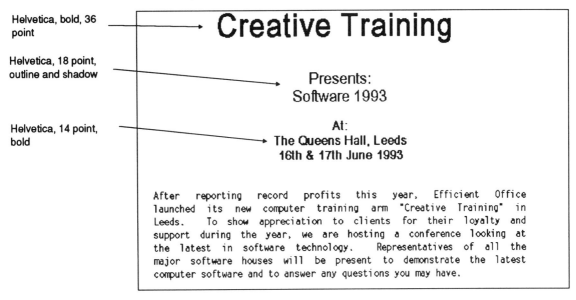

Creative Training

Presents:
Software 1993

At:
The Queens Hall, Leeds
16th & 17th June 1993

After reporting record profits this year, Efficient Office launched its new computer training arm "Creative Training" in Leeds. To show appreciation to clients for their loyalty and support during the year, we are hosting a conference looking at the latest in software technology. Representatives of all the major software houses will be present to demonstrate the latest computer software and to answer any questions you may have.

6 Save the document.

8.4   Line spacing

White space is left between each line of text in the document. The default amount of space is known as *single spacing*. This can be increased to *double spacing*, *triple spacing* etc, or some fraction in between.

To set the spacing, position the cursor at the beginning of the text and select the spacing icon from the ruler. Hold down the mouse button and select the required spacing from the list.

Alternatively, select the **Layout, Line, Spacing** options and, in the **Line spacing** dialog box, type in the required spacing or click the up or down arrow until the required spacing is selected. Line spacing depends very much upon your printer. Some printers may only be capable of printing standard line spacing such as single, double and triple.

⊃ Setting line spacing

1 Position the cursor at the beginning of the paragraph "After reporting record profits...".

2 Select the spacing icon on the ruler and hold down the mouse.

3 Select **1.5** as the spacing. All text from the first paragraph onwards should now appear with 1.5 spacing.

Pre-set tabulation (tab) positions can be set up within a document. Each time the [Tab] key is pressed, the insertion point will move from one tab position to the next. Tab positions help you to line up text in a columnar fashion and are most useful for itineraries or timetables.

You can create four different types of tab position, and each type of tab has a specific effect on the positioning of the text.

- A left tab will push all text to the right of the tab position.

- A right tab will push all text to the left of the tab position, so ensuring that text is right-aligned.

- A centre tab will centre text around the tab position.

- A decimal tab is used for accurately aligning numbers. The decimal points in a list of numbers will line up underneath the tab position.

Each of the above tab icons can be found on the ruler. To display the ruler, select the **Ruler** option from the **View** menu. To the left of the tab icons there is an icon displaying dots. If this icon is used at the same time as a tab, *leader dots* will appear before the tab position. You will notice from the ruler that left tabs have been set at every 0.5 inches along the ruler. These are the default tab settings and will remain in place unless you create new tab settings.

Once tabs have been created, they can be used to produce tables or to indent text.

Setting tabs through the ruler

Place the insertion point in the document at the position where you want new tabs to take effect. If you simply wish to change the position of existing tabs, position the mouse on a tab and drag the tab to a new location. To delete a tab, drag the tab down off the ruler. If you make a mistake, select the **Undo** option from the **Edit** menu.

To insert a new tab, click and drag the tab icon which represents the type of tab to be inserted to the desired location on the ruler.

Leader dots can be inserted before tab positions by clicking on the leader dot icon on the ruler. Tab icons will now display dots. Select the type of tab required and drag to the desired location on the ruler.

Once you have set tab positions on the ruler, press the [Tab] key to move to the first tab position and type the text. Press the [Tab] key a second time to move the insertion point to the second tab position and so on.

Setting tabs through the menu

Setting tabs through the menu gives you a greater degree of control over both the placing and deleting of tabs. Select the **Layout, Line, Tab set** options from the menu to access the **Tab set** dialog box.

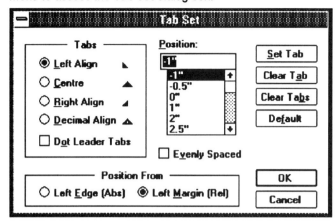

Select the type of tab that you wish to insert from the list of tab types, type the tab position in the **Position** box and click on the **Set tab** button to insert the tab into the **Position** box. You may find that you no longer require tabs at some of the positions set in the **Position** box. If this is the case, simply select the tab position to be deleted and click on the **Clear tab** button.

There are several other useful options available from this dialog box. Click on the **Clear tabs** button to delete all tabs from the ruler or the **Default** button to re-set tab positions back to the default setting of left tabs at every 0.5 inches. If you require tab positions to take effect from the left edge of the paper, select the **Left edge** option; otherwise select the **Left margin** option for tabs to take effect from the left margin.

8.6 Changing tabs

If you set tab positions before you begin to type, you may find that some text is too long to fit within the tab positions set. Before making changes to existing tab positions, complete the table first, making sure that you only press the `Tab` key once between each column of text. In other words, do not press the `Tab` key several times between columns in an effort to get text to line up. Having completed the table, select the entire table and drag the tabs to a new location on the ruler. This way, the entire table will adjust and not just the current row of the table.

If you are unsure as to what tab positions have been set, positioning the insertion point anywhere in the table or outside of the table will display the current tab settings in the ruler. You may wish to access the **Tab set** dialog box and re-set all tabs to the default.

Bullet points can be used in conjunction with tabs to improve the presentation of lists of text. To set a bullet point, select the **WP characters** option from the **Font** menu followed by the **Typographic symbols** option from the **Set** pop-up menu. Select the type of bullet point required. Select the **Insert and close** button to return to the document.

 Using bullet points and tabs

1   Open **CONFER.WP**.

2   Select the **Ruler** option from the **View** menu. Move to the end of the document and press Enter .

3   Access the **Layout** menu and select the **Page, Page break** options or press Ctrl Enter to create a page break.

4   Type "Conference Itinerary" and centre this line.

5   Select the heading "Conference Itinerary" and choose **Bold** from the **Font** menu.

6   With the heading still selected, choose the **Size** option from the **Font** menu and choose **Very large** as the **Size.**

7   Still with the heading selected, access the **Edit** menu and select the **Convert case** option followed by **Uppercase** to change the heading to upper case. Press Enter twice.

8   Press Ctrl L to set left justification and type "Representatives from the following software houses will be present to answer your questions:" and press Enter twice.

9   Press Ctrl W to insert WordPerfect characters and choose the **Typographic symbols** option from the **Set** box.

10 Select the square bullet shape and click on the **Insert and close** button. The bullet should now appear in the document. Press the Tab key and type "Software International".

11 Complete the exercise so that your document resembles the following example.

CONFERENCE ITINERARY

Representatives of the following software houses will be present to answer your questions:

- Software International
- Graphics Incorporated
- T.M.S
- Pentathalon Ltd

---

12 Save the document with the changes.

Using tab positions to create an itinerary

1 Using **CONFER.WP**, move to the end of the what you typed in the previous exercise. Press the Enter key twice and set left aligned tabs at 2.5" and 4.5".

2 Set a decimal tab at 6.5". Drag all other tabs off the ruler.

3 Type the following table, pressing the Tab key after each column and Enter at the end of each line. Do not worry if the lines of the table appear too long at this stage.

Speaker	Company	Subject	Time
Sam Smith	Software Int.	New Products	09.30 a.m.
Tim Elliot	Graphics Inc.	Electronic Mail	11.00 a.m.
Morning Break			11.30 a.m.
Celia Black	T.M.S.	Desktop Publishing	12.00 p.m.
Lunch			1.00 p.m.
Cait Jenkins	Pentathalon Ltd.	Graphic Design	2.00 p.m.
Peter Old	Creative Training	New Directions	3.00 p.m.
Afternoon Break			3.30 p.m.
Forum			4.00 p.m.

4 Select the entire table and pull down the **Font** menu.

5 Select the **Font** option and choose **CG Times [WN][Bold]** or some other suitable font and **12 points**.

6 Select the line containing the headings for the table and apply the same font but 14 points in size.

7 With only the headings still selected, drag the decimal tab off the ruler and replace it with a left aligned tab at 6.5". The table should resemble the example below.

Speaker	Company	Subject	Time
Sam Smith	Software Int.	New products	09.30 a.m.
Tim Elliot	Graphics Inc.	Electronic Mail	11.00 a.m.
Morning Break			11.30 a.m.
Celia Black	T.M.S.	Desktop Publishing	12.00 p.m.
Lunch			1.00 p.m.
Cait Jenkins	Pentathlon Ltd.	Graphic Design	2.00 p.m.
Peter Old	Creative Training	New Directions	3.00 p.m.
Afternoon Break			3.30 p.m.
Forum			4.00 p.m.

8   Save the document with the changes.

8.8   Indenting text

The appearance of a paragraph or group of paragraphs may be improved by indenting text to a particular position on the page. Indents may be applied to the first line of a paragraph or to an entire paragraph. To indent the first line, position the insertion point before the first character in the paragraph and press the `Tab` key. This will move the first character underneath the first tab position in the ruler. To indent the entire paragraph to this position, access the **Layout** menu and select the **Paragraph, Indent** options or press `F7`.

Double indent

You can indent both the left and right margins of the paragraph by the same amount by accessing **Layout** menu and selecting the **Paragraph, Double indent** options or by pressing `Ctrl Shift F7`. If the first tab has been set at 1.5", applying a double indent will indent both the left and right margins of the paragraph by 1.5".

Hanging indent

The first line of a paragraph may also be positioned to the left of the paragraph instead of being indented to the right. This is known as a hanging indent. To set a hanging indent access the **Layout** menu and select the **Paragraph, Hanging indent** options or press `Ctrl F7`. Hanging indents are useful for numbering paragraphs.

After setting a hanging indent you could type a number at the beginning of the paragraph and press the `Tab` key to indent the rest of the paragraph in line with the first tab position.

Margin release

If you wish the first line of the paragraph to begin within the left margin but the rest of the paragraph to line up with the left margin, use the margin release feature. Access the **Layout** menu and select the **Paragraph, Margin release** options or press `Shift Tab`. To return to normal paragraph layout, reveal codes and delete the appropriate codes.

Indenting text

1   Using **CONFER.WP**, position the insertion point on the first character of the first paragraph.

2   Press the `Tab` key to indent the first line to the first tab position at 1.5".

3   Position the insertion point on the first character of the second paragraph and press `Ctrl F7` to create a hanging indent.

4   Use **Reveal codes** to delete the [Tab] code from the first paragraph and the [Indent][Mar Rel] code from the second paragraph. The alignment of the paragraphs should return to normal.

8.9   Inserting dates

To insert a date into a document, position the insertion point where the date is to go and follow the steps below:

● access the **Tools** menu;

● select the **Date** option;

● select **Text** or **Code**.

The **Text** option will insert the current system date into the document. The **Code** option will insert the system date as a code and the date in the document will change as the system date changes. The **Code** option is particularly useful for sending standard letters because the document date will be the date the letter was printed and not the date the letter was created.

The date format can be set by accessing the **Tools** menu and selecting the **Date, Format** options. The **Document date/time format** dialog box will appear.

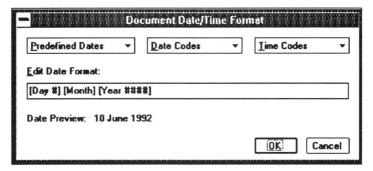

A predefined date format can be selected by clicking and holding the **Predefined dates** button and choosing a format from the pop-up list. Alternatively, date and time codes can be used in conjunction with ordinary text to create a customised format. To create a customised format, click and hold the **Date codes** or **Time codes** button and choose **Codes** from the pop-up lists. A copy of the selected codes will appear in the **Edit date format** box and may be edited using the usual editing keys.

The **Date preview** box provides an example of how the date will be displayed in the document.

⊃ Inserting dates

1   Open **CONFER.WP**.

2   Move to the top of the page containing the conference itinerary. Press the
    ⌷ **Enter** ⌷ key to create a blank line and then move the insertion point to the blank
    line.

3   Select the **Tools** menu followed by the **Date, Format** options.

4   Select the **Predefined dates** button and choose "Thursday, August 27, 1992" as
    an example of the date format required. The codes for this date format will
    appear in the **Edit date format** box. Click the **OK** button.

5   Access the **Tools** menu and select the **Date, Text** options. The current date will
    appear in the document. Select the date and set the font to **Times roman, 10
    points** in size.

6   Select the date with the mouse and then select the **Layout, Line, Flush right**
    options from the menu or press ⌷ **Alt F7** ⌷. The date should now be aligned with
    the right margin. Click away from the selected area.

7   Save the document with the changes.

8.10   Page breaks

When there is more text than can fit on a page, WordPerfect inserts a *soft page
break* represented by a single line across the document screen. The remaining text
will be typed onto the next page (below the line). This is known as a soft page
break because WordPerfect will make adjustments to the position of the page break
as new text is added or existing text removed.

If you want to force a page break at a particular point in a document, position the
insertion point where the page break is to go, pull down the **Layout** menu and

select the **Page** and **Page break** options. The keyboard shortcut is
| Ctrl Enter | . A double line will appear across the document screen.

```
┌─────────────────────────────────────────────────────────────┐
│ ▬        WordPerfect - [c:\wpwin\data\continfo.wp]            │
│ ▭  File  Edit  View  Layout  Tools  Font  Graphics  Macro  Window  Help │
```

into which text and numbers can be entered. The intersection of each column
and row is known as a cell and each cell has a unique address. For example,
the first cell on the spreadsheet will be the intersection of column A and row
1. Its address will therefore be cell A1. Information can be entered into the
spreadsheet which might normally be recorded on paper. For example, you
might record your annual budget or year to date sales figures. The major
advantage of using a spreadsheet is that figures can be easily calculated and
information quickly updated.

Hard (or forced) page break

Word Processors

A word processor is a computer program which replaces the typewriter

A *hard page break* will remain in place no matter what changes are made to the
document. To delete a hard page break, position the insertion point underneath the
double line and before the first character on the page. Press the | **Backspace** |
key. The current page will be indicated on the status bar.

9　Advanced editing

9.1　Preparing for this chapter

In order to complete this chapter you need the following document:

File name	File type	Chapter
CONFER.WP	Document	8

 If you have not created this document in the previous chapters you will need to refer back to the chapter number listed above and create the file.

 If you have purchased the disks that accompany this book you can copy the necessary files from the appropriate floppy disk. To do this complete the following instructions:

1　Make sure you have created a sub-directory on the hard disk called **C:\WPWIN\DATA** (*see* Creating a data directory, page xvi).

2　Load WordPerfect for Windows (*see* Loading WordPerfect for Windows, page xv).

3　Follow the instructions for Using the diskettes on page vii.

9.2　Spell checking a document

WordPerfect will spell check your document for the following errors:

- words which are misspelt

- words which have been repeated

- words which are incorrectly capitalised

- words which have numbers in them

WordPerfect will check each word in a document against the words contained within its own dictionary which is located in the file **WP{WP}UK.LEX**. There are two types of list within the dictionary, a list of commonly used words and a list of main words. It will search through the list of commonly used words first, so reducing the amount of time needed to identify many misspelt words.

Although the WordPerfect dictionary contains approximately 120,000 words there will be many words which are not in the dictionary and which will be identified as misspellings, even though they are not. Alternatively, there will be times when words are correctly spelt but out of context and are not picked up by WordPerfect. For example, in the sentence "I have bean shopping", the word "bean" is correctly spelt but out of context. WordPerfect will not therefore identify it as a misspelling.

To spell check a document or part of a document, position the insertion point at the beginning of the text to be checked or select the relevant portion and then select **Speller** from the **Tools** menu or press Ctrl F1 . The **Speller** dialog box will appear.

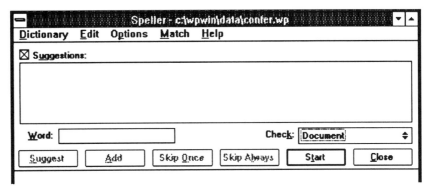

Select the **Check** button and choose the portion of the document to be checked from the pop-up list. You can choose to spell check the following:

- the current word

- the document

- from the current insertion point to the end of the document

- the current page

- from the insertion point to the end of the current page

- selected text

Having decided on the portion of the document to be checked, click the **Start** button. WordPerfect will identify the first word not found in its dictionary. There are several options open to you:

- The **Suggestions** box can be checked so that a list of alternative spellings will appear. Choose an alternative word from the list or edit the word in the **Word** box.

- Clicking the **Suggest** button will produce a list of alternative spellings if the **Suggestions** box has not been selected.

- The **Add** button can be used to add specific words to a supplementary dictionary so that WordPerfect recognises them thereafter as being correctly spelt. Spell checking will frequently highlight people's names and company names as being misspelt because they are not part of a standard dictionary. Add such names to a supplementary dictionary called **WP{WP}UK.SUP** which will also be searched at the time of spell checking.

- The **Replace** button can be used to replace the word in the document with the word in the **Word** box.

- The **Skip once** button instructs WordPerfect to ignore the word this time.

- The **Skip always** button instructs WordPerfect to ignore the word throughout the entire document.

Work your way through each of the words picked out from the document and select from the options listed above. When the spell check is completed, the following dialog box will appear. Click the **OK** button to confirm.

A special dialog box will appear if duplicate words or irregular capitalisation are found. When duplicate words are located you will be prompted to delete the second word, continue without making changes, or *disable checking*. If you choose to disable checking, WordPerfect will continue the spell check but will no longer search for duplicate words. Similar options are presented for irregular capitalisation. You may choose to continue without changing the word, replace the word with a correct form of capitalisation, or disable checking and so prevent WordPerfect from searching for incorrect capitalisation throughout the rest of the document.

Spell check can also be used to check the text in headers and footers, footnotes, endnotes and captions. Simply open the header, footer, footnote box etc before beginning the spell check.

 Spell checking a document

1 Open **CONFER.WP** and position the insertion point at the beginning of the document.

2 Select the **Speller** option from the **Tools** menu.

3 Select the option **To end of document** in the **Check** box.

4 Click the **Start** button.

---

5 The spell check will identify the word "Leeds" as a misspelling and produce a list of suggestions because the **Suggestions** box has been selected.

6 Select **Skip always** so that WordPerfect will ignore the word "Leeds" for the rest of the document.

7 Continue spell checking the document, choosing appropriate options until the spell check is complete. Save the document.

9.3 Using the thesaurus

The WordPerfect thesaurus offers alternative choices for words in your document. To use the thesaurus, position the insertion point within a word and select **Thesaurus** from the **Tools** menu or press ‎ Alt F1 ‎. A **Thesaurus** dialog box similar to the following example will appear.

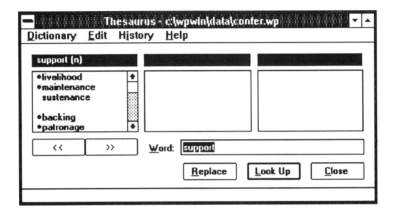

The dialog box is divided into three columns. The first column will display a list of *synonyms* (words with a similar meaning) and *antonyms* (words with the opposite meaning) to the current word in the document. The list of synonyms may be further divided into adjectives (a), nouns (n) and verbs (v).

Words preceded by bullet points are known as *headwords*. By double clicking the mouse on a headword, a list of synonyms for the headword will be displayed in the next column to the right. A pointing hand will appear in the current list to indicate the headword selected.

Alternatively, select a headword and then the **Look up** button. This will replace the current list with a list of synonyms for the headword selected. To return to a previous list of synonyms, access the **History** menu and select the list whose synonyms you wish to display.

Select a word from any list and then click the **Replace** button to replace the word in the document. Otherwise, click the **Close** button to close the thesaurus.

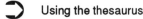 Using the thesaurus

1 Open **CONFER.WP** if it is not already open and position the insertion point in the word "support" in the first paragraph. Press | **Alt F1** |.

2 Select "backing" from the list and click the **Replace** button.

3 Change "demonstrate" to "show".

4 Find alternative words for "reserve" in the second paragraph and "representatives" on the conference itinerary page. Save the document with the changes.

9.4 Searching a document

Having created a long document, you may wish to search for and quickly move to a piece of text, symbol or code in it. For example, you may like to review a company name or date. Before beginning a search, position the insertion point at the start of the document and select the **Search** option from the **Edit** menu or press | **F2** |. The **Search** dialog box will appear.

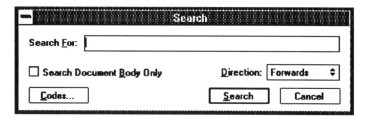

Type the text to be searched for in the **Search for** box and select the **Search** button to begin the search. You can type up to 80 characters which may include single characters, whole words or parts of sentences. WordPerfect will search forwards through the document for the first occurrence of the characters typed. Select the **Direction** button and the **Backwards** option to search backwards through the document from the insertion point.

To search for further occurrences, select the **Search next** option from the **Edit** menu or press | **Shift F2** |. If the *text string* cannot be found, a message will appear briefly to this effect, on the status bar.

Searching for whole words

Although the search feature provides a quick and easy method of moving to a specific part of a document, it can also prove frustrating because it may locate the specified characters in the middle of text other than the text you are searching for. For example, the word "test" will also be found in "testing", "contest", "testify" etc. To get around this problem, you can search for the whole word by pressing the | **Spacebar** | before and after typing the word in the **Search for** box.

Using case sensitivity

To find every occurrence of a set of characters, type the characters in lower case. For example, searching the document for "test" will locate "test", "Test" or "TEST". Characters typed in upper case will only be located if they are upper case in the document. For example, typing "TEST" in the **Search for** box will only locate "TEST" in the document. Similarly, "Test" will only locate "Test".

Special characters and codes

It is possible to search for WordPerfect characters or codes in the **Search** dialog box. To search for a WordPerfect character, move to the **Search for** box and press Ctrl W . Choose the character set and then the special character from the dialog box displayed. Select the **Search** button.

WordPerfect formatting codes can be located throughout a document. Select the **Codes** button and then the appropriate code from the list displayed. Select **Insert** to insert the code in the **Search for** box. For example, if you want to locate every piece of bold text, select the **Bold on** code from the **Codes** dialog box represented below.

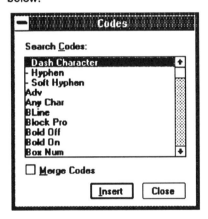

Insert the **[Any Char]** code if you wish to search for a string of characters but are unsure of any one character in the string. For instance, type "Sm" in the **Search for** box, choose the **Codes** button and select **[Any Char]** followed by **Insert**. Finally, type "th" as the last group of characters to search for. The string in the **Search for** box should read:

Sm[Any Char]th

This will search for all occurrences of "Smith", "Smyth" etc.

 Using **Search**

1   Using **CONFER.WP** you will now search for the start of the conference itinerary. Position the insertion point at the start of the document.

2   Select the **Search** option from the **Edit** menu or press F2 . Type **conference** in the **Search for** box and click the **Search** button.

3 The insertion point will jump to the first occurrence of "conference". Press Shift F2 to jump to the next occurrence.

4 Press Shift F2 until "Conference Itinerary" is located.

9.5 Using Search and replace

More often than not, you will wish to search for a piece of text and replace it with another. For example, you may have used a date or company name throughout a document and wish to replace it with a different one.

To carry out a search and replace, position the insertion point at the start of the document. Select **Replace** from the **Edit** menu or press Ctrl F2. The **Search and replace** dialog box will appear.

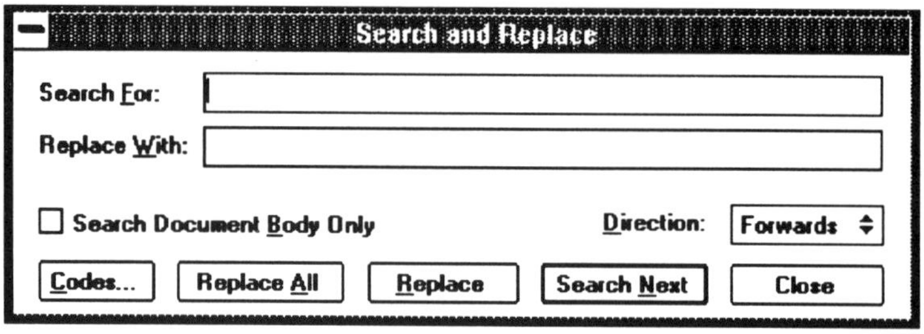
Search and Replace
Search For:
Replace With:
Search Document Body Only
Direction:
Forwards
Codes...
Replace All
Replace
Search Next
Close

Type the characters to be searched for in the **Search for** box and the characters to replace them in the **Replace with** box. To search for the first occurrence, click the **Search next** button. If you wish to replace these characters, click the **Replace** button. If not, click the **Search next** button to search for the next occurrence. Alternatively, click the **Replace all** button to replace every occurrence of the specified characters with the replacement text.

The **Replace all** option can prove disastrous and should only be selected after careful consideration. Let's say, for example, that you are part of a group which organises annual cat shows to raise money for charity. This year you intend to organise a baby show and replace all occurrences of "cat" with "baby" in your standard document. In this instance it would be unwise to use **Replace all** unless you have placed a space before and after the word "cat" because the word "cat" could be found in "catch", "cattle" and so on. These words would then be replaced with "babych" and "babytle". To prevent such a mistake, make sure you save your document first so that you can close the document without saving changes. If you realise your mistake straight away, select the **Undo** option from the **Edit** menu.

Replacing characters follows the same principles as searching for characters. If you wish to search for every occurrence, type the characters in lower case. When replacing the characters though, WordPerfect will try and put the replacement characters in the same case.

One word of warning: be sure to type something in the **Replace with** box otherwise the text to be searched for will be replaced with nothing. You may, of course, wish to do this deliberately to delete specified text from the document. For example, you might wish to use it to delete formatting codes from the document. To do this, click in the **Search for** box and then select the **Codes** button. Select the code to be replaced and then leave the **Replace with** box empty. Select **Replace all** to strip the codes out of the document.

⟳ Removing codes

1   Open **CONFER.WP** if it is not already open and select "Efficient Office". Select the **Italics** option from the **Font** menu.

2   Select "Creative Training" and apply italics. Click away from the selected area.

3   Select the **Replace** option from the **Edit** menu and, with the insertion point in the **Search for** box, select the **Codes** button. A list of codes will appear.

4   Scroll through the list of codes and select **Italic on**.

5   Click the **Insert** button and then the **Close** button. The code **[Italc on]** will appear in the **Search for** box.

6   Leave the **Replace with** box empty and click the **Replace all** button. This will remove italics from all words.

7   Click the **Close** button.

⟳ Using **Search and replace**

1   Using **CONFER.WP** position the insertion point at the beginning of the document.

2   Select the **Replace** option from the **Edit** menu or press ⌷ **Ctrl F2** ⌷. Type **1993** in the **Search for** box and **1992** in the **Replace with** box.

3   Click the **Replace** button. The insertion point will move to the first occurrence. Click the **Replace** button again.

4   Replace any other occurrences of 1993 with 1992.

5   Click the **Close** button when the status bar displays the message "Next occurrence not found" or "String not found".

6   Replace all occurrences of "Leeds" with "London" and save the document.

10   Simple mail merge

The term *mail merge* is usually used to describe the process of merging together a standard letter and a list of names and addresses. In practice, the mail merge capabilities are used for a much wider range of applications including the production of labels, envelopes, invoices and general lists. In this chapter you will concentrate on the mail merge letter and will adapt a general letter that can be merged with a list of customers, providing personalised mailing. In Chapter 14 you will look at further, more advanced, mail merge features.

10.1   Preparing for this chapter

In order to complete this chapter you need the following document:

Filename	File type	Chapter
NEWLETT.WP	Document	2

 If you have not created this document in the previous chapters you will need to refer back to the chapter number listed above and create the file. Please note, this file has been modified in subsequent chapters.

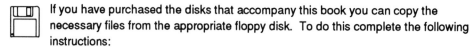 If you have purchased the disks that accompany this book you can copy the necessary files from the appropriate floppy disk. To do this complete the following instructions:

 1   Make sure you have created a sub-directory on the hard disk called **C:\WPWIN\DATA** (*see* Creating a data directory, page xvi).

2   Load WordPerfect for Windows (*see* Loading WordPerfect for Windows, page xv).

3   Follow the instructions for Using the diskettes on page vii.

10.2   Creating a primary merge file

To create a *primary merge file*, you need to enter a set of merge fields into a standard letter. This is achieved by first moving to the position where the *variable field information* is to be inserted. Select the **Merge** option from the **Tools** menu and then select the **Field** option. The **Insert merge code** dialog box will appear.

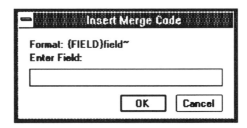

Format: {FIELD}field~
Enter Field:

```
[                              ]
```

```
[   OK   ]    [ Cancel ]
```

Type the name of the field to be used in the **Insert merge code** dialog box. Alternatively, press **Ctrl F12**, select **Field** and type the field name.

You have already created a general letter in Chapter 2. You can now use this as the basis for a primary merge file.

Creating a primary merge file

1   Open the document **NEWLETT.WP**. Edit the date to read 17 April, 1993. To add the customer address block, move the cursor to the end of the date. Press **Enter** twice.

2   Select the **Merge, Field** options from the **Tools** menu and type **Title** in the **Insert merge code** dialog box. Click the **OK** button.

3   Press the **Spacebar** once to leave a space between the title and surname.

4   Press **Ctrl F12**, select the **Field** option and type **Surname** to insert the surname field. Press **Enter**.

5   Type in the remaining fields as shown in following example.

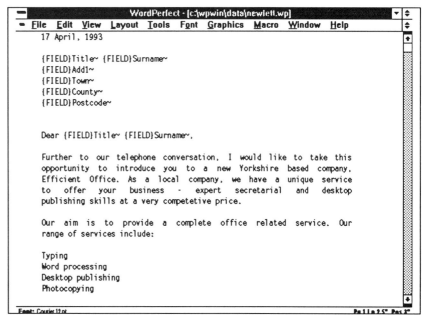

6   Save the file.

A *secondary merge file* is the document containing the names and addresses of the people you want to send the letter to. Each item of information you require for your letter, ie name, address, town, is referred to as a *field*. Each group of fields is termed a *record*. So, if you have 50 clients to write to, you will need to enter 50 records with each record being made up of a series of fields.

Before entering the data for the secondary file it is a good idea to write down all of the field names you require. Having noted the field names, select the **Merge** option from the **Tools** menu. Select the **Merge codes** option followed by the {FIELD NAMES}name1~...nameN~~ option. Click on the **Insert** button.

In the **Merge field name(s)** dialog box, type the name of the field you wish to insert and click on the **Add** button. Click in the **Field name** box and the previous field name should become highlighted. Type the next field name and click the **Add** button.

Repeat the above steps until all field names have been added to the list.

Click the **OK** button and then the **Close** button in the **Insert merge codes** dialog box when the list is complete.

The field names specified will now be displayed across the top of the screen with a page break underneath the list. It is a good idea to have each field name appear on a line of its own so making the document easier to read. Move to the beginning of each field name and press the Enter key to place the field on a separate line, but make sure that at the start of the list you have the {FIELD NAMES} command, that each field name is followed by the tilde character (~), that the last field has two tildes (~~) after the field name and that an {END RECORD} command appears at the end of the list. See the following example:

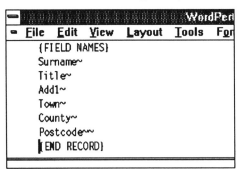

Now that the field names have been identified, the information for each field can be typed into the document. Move the cursor to the line below the page break by pressing Ctrl End. The status bar will indicate which field information to type in. Type the information. It may be as long as several paragraphs or as short as one line. Select the **Merge, End field** options from the **Tools** menu or press Alt Enter to end the information for a field. {END FIELD} will appear after the field name.

The name of the next field will now appear in the status bar. Enter the corresponding information and press $\boxed{\text{Alt Enter}}$ to end the field. Repeat these steps until information has been entered for each field. If a field is to be left blank, you must still press $\boxed{\text{Alt Enter}}$ to end the field.

After the last field information has been entered, press $\boxed{\text{Alt Shift Enter}}$ to end the record or select the **End record** option from the **Tools, Merge** menu. An **{END RECORD}** message will appear, followed by a page break. Complete the next record using the techniques described above.

⊃   Creating the secondary file

1   To create the secondary file, create a new document inserting the following fields:

Surname
Title
Add1
Town
County
Postcode

2   Press $\boxed{\text{Enter}}$ at the end of each of the field names displayed across the top of the screen. Position the insertion point below the page break. Make sure that you do not leave any blank lines. Type in the first record using the following information, remembering to press $\boxed{\text{Alt Enter}}$ at the end of each field. Follow the prompts in the status bar at the bottom of the screen.

Hall
Mr.
20 The Rise
Leeds
West Yorkshire
LS6 8YT

3   To complete the record, press $\boxed{\text{Alt Shift Enter}}$. An **{END RECORD}** message followed by a page break will appear.

4   Enter another record as shown in the following example.

```
       20 The Rise{END FIELD}
       Leeds{END FIELD}
       West Yorkshire{END FIELD}
       LS6 8YT{END RECORD}

       Scribbens{END FIELD}
       Ms.{END FIELD}
       6 The Oaks{END FIELD}
       Bradford{END FIELD}
       West Yorkshire{END FIELD}
       BD12 8PQ{END RECORD}
```

5 Add two more records to the list. Save the list as **CUSTOMER.WP** and close the window.

10.4   Merging the primary and secondary files

Merging the primary and secondary files is a simple task. First, make sure that the primary and secondary files have been saved. Select the **New** option from the **File** menu. Access the **Tools** menu and select the **Merge** option. Select the **Merge** option again and, in the **Merge** dialog box, type the names of the primary and secondary files (including extensions). Click the **OK** button to complete.

Once the " * Merging * " message has disappeared from the bottom of the screen, the merged letter will be displayed. The insertion point will be at the end of the document. Press $\boxed{\textbf{Ctrl Home}}$ to move to the top of the document. Use $\boxed{\textbf{Alt PgUp}}$ and $\boxed{\textbf{Alt PgDn}}$ to move through the letters. The merged document can then be printed in the usual way.

When closing the document or exiting from WordPerfect for Windows select the **No** option for saving unless you want to print the same letters at a later time. Both the primary and secondary files are still on disk and the merge may be carried out again, if required.

Merging the primary and secondary files

1 With a clean document window access the **Tools** menu and select the **Merge, Merge** options.

2 Type **NEWLETT.WP** as the primary filename and **CUSTOMER.WP** as the secondary filename. Click the **OK** button.

3 When merging is complete, print the letters by accessing the **File** menu and selecting the **Print** option. Select the **Full document** option from the **Print** dialog box.

4 Close the document without saving.

11   Consolidation

This last chapter in Part 1 is designed to reinforce a number of the topics covered so far. It is strongly recommended that you complete this exercise before moving on to Part 2. For those working without the disks, it should be noted that **NEWS.WP** will be referred to later in the book.

The aim of this exercise is to create a newsletter which can be enhanced using the features covered in Part 1 of this book. You will continue to work to improve the appearance of the newsletter in Parts 2 and 3.

1   If working with the disks, load **NEWS.WP**.

If working without the disks, close all documents and create a new document. Enter the following information and save the document as **NEWS.WP**.

Creative Training

Happy New Year!

Creative Training would like to thank all customers for their help and support throughout 1993 and wish you all a successful and prosperous 1994.

Staff

Two new members of staff have recently joined the team. Brenda Smithson has taken up the post of Sales and Marketing Director and comes to us with a wealth of experience in these fields. Brenda has spent the last 15 years as the European Marketing Director for Pickson & Co and has acted as a business consultant on the European Business Commission for the last five years. She is also the author of "Women in Business". We are delighted that she has chosen to work with Creative Training and we wish her every success in her new post. Our other new team member is Trudy Lilley who has joined Creative Training in the capacity of Training Co-ordinator. For the past seven years Trudy has been the Administrative Officer in the Information Technology department of our parent company, Efficient Office. She is looking forward to the challenge of her new position.

Awards

**We were very pleased to be given the SPECO award for Outstanding
Customer Service. We are always striving to improve the services on offer
to our clients and in the next quarter we will be asking for your help in
completing a questionnaire.**

Certificates

**We have recently developed a new booking and confirmation system
which will be implemented from the 1st February. Due to customer
demand, we have also introduced a system of certification. Certificates
will be issued to all training customers who attain a specific level of
product knowledge.**

Schedule

**Last year we published a training schedule for the first quarter of 1993.
This proved to be very popular and a schedule will now be produced
quarterly throughout the year.**

New Courses

**In addition to the graphics products which we have recently added to our
training schedule, we are now able to offer training on all Windows
products. We are also in the process of developing a range of general
courses such as Time Management, Presentation Skills and Customer
Care. Do remember, if you have a requirement for training in areas which
do not currently appear on our training list, please give us a call. We will
do our best to accommodate your requirements.**

2   Make all text in the document **Bold**.

3   Spell check the document.

4   Select the title "Creative Training" and set the font to **New Century Schoolbook**
    (or a font of your choice if this is not available), **24 points** in size, **Bold** and **Very
    Large**.

5   Centre the title "Creative Training".

6   Select the text "Happy New Year" and set the font to **ITC Zapf Chancery
    medium italic** (or another font of your choice), **24 points** in size and **Very large**.

7   Change "Smithson" to "Dickinson" and "Pickson & Co" to "Wattles International".

8   Move the **Schedule** paragraph above the **Certificates** paragraph.

9   In the paragraph beginning "Our other new team member" change the "past
    seven years" to "past five years".

10 Alter the last paragraph until it resembles the following example.

```
New Courses

In addition to the graphics products which we have recently
added to our training schedule, we are now able to offer
training on all Windows products.  We are also in the
process of developing a range of general courses.

The following courses will be available from March 1st:

Recruitment Skills
Leadership
Time Management
Customer Care
Presentation Skills
Sales and Marketing
The European Market

If you have a requirement for training in areas which do not
currently appear on our training list, please give us a
call.  Courses can be developed to your specific
requirements given sufficient demand.
```

11 Save the document and check it in **Print preview**. Click the **Next page** or **Previous page** buttons to move between pages of the document in **Print preview**. Close **Print preview** and return to normal document view.

12 Close the document.

13 Select the **Open** option from the **File** menu. Select **NEWS.WP** from the list of files in the current directory and **View** the file. Your screen should be similar to the following example.

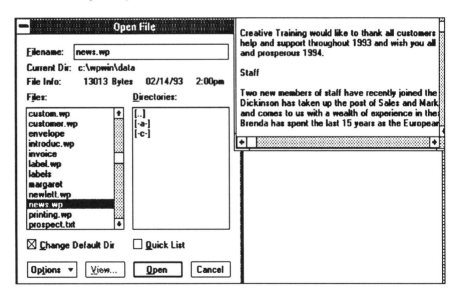

14 Maximise the view of the file until your screen resembles the following example.

Creative Training would like to thank all customers for their
help and support throughout 1993 and wish you all a successful
and prosperous 1994.

Staff

Two new members of staff have recently joined the team. Brenda
Dickinson has taken up the post of Sales and Marketing Director
and comes to us with a wealth of experience in these fields.
Brenda has spent the last 15 years as the European Marketing
Director for Wattles International and has acted as a business
consultant on the European Business Commission for the last five
years. She is also the author of "Women in Business". We are
delighted that she has chosen to work with Creative Training and
we wish her every success in her new post.

Our other new team member is Trudy Lilley who has joined Creative
Training in the capacity of Training Co-ordinator. For the past
five years Trudy has been the Administrative Officer in the
Information Technology department of our parent company,
Efficient Office. She is looking forward to the challenge of her
new position.

Awards

We were very pleased to be given the SPECO award for Outstanding
Customer Service. We are always striving to improve the services

15 Restore the view window to its previous size and copy the document from the
C:\WPWIN\DATA directory to a floppy diskette in drive A.

16 Double underline all headings starting with **Staff**.

17 Set the line spacing to double for the list of new courses.

18 Place a page break before the paragraph on **Certificates**.

19 Insert a table at the bottom of the document using the following as an example.

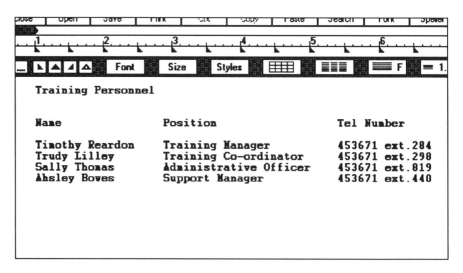

Name	Position	Tel Number
Timothy Reardon	Training Manager	453671 ext.284
Trudy Lilley	Training Co-ordinator	453671 ext.298
Sally Thomas	Administrative Officer	453671 ext.819
Ahsley Boves	Support Manager	453671 ext.440

20 Save and print the full document.

Part 2

Intermediate level

12   Working with large documents

The layout or design of a page is of paramount importance in creating professional documents. This section will cover setting paper size, setting margins, numbering pages, headers, footers and notes. Eventually you will be able to implement these skills to produce desktop published documents.

12.1   Setting paper size

A4 is the standard paper size set at installation. This corresponds to a width of 8.27" and a length of 11.69". If you have selected to print with a WordPerfect printer driver you can change the paper size for each page of the document if you wish. If you have chosen a Windows printer driver then you can only change the paper size for the whole document. Any new settings will be saved with the document.

To set a specific paper size for each new document created, select the **Preferences** option from the **File** menu followed by **Initial codes**. Access the **Layout** menu and select the **Page, Paper size** options.

To set a paper size to be used in a document, position the insertion point on the page where you would like the new size to take effect. Pull down the **Layout** menu and select the **Page** option followed by **Paper size**. Select the option which represents the required paper type, size and orientation, and click the **Select** button. To create your own paper sizes refer to section 13.3.

12.2   Setting margins

A margin is the amount of space between the text and the edge of the paper. Although the text on the screen may appear to start at the top left-hand corner of the page, the line and position codes at the bottom of the screen indicate the amount of margin to be left. Unless you specify otherwise, a standard margin of 1" will be left at the top, bottom, left and right of a document.

Margins will take effect from the current insertion point and will affect all text below. Changes to a left or right margin will take effect from the current paragraph, changes to the top or bottom margin will take effect from the current page onwards. To change margins, select the **Margins** option from the **Layout** menu or press ⸢ **Ctrl F8** ⸥. A dialog box will appear into which you can type new margin specifications.

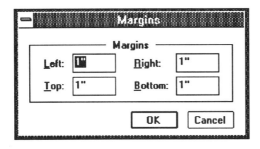

Using the ruler

The left and right margins can also be set on the ruler. Select the **Ruler** option from the **View** menu if it is not already visible.

Left margin marker   Right margin marker

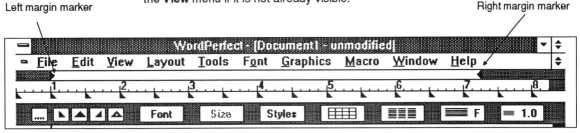

Drag the left and right margin icons to a new position on the ruler.

Margin codes

Changes to the left or right margin can be seen in **Reveal codes** as **[L/R Mar:]**. The colon will be followed by the new margin setting. Changes to the top or bottom margin will be displayed as **[T/B Mar:]** in **Reveal codes**. To delete margin codes, position the insertion point in the region of the document where the changes took place and reveal the codes by pressing $\boxed{\textbf{Alt F3}}$. Move the insertion point into the code to be deleted. The code will become highlighted. Press the $\boxed{\textbf{Delete}}$ key to delete the code.

 Working with long documents

1   Create a new document and type in the following information. Save the document as **CONFINFO.WP**.

Product information

Please find enclosed some general information on the range of software products available.

Spreadsheets

A spreadsheet is primarily used to perform financial calculations. The computer screen represents a piece of paper divided into columns and rows into which text and numbers can be entered. The intersection of each column and row is known as a cell and each cell has a unique address. For example, the first cell on the spreadsheet will be the intersection of column A and row

1. Its address will therefore be cell A1. Information can be entered into the spreadsheet which might normally be recorded on paper. For example, you might record your annual budget or year-to-date sales figures. The major advantage of using a spreadsheet is that figures can be easily calculated and information quickly updated.

Word processors

A word processor is a compuriter program which replaces the typewriter. Information can be quickly entered at the keyboard and changes can be made efficiently. For example, most word processors allow information to be easily moved or copied in the document. Many also have special formatting features which improve the quality of printed material.

Databases

A database is a collection of information. Common examples of databases include telephone directories, library cards and address books. Many businesses use databases to record information such as clients' names and addresses, product codes, stock levels and so on. The advantage of using an electronic database is that information can be quickly recorded, changed and extracted.

Desktop publishing

Traditionally, material to be published would be written by an author, typeset by a typesetter, designed by a designer and printed by a printer. With the introduction of desktop publishing software, all aspects of publishing can be achieved with a 386 or 486 computer and laser printer.

Presentation software

There are several products on the market designed to produce high quality presentation slides and OHPs. You can produce bulleted lists, tables, title slides, charts and drawings. Slides can then be printed, plotted, put onto 35mm slides or presented in a screenshow.

2   Select the **Margins** option from the **Layout** menu. Set the top margin to **2.5"**, the bottom margin to **2"** and the left and right margins to **1.5"**.

3   Position the insertion point at the start of the document and select **CG Times [WN], 12 points** as the font (if this font is not available select a font of your choice).

4   Set the font for the title to **CG Times [WN] 18 points** and **Very large**. Centre the title. Change the format of all subtitles to **CG Times [WN], 14 points** and **Large**.

5   Position the insertion point at the start of the paragraph on spreadsheets. Select the spacing icon from the ruler and choose 1.5 as the spacing. This should affect the entire document from the insertion point onwards. WordPerfect will have inserted an automatic page break as the document will now be too long to fit onto one page.

6   Save the document to include the changes.

12.3 Page numbering

Automatic page numbering can be inserted into a document by positioning the insertion point at the start of the first page where page numbering is to take effect and selecting the **Page, Numbering** options from the **Layout** menu. The **Page numbering** dialog box will appear.

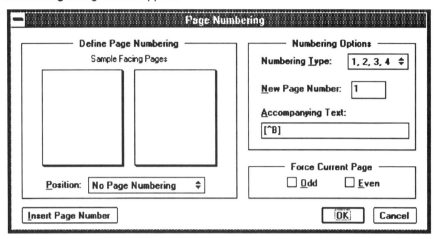

To set an appropriate type of page numbering, click the **Numbering type** button and choose the type of page numbering from the pop-up list. Click the **Position** button and choose the position for the page number from the pop-up list.

The **Sample facing pages** in the **Define page numbering** box will display the type and position of the page numbering chosen. If you want page numbering to begin on a page other than the first page, position the insertion point at the start of the first page to display numbers and follow the steps above. For example, suppose the first few pages are title pages and do not require page numbers, but you want the third page to display page number 1. Move the insertion point to the start of page 3, access the **Layout** menu and select the **Page** followed by **Numbering** options. In the **Page numbering** dialog box, select the numbering type and position, click in the **New page number** box and type **1**. Finally click the **OK** button.

A code representing the page number will appear in the **Accompanying text** box as **[^B]**. If you want the page number to be accompanied by text or any symbols, type them into the **Accompanying text** box in the correct position. For instance, **-[^B]-** will produce **-1-** as the page number.

 Page numbering

1   Position the insertion point at the start of **CONFINFO.WP**.

2   Select the **Page, Numbering** options from the **Layout** menu.

3   Click the **Position** button and select **Bottom centre** from the pop-up menu.

4   Select the **Numbering type** button and **Upper case roman numerals** from the pop-up list.

5 Move to the **Accompanying text** box and type a hyphen either side of the page number code so that the code reads **-[^B] -**.

6 Click the **OK** button and preview the document.

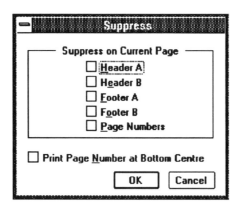

Product Information

Please find enclosed some general information on the range of software products available.

Spreadsheets

A spreadsheet is primarily used to perform financial calculations. The computer screen represents a piece of paper divided into columns and rows into which text and numbers can be entered. The intersection of each column and row is known as a cell and each cell has a unique address. For example, the first cell on the spreadsheet will be the intersection of column A and row 1. Its address will therefore be cell A1. Information can be entered into the spreadsheet which might normally be recorded on paper. For example, you might record your annual budget or year to date sales figures. The major advantage of using a spreadsheet is that figures can be easily calculated and information quickly updated.

Word Processors

A word processor is a computer program which replaces the typewriter. Information can be quickly entered at the keyboard and changes can be made efficiently. For example, most word processors allow information to be easily moved or copied in the document. Many also have special formatting features which improve the quality of printed material.

- 1 -

Page numbers can be entered anywhere in a document by positioning the insertion point and then clicking the **Insert page number** button in the **Page numbering** dialog box. To prevent a page number from being displayed on the current page, select the **Page, Suppress** options from the **Layout** menu and choose **Page numbers** from the **Suppress** dialog box.

A *header* is a piece of text which appears at the top of every page, or of every even or odd page of a document. A *footer* is a piece of text which appears at the bottom of every page of a document. Header or footer text can be as little as a single character or as much as a whole page of text. For most documents, however, one or two lines will be sufficient.

Headers and footers can contain page numbers, dates, graphical lines and boxes and special characters. They can also be formatted using some of the special formatting features covered in earlier sections.

To insert a header or footer, position the insertion point at the start of the page where the first header or footer is to take effect. Select the **Page, Headers** or **Footers** options from the **Layout** menu. A dialog box will appear prompting you to choose to discontinue, edit or create one of two headers or footers, as below.

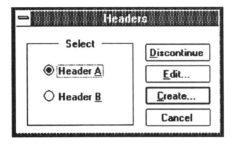

Select **Header A** or **Header B** or **Footer A** or **Footer B** and click the **Create** button. An empty screen will appear with the words "Header" or "Footer" in the title bar as can be seen in the following example.

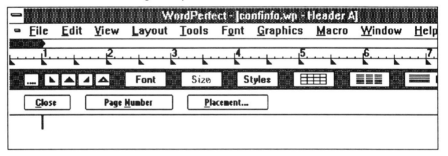

Click the **Placement** button. The **Placement** dialog box will appear.

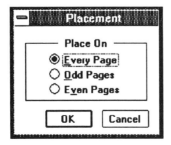

From the **Placement** dialog box, choose to print the header or footer either on every page of the document, or only on odd pages or only on even pages.

Type the header or footer text and select any formatting options from the menu, button bar or ruler in the normal fashion. A page number can be quickly inserted at the insertion point by clicking the **Page number** button. If you insert a page number via the header or footer dialog box, turn off automatic page numbering otherwise you will end up with two page numbers. The date or time can be inserted in the usual way by selecting the **Date, Code** options from the **Tools** menu. Click the **Close** button when the header or footer is complete.

Headers and footers may be turned off from the current page onwards by clicking the **Discontinue** button.

Headers are printed on the first line below the top margin and a line is then left between the header and the main body of text. Similarly, a footer is printed above the bottom margin, with a line of space left between the footer and the bottom of the main body of text.

To reposition headers and footers either change the top and bottom margins or press the ⟦ **Enter** ⟧ key as many times as required after typing the header or before typing the footer, so creating more space between the header or footer and the main body of text.

If headers and footers fail to appear, check that the codes precede any text on the page.

Inserting a header

1 Move to the start of the first page of **CONFINFO.WP** and select the **Page, Headers** options from the **Layout** menu.

2 Select **Header A** and then click the **Create** button.

3 Once into the empty header screen click the **Placement** button and then choose **Odd pages**. Click the **OK** button.

4 Select the **Line, Flush right** options from the **Layout** menu to place text on the right-hand side of the page. Select the font **CG Times [WN]**, **10 points** and **Bold** from the **Font** dialog box. Type **Product information** and press ⟦ **Enter** ⟧.

5 Select the **Line, Horizontal** options from the **Graphics** menu to see the following dialog box.

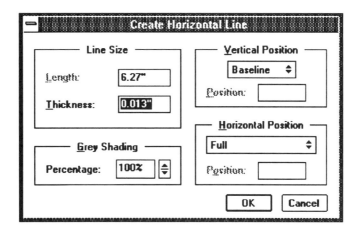

6   Press [Enter] to create a graphic line underneath the heading and click the **Close** button.

7   Follow the steps above but this time create **Header B**. Type **Creative Training** as the header.

8   Change **Header B** to **CG Times [WN]**, **10 points** and **Bold**. Leave the header left justified and press the [Enter] key.

9   Select the **Line, Horizontal** options from the **Graphics** menu and click the **OK** button. Click the **Close** button.

10 Print preview the document.

12.5   Footnotes and endnotes

Footnotes are numbered pieces of text which appear at the bottom of a page and make reference to some text contained on the page. *Endnotes* appear at the end of a document. For example, you may wish to expand upon a particular point without making the extra information part of the main body of text. Creating a footnote or endnote will place a superscripted number in the main body of text and a corresponding number with the additional information at the bottom of the page or document.

Move the insertion point to the part of the document where the footnote or endnote is to be inserted. Access the **Layout** menu and choose **Footnote** or **Endnote** followed by **Create**. The **Footnote** or **Endnote** screen will appear.

The number of the footnote will appear on the screen. Press the [Spacebar], [Tab] or [F7] key to indent the footnote text as required. Type the footnote text and click the **Close** button. As with headers and footers, many of WordPerfect's formatting features can be used along with graphics and WordPerfect characters.

Creating a footnote

1 Using **CONFINFO.WP**, position the cursor at the end of the paragraph on word processing.

2 Select the **Footnote, Create** options from the **Layout** menu.

3 Press F7 to indent the text. Type the footnote displayed in the following example. Format the text to **Times roman**, **8 points** and **Bold** and click on the **Close** button.

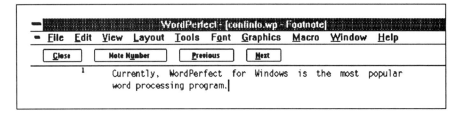

4 Move to the end of the paragraph on presentation software. Select the **Endnote, Create** options from the **Layout** menu.

5 Press the Enter key twice. Press the Tab key and type the following information. Format the text to **Times roman**, **8 points** and **Bold** and click on the **Close** button.

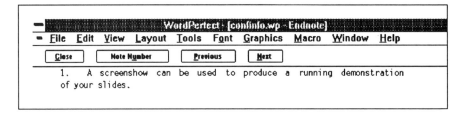

6 Select **Print preview** from the **Print** menu. The first footnote should appear at the bottom of the page containing the paragraph on word processing as illustrated in the following example.

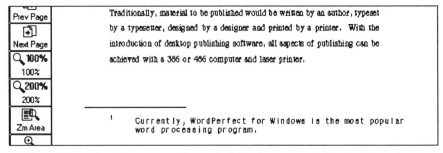

7 The endnote should appear at the end of the document. Click the **Close** button and save the document.

Changing a footnote or endnote

Move the insertion point to the beginning of the page containing the footnote or endnote to be changed. Select the **Footnote** or **Endnote, Edit** options from the **Layout** menu. You will be prompted to enter the number of the note to be changed and then taken to the **Footnote** or **Endnote** screen. Make changes using the usual WordPerfect editing keys and click the **Close** button.

There are several options available in the **Footnote** or **Endnote** screen. Click the **Note number** button if you want to place a copy of the note number in the text. Click the **Previous** button to see the previous note and the **Next** button to see the next note. Make the editing changes and click the **Close** button.

Options

Footnote and endnote options are available to control the type and style of numbering used for the notes, the position of notes and the line spacing within and between notes. Changes to the footnote options will affect new footnotes created from this point onwards.

Select the **Footnote** or **Endnote, Options** commands from the **Layout** menu before creating the note. A dialog box similar to the following will appear.

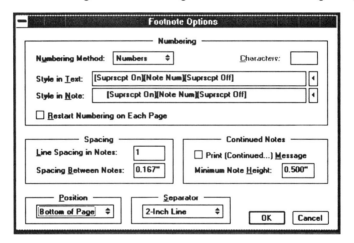

To choose a different type of numbering, click the **Numbering method** option and choose to have numbers, letters or special characters from the pop-up menu. If you choose to mark notes with characters, position the insertion point in the **Characters** box and press Ctrl W to select the type of character required from the **WordPerfect characters** dialog box. Click a character in the **Characters** box and click the **Insert and close** button. If there is still a number in the **Characters** box in the **Footnote options** dialog box, delete it. Click the **OK** button to complete.

The **Style in text** and **Style in note** options control how the number will appear in the main body of the text and in the note. Click in the arrow to the right of the option to see a list of available styles. An example is shown on the following page.

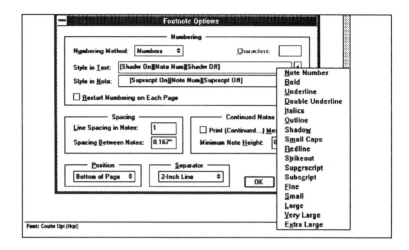

Select new styles from the pop-up list but be careful not to delete the **[Note Num]** code which represents the current note number. If you do delete it by accident, press `Alt Shift Backspace` to bring it back.

Check the **Restart numbering on each page** option if you wish notes numbers to start at 1 on each page, otherwise notes will be numbered sequentially throughout the document. Notes may be positioned to appear at the bottom of a page (this is the default setting) or at the end of a page if there is some space available, by choosing **Bottom of page** or **After text** from the **Position** box.

The **Separator** option displays a **2-inch line** between the main body of text and the note, **No line**, or a line from **Margin to margin**.

1   Using **CONFINFO.WP** create a footnote at the end of the Databases section saying "Refer to reference manual". Change the numbering method of the footnote to letters.

2   Set the line spacing in notes to **1.5**.

3   Set the font of the note to **CG Times [WN], 8 points, Bold**.

4   Position the note after text and set the separator to be a line extending from the left to right margin. Close the document without saving.

Changing the position of notes

Notes can be moved to another location in a document by revealing codes, selecting the number of the note to be moved and pressing the `Delete` key. The insertion point should then be placed at the new location for the note and the **Edit, Undelete, Restore** options chosen from the menu. Notes will be renumbered automatically and printed in sequence.

Deleting notes

To delete a note, look for the **[Footnote]** or **[Endnote]** code in **Reveal codes** and press the `Delete` key. Notes will be re-numbered to take account of this change.

13   Hints and tips for printing

Simple printing options were covered in Part 1 of this book. In this part you will look at more sophisticated features involved in printing such as creating new paper sizes, paper orientation, printing multiple pages and printing double-sided publications.

13.1   Preparing for this chapter

In order to complete this chapter you need the following documents:

Filename	File type	Chapter
NEWLETT.WP	Document	2
PRINTING.WP	Document	4
REPLY.WP	Document	7
CONFER.WP	Document	8

 If you have not created these documents in the previous chapters you will need to refer back to the chapter numbers listed above and create the files. Please note, these files have been modified in subsequent chapters.

 If you have purchased the disks that accompany this book you can copy the necessary files from the appropriate floppy disk. To do this complete the following instructions:

 1 Make sure you have created a sub-directory on the hard disk called **C:\WPWIN\DATA** (*see* Creating a data directory, page xvi).

2 Load WordPerfect for Windows (*see* Loading WordPerfect for Windows, page xv).

3 Follow the instructions for Using the diskettes on page vii.

13.2   Printer drivers

As part of the installation process you are prompted to install one or several printers. To enable WordPerfect to print effectively with each selected printer, special *printer driver files* are installed. Installed printers are then available for selection from the **Select printer** option on the **File** menu.

The font and formatting options available with each printer depend on whether you have chosen to use WordPerfect printer drivers or Windows printer drivers in the **Select printer** dialog box. Generally there will be fewer formatting features available with Windows printer drivers and only one paper size can be set for the whole document.

When you apply formatting changes to a document, the document will be formatted to print with the current printer and formatting information will be saved with the document. If at any time you choose to print the document with a different printer, WordPerfect may have to re-format the document to take account of current printer capabilities.

13.3　Creating paper sizes

If the current printer driver is a WordPerfect driver several different paper sizes may be used within a document. To set a paper size with **Auto code placement** selected, position the insertion point at the point where the new paper size is to take effect and access the **Layout** menu. Choose the **Page** option followed by **Paper size**. If **Auto code placement** has not been selected, the paper size code should be the first code at the start of a page.

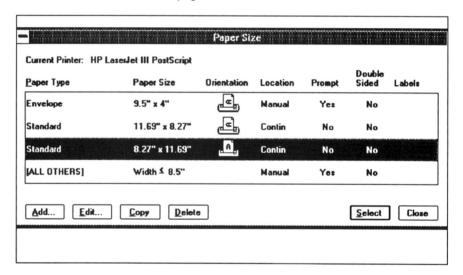

The list of available paper sizes in the **Paper size** dialog box will depend upon the printer currently selected. Click on a paper size (or highlight it using the cursor arrow keys) and click the **Select** button to set the document or part of the document to print on this paper size. If your printer is capable of printing on a paper size not currently in the list, you can add it to the list by clicking the **Add** button in the **Paper size** dialog box. The **Add paper size** dialog box will appear.

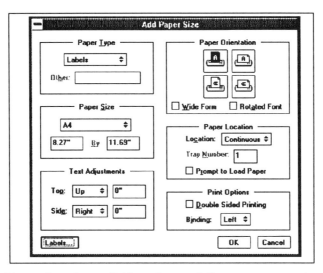

Choose from the available options to define new paper settings.

Paper type

To create a new paper definition, click the **Paper type** button and choose a type of paper from the pop-up list. The selected paper type will appear as the name in the list of available paper sizes. If you want to create a more meaningful name for the paper size, select the **Other** option and type a name in the **Other** box. To define a paper size, click the **Paper size** button and choose a standard size from the list or choose the **Other** option and enter your own specifications for the width and height.

Paper orientation

There are four buttons in the **Add paper size** dialog box (paper orientation section) which represent paper feeding and text orientation. The top left-hand button should be selected if you feed the short edge of the paper into the printer first and want the text to be printed across the short edge of the paper. This is known as *portrait printing*. The top right-hand button should be selected if you normally feed the wide edge of the paper into the printer and want the text to appear from left to right across the widest part of the paper (*landscape printing* - not all printers are capable of this). The bottom left-hand button should be selected if you feed the short edge of the paper in first but want the text to be printed parallel to the widest edge of the paper and the bottom right-hand button should be selected if you feed the wide edge of the paper into the printer and also want the text to be printed parallel to the widest edge of the paper.

If you are using a Windows printer driver you will have to follow a different set of steps. Refer to your Windows manual and Printer: Setup in the WordPerfect reference manual.

Paper location

The **Paper location** option allows you to select how the paper is fed into the printer. Select **Continuous** if your printer uses continuous paper. Select **Manual** if you need to feed each sheet of paper separately into the printer or if you want WordPerfect to prompt you to feed paper into the printer. Select **Bin** if you want paper to be fed into the printer from a different tray to normal. If you select this option you will need to enter the tray number. Check the **Prompt to load paper** option if you want WordPerfect to beep and wait before printing the document. It may be useful to use this option to remind you to load a different type of paper. If this option is left unchecked, printing will begin as soon as the **Print** option is selected from the **Print** dialog box.

Printing options

If your printer is capable of printing on both sides of the paper, you can select the **Double sided printing** option in the **Add paper size** dialog box. You should also select whether an extra margin should be left at the top or left side of the page to take account of binding. The amount of binding space can be set in the **Print** dialog box. If you have selected the **Double sided printing** option, the position of the binding offset may change. For example, the binding offset will be on the right-hand side for a left page and the left-hand side of a right page.

13.4   Editing paper sizes

If you need to change the definition for a particular type of paper, select the paper definition in the **Paper size** box and click the **Edit** button. Make changes as appropriate.

13.5   Using the advance feature

WordPerfect for Windows incorporates a special feature which *advances* the insertion point to an exact location in the current page. This feature is particularly useful if you have to enter text onto pre-printed forms. To use the advance feature, select the **Advance** option from the **Layout** menu. The **Advance** dialog box will be displayed.

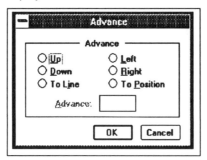

To place text a set distance to the left, right, above or below the current insertion point, choose the appropriate option (**Up**, **Down**, **Left** or **Right**) from the **Advance** dialog box and enter the distance. You may find it useful to display the ruler to gauge distances. For example, if the insertion point was 4" across the page and you choose to advance the insertion point **2"** to the **Right** of the current position, the insertion point would move to the 6" position.

If you choose one of the remaining options, **To line** or **To position**, the insertion point will be placed in an exact location on the page irrespective of the current cursor position. The **To line** option will advance the insertion point a set distance from the top edge of the page. For example, if the **To line** option is set at 2", the top of the next line of text will then be printed 2" down from the top edge of the page.

If you are working with pre-printed forms you may prefer the bottom of the text (known as the *baseline*) to be printed at the 2" position. If so, select the **Typesetting** option from the **Layout** menu and click the **First baseline at top margin** option. Usually the position of the baseline of the first line of text on the page is dependent upon the font set for the text. This means that if different fonts have been set the text baseline might differ from one page to the next. This will then make it difficult for you to use the advance feature to print text at specific locations. By selecting the **First baseline at top margin** option, the baseline of the first line of text will always be printed in line with the top margin.

The **To position** option will advance the insertion point horizontally across the page a set distance from the left edge of the page. To return the insertion point to its original position remove the advance code using **Reveal codes**.

 Adding a paper size for envelopes

1   Standard envelopes have an approximate width of 8.5" and height of 4.3". Text would normally be placed 2" from the top of the envelope and 3" in from the left.

2   Create a new document. Pull down the **File** menu. Select the **Preferences** option followed by **Environment**. Check the **Auto code placement** option if it is not already checked.

3   Pull down the **Layout** menu and select the **Page** option followed by **Paper size**. The **Paper size** dialog box will appear. Click the **Add** button to display the **Add paper size** dialog box.

4   Select **Envelope** as the **Paper type** and **Envelope** as the **Paper size**. The paper orientation will change accordingly.

5   Set the appropriate **Paper location** and click **OK**. This new paper size should be added to the list in the **Paper size** dialog box. Click on the paper size and click the **Select** button. You will be returned to the document screen.

6   To print text 3" in from the left edge of the envelope, pull down the **Layout** menu and select the **Margins** option. Type **3"** as the left margin setting and **0"** as the setting for the other margins. If WordPerfect displays a message saying that the values entered for the margins are invalid, change the margin settings to **0.3"**. WordPerfect will probably change these for you, in which case simply click **OK** to accept each new setting.

7 To advance the text 2" down from the top of the page, access the **Layout** menu and select the **Advance** option. In the **Advance** dialog box select the **To line** option and type **2"** as the measurement. Click the **OK** button.

8 The insertion point should now be in the correct position on the page. Type the following address:
Mr P.K. Hillary
17 The Eves
Jesmond
Newcastle
NN1 6AT

9 Print preview the document. Your document should resemble the example below.

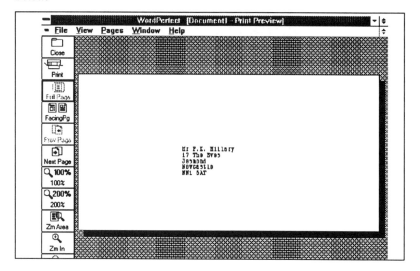

10 Save the document as **ENVELOPE.WP**.

13.6 Printing labels

Once the correct paper size for labels has been set, you may choose to enter the text for each label as a separate item or create a label document as a primary merge file and merge it with names and addresses contained in a secondary merge file. The important thing is to set the correct paper size in the primary file otherwise the information for one label may spill over onto the next label.

There are three steps to creating labels. The first step is to ensure that you have the correct printer selected (the following instructions only apply if you have selected a WordPerfect printer driver). The second step is to create a suitable paper definition and the third step is to position text accurately on each label.

Defining a paper size for labels

To define a paper size for labels in the primary file, select **Document**, **Initial codes** from the **Layout** menu and follow the steps in section 13.3 to add a new paper size. Click the **Paper type** button and select **Labels** as the type.

Complete the information for each option in the dialog box, referring to section 13.3 for explanations of specific options if necessary. Pay particular attention to setting the paper size. If you are printing on an A4 sheet of labels, select **A4** as the **Paper size**. If you are printing onto a continuous sheet of tractor-fed labels (special paper with holes in the side which fits onto rollers and feeds into the printer), select the **Other** option and specify the paper size as the width of the sheet and the height of one label. Click the **Labels** button at the bottom of the **Add paper size** dialog box and complete the **Edit labels** dialog box with information relevant to the type of labels being used.

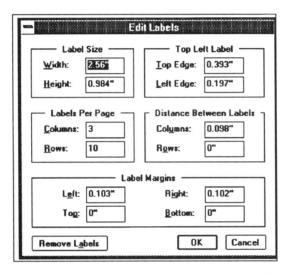

Printing labels can prove time-consuming and fiddly. If you are printing onto standard A4 sheets of labels and you choose an appropriate paper size, location, orientation and so on, then the correct label specifications may have already been entered in the **Edit labels** dialog box by WordPerfect. If, on the other hand, you are printing on non-standard paper or using tractor-fed labels, you may have to measure each label carefully and enter the appropriate information in the **Edit labels** dialog box. Some of the less obvious options are explained below.

With tractor-fed labels it is important to position the labels correctly in the printer. It is a good idea to position the labels, set the label margins to 0" and print a test batch of labels. You should aim for the first character to be printed in the top left-hand corner of the label. If this doesn't work, then move the label in the right direction and try again. The **Label width** and **height** for tractor-fed labels should include the space between columns and rows of labels. For example, if a sheet contains three columns of labels, each 2.5" wide with 1" of space between them, the **Label width** should be entered as **9.5"** (2.5" + 1" + "2.5" + 1" + 2.5"). The **Label height** should be the height of one label plus the distance to the next label down.

On a standard sheet of labels you may have three columns and ten labels per column. These numbers would be entered into the **Column** and **Row** options. If you are using tractor-fed labels the number of rows would be **1**. The **Top edge** of the **Top left label** would be the position of the top of the first label from the top of the page. The **Left edge** would be the distance position of the left edge of each label from the left edge of the paper.

The **Distance between labels** is fairly self-explanatory but if printing onto tractor-fed labels, enter **0** as the distance between both columns and rows as this distance has already been taken account of in the measurement entered for the label width and height.

Positioning text on labels

You can centre each line of text on a label by accessing the **Layout** menu and selecting the **Line** option followed by the **Centre** option before typing text. You can advance the text to a certain position on the label using the options available in the **Advance** dialog box. You can also set margins in the **Edit labels** dialog box to force text away from each edge of a label or position text vertically in the centre of each label by choosing the **Page** and then **Centre page** options from the **Layout** menu. When printing the labels be sure to select the **Full document** or **Multiple pages** options because the **Current page** option will only print a single label.

Creating mailing labels

1   Create a new document. Pull down the **Layout** menu and choose the **Document** and **Initial codes** options. Select the **Layout** menu again and select the **Page** followed by **Paper size** options.

2   Click the **Add** button and, in the **Add paper size** dialog box, select **Labels** as the **Paper type** and **A4** as the **Paper size**. Click the **Labels** button.

3   Enter **3** as the number of **Columns per page** and **10** as the number of **Rows**. Click the **OK** button.

4   In the **Add paper size** dialog box select the **Labels** paper definition and click the **Select** button to return to the document screen.

5   Position the insertion point at the top of the document, pull down the **Layout** menu and select the **Page** option followed by **Centre page** to centre the label text vertically on each label.

6   Save the document as **LABEL.WP**.

13.7   Print options

You have already seen that there are a number of ways to access the **Print** dialog box. You can either select the **Print** option from the **File** menu, press $\boxed{\text{F5}}$ or click on the **Print** button on the button bar.

Multiple pages

The dialog box displays various print options, the default being to print the full document. However, when working with longer documents you may want to print only a selection of pages. To do this, select the **Multiple pages** option and type the numbers of the pages you want to print into the **Multiple pages** dialog box.

There are several techniques available to specify the range of pages to print. Single pages can be specified by typing the page numbers separated by commas. For example, typing **1,7,10** would print only pages **1,7** and **10**. A range of pages can be specified by typing the page numbers separated by hyphens. For example, **2-4 10-14** would print pages **2** through to **4** and pages **10** through to **14**. You can also specify ranges and lists of pages, for example, **1,7,10, 15-20**. Typing **-20 40-** would print pages **1** to **20** and pages **40** to the end of the document.

Printing double-sided documents

If you want to print on both sides of your paper you can print all the even-numbered pages on one side of the paper, turn the paper over and print the odd-numbered pages on the other side. To do this, select **Multiple pages** from the **Print** dialog box and then the **Print** option. From the pop-up list choose to print **Even** pages. When printing is complete, turn the paper over and choose to print **Odd** pages.

Printing a document on disk

You do not have to open a document to print it. You can print the document straight from the disk by selecting the **Document on disk** option from the **Print** dialog box. Click on the **Print** button and type the path and filename of the document to be printed. Alternatively, click on the button next to the **Filename** option and select a filename from the list. Click on the **Print** button to print the full document or specify the pages to print in the **Range** box.

Printing multiple copies

If you need to print multiple copies of a document select an option relating to the amount of the document to be printed and then the **Number of copies** option. Enter the number of required copies and select **Printer** from the **Generated by** pop-up list. If your printer is capable of generating multiple copies by itself then the process will be completed quicker than if WordPerfect has to instruct the printer to print each successive copy separately. Note, this setting will remain in effect until you change it or exit from WordPerfect and you may end up printing unwanted copies of other documents.

Binding offset

If you are intending to have a document bound you may need to allow extra space for the binding, in addition to the amount set for margins. If a binding offset is specified it will usually be added to the left margin of odd-numbered pages and the right margin of even-numbered pages. This amount will then be taken off the opposite margin. The following illustration shows a document with 1" margins all the way around.

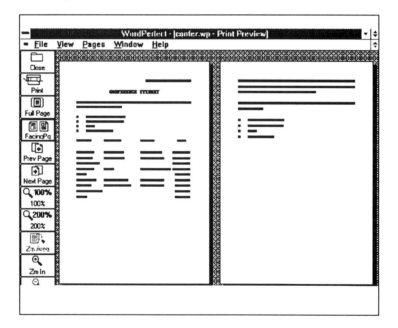

In the following example the same document has a binding offset of 0.5". As you can see, this has been added to the appropriate margin on each page and taken off the opposite margin.

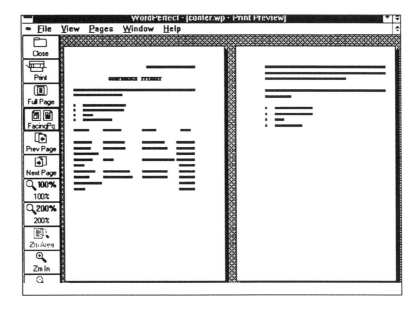

A binding offset may be added to the top margin instead of the left or right margins. To change its location, select the **Binding** button in the **Add paper size** dialog box and then the **Top** option from the pop-up menu.

13.8 Print Manager

When you choose the **Print** option in the **Print** dialog box, WordPerfect sends the information to be printed via the Windows Print Manager. The Print Manager will take control of printing your document, giving you the option to continue editing or using other WordPerfect features. When you first send the document to the printer the **Current print job** dialog box will display information concerning the current print job, such as which page is currently being printed and how many copies. You can click the **Cancel print job** button if you want to cancel the printing operation.

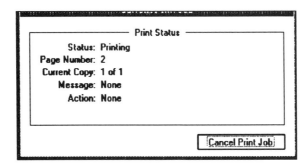

Several documents may be sent to the printer in succession and the Windows Print Manager will then place each of them in a queue. You can access the Print Manager and choose to delete a print job or temporarily pause a print job and then resume printing when ready. You can also prioritise printing by changing the order in which the documents are printed.

To access Print Manager, click in the **Application control** menu (the hyphen to the left of the title bar) and select the **Switch to** option. The **Task list** dialog box will display the applications which have been accessed during the current session and provides a way of accessing frequently used applications quickly.

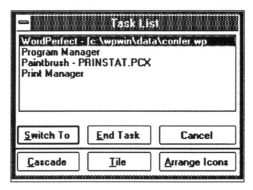

To access an application, select the application from the list and click the **Switch to** button. For example, to access the Windows Print Manager click on **Print Manager** in the task list and then click on the **Switch to** button. If **Print Manager** does not appear in the task list you will need to *switch to* the **Program Manager**, and double click the **Print Manager** icon in the **Main** group of programs. You should then be able to select **Print Manager** from the task list for future print jobs.

The Print Manager screen will vary depending upon the current printing tasks.

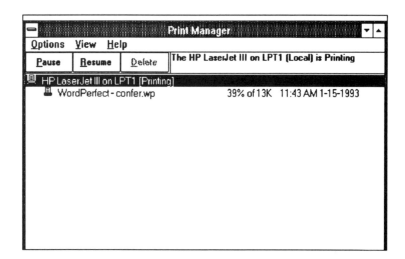

At the top right-hand side of the Print Manager screen you will see information relating to the current printer, the port to which the printer is attached and the printer status. If there is a problem with the printer the word "stalled" will appear. Print Manager will halt the printing process until the error has been rectified and you have clicked the **Resume** button.

Changing print order

The Print Manager screen will also display a list of documents to be printed in order of printing. A printer icon to the left of the document name indicates that a document is currently printing. You can change the order in which the documents print by clicking and holding the mouse on a line containing a print job and dragging the print job to a new location in the list. Alternatively you can select the print job, hold down the $\boxed{\text{Ctrl}}$ key and press the $\boxed{\uparrow}$ or $\boxed{\downarrow}$ arrow keys to move the job in the desired direction.

Cancelling a print job

To cancel a print job, select the line containing the print job information and click on the **Delete** button.

Stopping and starting a print job

Instead of cancelling a print job you may prefer to have a temporary pause and continue printing at a later stage. To do this, select the relevant print job and click on the **Pause** button. The Print Manager will indicate that the job has been paused. Click the **Resume** button when you are ready to continue.

Using **Print Manager**

1 Select the **Print** option from the **File** menu. Select the **Document on disk** option from the **Print** dialog box and then click the **Print** button.

2 The path should already be set to **C:\WPWIN\DATA** so type **PRINTING.WP** as the file to print. If WordPerfect cannot find the file, type the full path and filename or click on the icon to the right of the filename box and choose the file from the list.

3 Click the **Print** button to print the entire document.

4 Repeat the steps above to send the following three files to the printer:
NEWLETT.WP
CONFER.WP
REPLY.WP

5 Access the **Application control** menu and select the **Switch to** option.

6 Select **Print Manager** from the **Task list** box and click the **Switch to** button. If **Print Manager** does not appear in the list, select the **Program Manager** and double click the **Print Manager** icon in the **Main** group of programs.

7 Select the print job for **REPLY.WP**, hold down the mouse button and drag the print job to the top of the list.

8 Select the print job for **CONFER.WP** and click the **Pause** button.

9 Select the print job for **NEWLETT.WP** and click on the **Delete** button.

10 Select the print job for **CONFER.WP** and click on the **Resume** button.

14   Further mail merge features

14.1   Preparing for this chapter

In order to complete this chapter you need the following documents:

Filename	File type	Chapter
INTRODUC.WP	Document	4
CUSTOMER.WP	Document	10
ENVELOPE.WP	Document	13
LABEL.WP	Document	13

 If you have not created these documents in the previous chapters you will need to refer back to the chapter numbers listed above and create the files. Please note, these files have been modified in subsequent chapters.

 If you have purchased the disks that accompany this book you can copy the necessary files from the appropriate floppy disk. To do this complete the following instructions:

 1   Make sure you have created a sub-directory on the hard disk called **C:\WPWIN\DATA** (*see* Creating a data directory, page xvi).

2   Load WordPerfect for Windows (*see* Loading WordPerfect for Windows, page xv).

3   Follow the instructions for Using the diskettes on page vii.

14.2   Mail merge overview

Part 1 examined the steps required to perform a simple mail merge. There are three stages involved in the merging process. The first is to create a standard letter and insert special merge codes throughout the document in place of variable information such as a customer's title, surname and address. This becomes known as the primary merge file, an example of which can be seen on the following page.

```
{FIELD}Title~ {FIELD}Surname~
{FIELD}Add1~
{FIELD}Town~
{FIELD}County~
{FIELD}Postcode~


Dear {FIELD}Title~ {FIELD}Surname~,

Further to our telephone conversation, I would like to take this
opportunity to introduce you to a new Yorkshire based company,
Efficient Office.  As a local company, we have a unique service
to  offer  your  business  -  expert  secretarial  and  desktop
publishing skills at very competitive prices.

Our aim is to provide a complete office related service.   Our
range of services include:

Typing
Word processing
Desktop publishing
Photocopying
```

The second stage is to prepare a document (a secondary merge file) which holds
the information relating to each individual customer or product etc. An example of a
secondary merge file is shown below.

```
{FIELD NAMES}
Surname~
Title~
Add1~
Town~
County~
Postcode~~
{END RECORD}

Hall{END FIELD}
Mr.{END FIELD}
20 The Rise{END FIELD}
Leeds{END FIELD}
West Yorkshire{END FIELD}
LS6 8YT{END RECORD}

Scribbens{END FIELD}
Ms.{END FIELD}
6 The Oaks{END FIELD}
Bradford{END FIELD}
West Yorkshire{END FIELD}
```

The third stage is to create a new document into which the results of the merge can
be placed. When the primary and secondary files are merged, information relating
to a specific customer or product is substituted in place of the merge codes,
resulting in the printing of a set of personalised letters. There is no need to save the
new document once the letters have printed because you can always open another
new document window and perform the merge again if you need to.

```
Mr. Hall                          Ms. Scribbens
20 The Rise                       6 The Oaks
Leeds                             Bradford
West Yorkshire                    West Yorkshire
LS6 8YT                           BD12 8PQ


Dear Mr. Hall,                    Dear Ms. Scribbens,

Further  to  our  telephone  conversati    Further  to  our  telephone  conversati
opportunity  to  introduce  you  to        opportunity  to  introduce  you  to  a
Efficient  Office.  As  a  local  comp      Efficient  Office.  As  a  local  comp
to    offer    your    business   -   ex    to    offer    your    business   -   exp
publishing skills at a very competetiv      publishing skills at a very competetiv

Our  aim  is  to  provide  a  complet       Our  aim  is  to  provide  a  complet
range of services include:                  range of services include:

Typing                                      Typing
Word processing                             Word processing
Desktop publishing                          Desktop publishing
Photocopying                                Photocopying
```

The term mail merge usually describes the process of merging a standard letter and
a list of names and addresses. In practice, mail merge has a much wider range of
applications, including the production of labels, envelopes and specially designed
forms. In this chapter we will look at some of the wider applications of mail merge
and how to improve a mail merge using some of WordPerfect's more sophisticated
features.

14.3   Using merge with envelopes

The general procedure for setting up the primary and secondary files remains the
same but different paper sizes and formats are required for the primary file. For
example, to print customised envelopes you would need to insert the appropriate
paper size codes at the beginning of your primary file and then insert merge codes
where names and addresses should be printed. It may be useful to display the
secondary file on the screen whilst creating the primary file. To do this, close all
open documents and open the secondary file. Select the **New** option from the **File**
menu to open a document window where you can create the primary file. To
display both windows at the same time, select the **Tile** option from the **Window**
menu.

1   Open **CUSTOMER.WP** and familiarise yourself with the merge codes used in
     this file.

2   Open **ENVELOPE.WP** and make this the current file.

3 Select the name and address in **ENVELOPE.WP** and delete it. Because you previously used the **Advance** feature with this document, the insertion point should appear at the correct location for typing the name and address.

4 Access the **Tools** menu and choose the **Merge** option followed by the **Field** option. The **Insert merge code** dialog box will be displayed.

5 Type **Title** into the **Enter field** box and click the **OK** button.

6 Press the Spacebar , pull down the **Tools** menu and select the **Merge** option followed by the **Field** option. Type **Surname** in the **Enter field** box and click the **OK** button. Repeat the above steps until your document resembles the example below. (Note, it is not necessary to use all the merge fields. In this example **County** is not included in the label.)

```
{FIELD}Title~ {FIELD}Surname~
{FIELD}Add1~
{FIELD}Town~
{FIELD}Postcode~
```

7 Save the document with the changes.

8 Create a new document and set the paper size to **Envelope**.

9 Access the **Tools** menu and select the **Merge** option followed by the **Merge** option again. Enter **ENVELOPE.WP** as the primary file and **CUSTOMER.WP** as the secondary file and click the **OK** button.

10 Print preview the document. Your screen should resemble the example below.

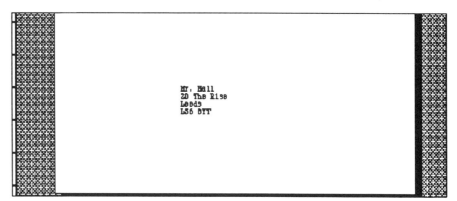

11 Print the document and then close the file without saving.

14.4 Using merge with mailing labels

There is very little difference between creating customised envelopes and creating customised mailing labels. The main difference is in the setting up and formatting of the primary file. As explained in the section on printing labels, the important thing is to create the correct paper definition for the labels being used. You can then enter the merge codes in the appropriate position in the labels document.

1 Open **LABEL.WP** if it is not already open and make it the current document. In a previous exercise you created the following paper definition for this document:

The **Paper type** was set to **Labels.**
The **Paper size** was set to **A4**.
The number of **Columns per page** was set to **3** and the number of **Rows** was set to **10**.
Text was centred vertically on each label.

2 Type the following merge codes (refer to the previous exercise if you are unsure how to do this) and save the document.

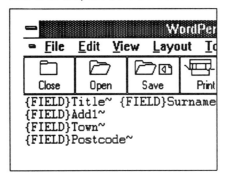

3 Create a new document, access the **Tools** menu and select the **Merge** option followed by the **Merge** option again.

4 Enter **LABEL.WP** as the primary file and **CUSTOMER.WP** as the secondary file.

5 Print preview the document. It should resemble the following example. Close the document without saving the changes.

```
Mr. Hall           Ms. Scribbens      Mrs Wright
20 The Rise        6 The Oaks         18 Oldfield La
Leeds              Bradford           Sheffield
LS6 8YT            BD12 8PQ           SH2 5NJ

Ms. Trinn
8 Albert Oaks
Luton
LU4 1NA
```

To add records into an existing secondary merge file, press Ctrl End to move the insertion point past the last page break. The status bar will indicate which field information to enter. Make sure the insertion point is on the current line - do not leave a blank line underneath the page break. Type the information and press Alt Enter to add the end of field code. Type the information for the remaining fields pressing Alt Enter at the end of each set of field information and Alt Shift Enter at the end of the record. Don't forget to press Alt Enter for every field, even if the field is to be left blank. Save the document to incorporate the new additions.

Adding records

1 Open and make **CUSTOMER.WP** the current file.

2 Press Ctrl End to move the insertion point past the last page break. Move the insertion point to the line below the page break. The status bar will indicate that the **SURNAME** field needs to be entered.

3 Type **Michaels** and press Alt Enter to add the end of field code. Enter the following information, pressing Alt Enter at the end of each set of field information and Alt Shift Enter at the end of the complete record:

Mr.
4b Sycamore Grove
Nottingham
Nottinghamshire
N08 1BY

4 Add four more records, two for people living in Leeds, and two for people living in Nottingham. Save **CUSTOMER.WP** with the changes.

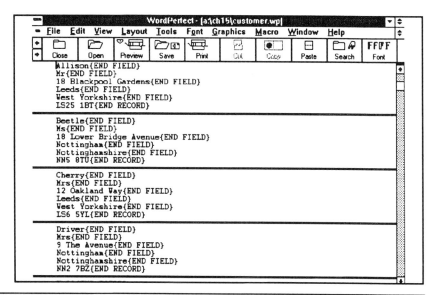

WordPerfect has the capability to sort a document in three ways.

- List - if a document contains a list, WordPerfect can sort the list line by line.

- Paragraph - paragraphs can be sorted into numeric or alphabetic order.

- Secondary merge file - the records of a secondary merge file can be sorted based on any field.

To sort a merge file, access the **Tools** menu and select the **Sort** option. The **Sort** dialog box will appear.

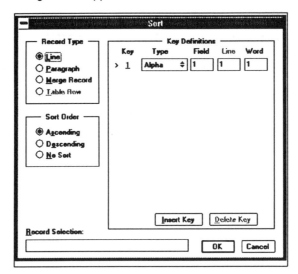

Select the **Merge record** option from the **Record type** box followed by the order in which the records should be sorted from the **Sort order** box. The **Ascending** option will sort the records in alphabetic or numeric order from A to Z or 1 to 10 if there are ten fields. The **Descending** option will sort in reverse order, from Z to A, for example.

In the **Key definitions** area you need to provide more information relating to the type of sort to be performed. Select **Alpha** or **Numeric** as the **Type** of sort (depending on whether the information contained in the field to be sorted is alpha or numeric). Type the number of the field to be sorted in the **Field** box. For example, if you want to sort a file into SURNAME order, type the number that the **SURNAME** field appears in the file. If a field contains more than one line of information, type the number of the line that you want to be sorted in the **Line** box. For example, an address field might contain three lines, one for the street, one for the area and one for the town. You would type **2** into the **Line** box if you wanted to sort the file into area order. A line may also be made up of several words. For example, a name field could contain first name and surname. To sort on surname, the **Word** option would need to be set to **2**. Click the **OK** button when complete.

Up to nine sort keys can be specified by selecting the **Insert key** option. Key **1** is the primary sort key, key **2** is the secondary sort key and so on. For example, if you had a surname and a first name field you could select surname as the primary key with first name as the secondary key. If you had a duplicate surname, for instance Smith, by selecting the first name as the secondary key, David Smith would be listed before Peter Smith.

↪ Sorting a secondary merge file

1 Open **CUSTOMER.WP** if it is not already open and make it the current file.

2 Select the **Sort** option from the **Tools** menu. The **Sort** dialog box will appear.

3 Click the **Merge record** button as the **Record type** and click the **Ascending** button as the **Sort order**.

4 In this example, you will sort the secondary file by **SURNAME**. Move to the **Key definitions** box and complete the entry as follows:

Set the **Type** to **Alpha**.
Set the **Field** number to **1**.
Set the **Line** and **Word** options to **1**.

5 Click the **OK** button to initiate the sort. The records in **CUSTOMER.WP** should now be sorted into alphabetical order based on the **SURNAME** field. See the following example.

```
Add1~
Town~
County~
Postcode~~
{END RECORD}

Allison{END FIELD}
Mr{END FIELD}
18 Blackpool Gardens{END FIELD}
Leeds{END FIELD}
West Yorkshire{END FIELD}
LS25 1BT{END RECORD}

Beetle{END FIELD}
Ms{END FIELD}
18 Lower Bridge Avenue{END FIELD}
Nottingham{END FIELD}
Nottinghamshire{END FIELD}
NN5 8TU{END RECORD}

Cherry{END FIELD}
Mrs{END FIELD}
12 Oakland Way{END FIELD}
Leeds{END FIELD}
```

6 Save the document and close the window.

14.7 Adding and deleting fields

The structure of the secondary file may be amended by adding and deleting fields. To add a new field name, look at the list of {**FIELD NAMES**} at the start of the document and decide where the additional field should be inserted. Move the insertion point after the tilde character (~) at the end of a field name and press the Enter key to start a new line. Type the name of the additional field followed by a tilde character. Save the document to include the changes to the structure and close it.

Open the secondary merge file and, as you move through the existing fields, you will be prompted (in the status bar) to enter the information for each field. The new field name should be included in the prompt at the bottom of the screen. Position the insertion point at the start of the field *below* the new field, type in the information relating to the new field and press Alt Enter to complete the field. Scroll through each record and add new information when appropriate. If the field is to be left empty make sure you press Alt Enter in the appropriate place to prevent information being incorrectly merged. Be sure to save the document when you have finished.

To delete a field from a secondary merge file, delete the name of the field and the tilde character from the list of {**FIELD NAMES**} at the top of the document. Save and close the document and then re-open it. Move through each record and position the insertion point at the start of the information to be deleted. Press Ctrl Delete to delete the current line of information and Delete to delete the blank line. Save the document. If you delete a field from a secondary file make sure that you also delete any reference to the field in the primary file.

 1   Open **CUSTOMER.WP** (the secondary file) and move the insertion point into the {**FIELD NAMES**} at the top of the document. Insert an extra field name "**POSITION**" on the line below **TITLE** as in the following example.

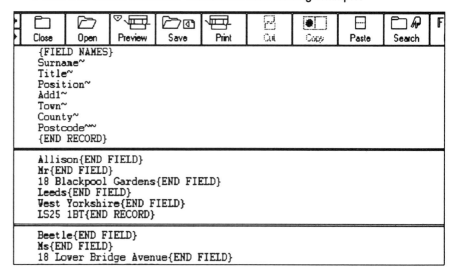

2   Save and close the document.

3   Open **CUSTOMER.WP** again and move the insertion point into the first record. Click the mouse at the start of "18 Blackpool Gardens", type **Managing Director** and press Alt Enter to complete the field.

4   Move into the next record and click the mouse at the start of "18 Lower Bridge Avenue", type **Personal Assistant** and press <u>Alt Enter</u>.

5   Move into the next record, click before the first line of the address, type **Senior Executive** and press <u>Alt Enter</u> to complete the record.

6   Complete job titles for the remaining records except for the last two. Press <u>Alt Enter</u> in the last two records, at the place where the job position should go.

7   Save the document.

8   Open **LABEL.WP** (the primary file) and move the insertion point after the field name **{FIELD}SURNAME~** and press <u>Enter</u>. Access the **Tools** menu and select the **Merge** option followed by the **Field** option.

9   Type **POSITION** in the **Enter field** box and click the **OK** button. Delete the line containing the **{FIELD}POSTCODE~** code and save the document.

10   Create a new document and merge **LABEL.WP** with **CUSTOMER.WP**.

11   Print preview the document and then close without saving changes.

14.8   Eliminating blank lines and fields

You may have noticed that some of the addresses in the previous exercise contained blank lines. This is because the corresponding field in the secondary file was empty. WordPerfect provides several solutions to this type of problem. The easiest solution is to type a question mark (**?**) at the end of a field name but before the tilde character (**~**) in the primary file. This would eliminate a blank line if the field in the secondary file was empty. For example, the following code entered in the primary file would eliminate a blank line if the **TOWN** field in the secondary file was empty.

{FIELD}TOWN?~

1   Open **LABEL.WP**

2   Add a question mark to the end of the **POSITION** field (but before the tilde character) and save the file.

3   Create a new document window and merge **LABEL.WP** with **CUSTOMER.WP**.

4   Print preview the document and make sure that there are no blank lines in the labels.

5   Close the new document without saving.

14.9   Eliminating blank fields

There may be occasions when you need to place several field codes on the same line in a primary merge file and where it is important that any gaps are closed if one of the fields appears empty. In **LABEL.WP** and **ENVELOPE.WP** the first line of the file includes the codes for **TITLE** and **SURNAME**. If the **TITLE** field in the secondary file was blank, a space would appear in the address before the surname. Inserting a question mark at the end of the **TITLE** field would not solve the problem on this occasion because the question mark would eliminate the entire line containing the title and surname. To get around the problem you would have to insert an **{IF}** command into the primary file.

The If command

The **{IF}** command tests to see if certain conditions are met. If they are met then WordPerfect will carry out any commands appearing after the **{IF}** command. If they are not met, the commands appearing after the **{IF}** command will be ignored. There is a special adaptation of the **{IF}** command called the **{IF NOT BLANK}field~** command. If this code is inserted in the primary file WordPerfect will check to see whether a particular field is blank and, if so, what action to take. A typical code might be as follows:

{IF NOT BLANK}title~{FIELD}title~ {END IF}

This can be analysed in three parts.

- **{IF NOT BLANK}title~** instructs WordPerfect to search the **TITLE** field.

- **{FIELD}title~** instructs WordPerfect to insert the contents of the **TITLE** field followed by a space if the condition is met; in other words, if the **TITLE** field contains information.

- **{END IF}** ends the command.

If the **TITLE** field *is* blank, then both the **TITLE** field and the space which follows it will be ignored when printing. To enter this code in the primary document, move the insertion point to where you want the code to appear. Pull down the **Tools** menu and select the **Merge** option followed by **Merge codes**. Select the **{IF NOT BLANK}field~** code from the **Insert merge codes** dialog box and, when prompted, type the name of the field to be tested and click the **OK** button. Enter the information which is to appear if the condition is true. If you want field information to be used, access the **Tools** menu and select the **Merge** and **Field** options to enter the name of the field. Finally, select the **{END IF}** code from the **Insert merge codes** dialog box to mark the end of the code. Add a space after the field tilde character if you want a space to be displayed after the field name.

1 Open **CUSTOMER.WP** and make it the current file. Delete titles from the first two records but leave the **{END FIELD}** code intact. Save the document.

2 Create a new document and merge **LABEL.WP** with **CUSTOMER.WP**. Print preview the results. Notice that a space appears in the first line of the first two addresses where the titles should go. Close the file without saving changes.

3 Open **LABEL.WP** and insert a question mark after the **TITLE** field but before the tilde character. Save the document.

4   Create a new file and merge **LABEL.WP** with **CUSTOMER.WP**. Due to inserting the question mark, the first line of the first two addresses should have been eliminated. Close the document without saving changes.

5   Make **LABEL.WP** the current document and delete the line containing the **TITLE** and **SURNAME** codes.

6   Access the **Tools** menu and select the **Merge** option followed by **Merge codes**. The **Insert merge codes** dialog box will be displayed.

7   Select the **{IF NOT BLANK}field~** code and click the **Insert** button. The following **Insert merge code** dialog box will prompt you to enter the name of the field to be tested.

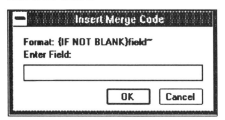

8   Type **TITLE** and click the **OK** button. Select the **Tools** menu and then the **Merge** option followed by the **Field** option. Type **TITLE** and click the **OK** button.

9   Select the **Tools** menu followed by the **Merge** and **Merge codes** options. Select the **{END IF}** code and click the **Insert** button.

10   Access the **Tools** menu and select the **Merge** option followed by the **Field** option. Type **SURNAME** and click the **Close** button. Add a space before the **{END IF}** code. If the **TITLE** field is not blank then WordPerfect will insert the title followed by a space.

11   Save the document and merge **LABEL.WP** with **CUSTOMER.WP** into a new document. Print preview the document. If the **TITLE** field is blank only the surname should appear in the address.

12   Close the document without saving changes.

14.10   Selecting records for a mail merge

If you need to send a letter to a sub-set of records, you can create a new list containing only those records that meet your criteria. For instance, if you need to send a letter to all Sales personnel, you can create a new list document by specifying that field number **3**, the **POSITION** field, must contain the words "Sales".

It is important to remember that WordPerfect actually *deletes* records that do not match the selection criteria. Therefore, the selected records that are the result of the search should always be sent to a new file, leaving the original secondary file intact.

To produce a sub-set of records, select the **Sort** option from the **Tools** menu. The **Sort** dialog box should be completed in much the same way as it would be for a normal sorting operation. Select the **Merge record** option in the **Record type** box, specify the field to be sorted in the **Key definition** box and the order in the **Sort order** box. However, in the **Record selection:** box you will need to specify the criteria to be used in making the sort. In the **Record selection:** box type the number of the field (key) to be tested followed by the *operator* to be used and, finally, the criteria to be searched for. For example, if you were to choose **5** as the number of the field to be searched and **Key1=Leeds** as the **Record selection**, WordPerfect would search the secondary file for all records where field 5 (Town) is equal to Leeds.

There are several operators available:

- = equal to

- <> not equal to

- > greater than

- < less than

- >= greater than or equal to

- <= less than or equal to

So, for example, if you were searching a numeric field you could specify that you were looking for all records where the number was greater than a certain amount by using the greater than > symbol as part of the criteria.

 Producing a sub-set of records

1 Open **INTRODUC.WP** and make it the current file. Edit the document until it resembles the example below.

```
{FIELD}Title~ {FIELD}Surname~
{FIELD}Position~
{FIELD}Add1~
{FIELD}Town~
{FIELD}Postcode~


21st May, 1993


Dear {FIELD}Title~ {FIELD}Surname~,

Further to our recent conversation, I would like to take this opportunity to introduce you to
a new Manchester based company, Future Printing. As a local company, we have a unique
service to offer your business - expert printing and desktop publishing skills at very
competetive prices.

Future Printing's range of services include:
```

2 Save the document as **NOTTING.WP**.

3   Open **CUSTOMER.WP**, access the **Tools** menu and select the **Sort** option.

4   Change the **Key definitions** option for **Key 1** so that the sort field is field **5**, the **TOWN** field.

5   Click in the **Record selection**: box and type **Key1=Nottingham**. The sort screen should resemble the following example.

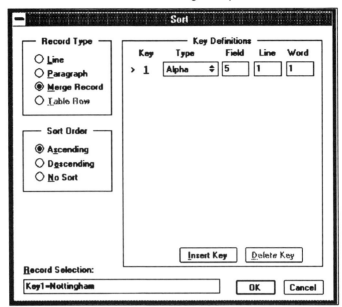

6   Click the **OK** button. WordPerfect should only display records for customers living in Nottingham.

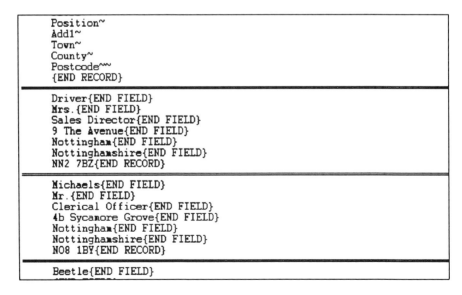

```
     Position~
     Add1~
     Town~
     County~
     Postcode~~
     {END RECORD}

     Driver{END FIELD}
     Mrs.{END FIELD}
     Sales Director{END FIELD}
     9 The Avenue{END FIELD}
     Nottingham{END FIELD}
     Nottinghamshire{END FIELD}
     NN2 7BZ{END RECORD}

     Michaels{END FIELD}
     Mr.{END FIELD}
     Clerical Officer{END FIELD}
     4b Sycamore Grove{END FIELD}
     Nottingham{END FIELD}
     Nottinghamshire{END FIELD}
     NO8 1BY{END RECORD}

     Beetle{END FIELD}
```

7   Select the **Save as** option from the **File** menu and save the file as **NOTTLIST.WP**. Close all files.

15   Tables

The table feature can be used to organise text into columns and rows without having to set tabs. Tables are commonly used to produce invoices, minutes and purchasing requests. The width of columns and the height of rows can be adjusted to improve the layout and appearance of the table.

It is a good idea to sketch the layout of the table on paper and then decide on the number of rows and columns you require. There are two ways to create a table in WordPerfect for Windows; through the ruler or through the menu. Both methods are outlined below.

15.1   Using the ruler

To create a table using the ruler, select the **Ruler** option from the **View** menu and locate the **Table** icon. Point the mouse into the **Table** icon and hold the mouse button down.

WordPerfect will display a table grid consisting of ten rows and ten columns, with the words "No Table" at the top.

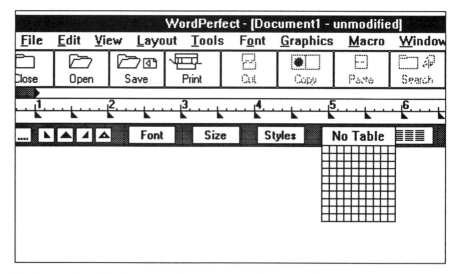

To change the table size, point the mouse into the table grid, hold the mouse button down and drag across and down the grid until the required number of rows and columns become highlighted. Release the mouse button when the required number of columns and rows are displayed in the icon. In the following example, twenty columns and two rows have been selected.

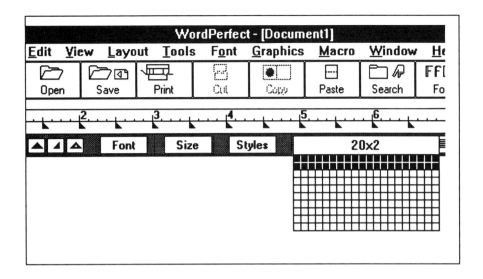

15.2 Using the menu

If using the menu to create the table, access the **Layout** menu and select the **Tables** option followed by the **Create** option. The **Create table** dialog box will appear.

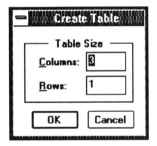

To set the table size, type the number of columns required for the table. Press the Tab key and type the number of rows for the table. Press Enter or click the **OK** button to confirm your choice.

The table will appear with the specified number of columns and rows. It doesn't really matter how many rows and columns you specify at this stage because you can add and delete rows and columns at a later stage if you need to. WordPerfect assigns a letter to each column of the table and a number to each row. The far left column takes the letter **A**, the next column to the right takes the letter **B** and so on. Rows are numbered consecutively. The top row is row number **1**, the next row down is row number **2** and so on.

At the intersection of each column and row is a box known as a *cell*. Each cell has a unique address which appears in the status bar when the insertion point is in it. The cell address is taken from the column letter and row number. For example, the top left cell of a table is cell **A1**, the next cell to the right is cell **B1** and so on.

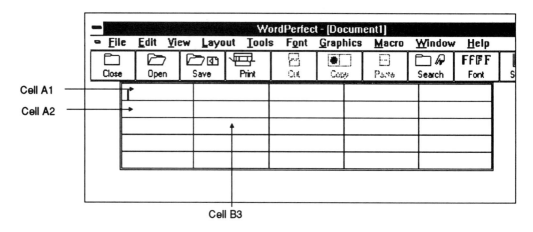

Cell A1

Cell A2

Cell B3

15.3   Moving around a table

The easiest method of moving around a table is to point the mouse I -Beam into a cell and click the left mouse button. The insertion point will then be positioned in the cell ready for you to type. A set of keyboard shortcuts is also available:

Alt ↑ or ↓	to move up or down one row
Alt ← or →	to move one cell to the left or right
Home Home	to move to the first cell in a row
End End	to move to the last cell in a row
Tab	to move one cell at a time through the table
Shift Tab	to move one cell at a time back through the table

Alternatively, with the insertion point somewhere in the table, access the **Edit** menu followed by the **Go to** option or press Ctrl G . The **Go to** dialog box will appear.

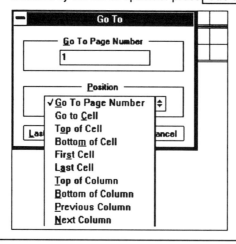

A set of arrows is displayed within the **Position** box. Point and hold the mouse on the arrows to see the areas of the table to which you may quickly move. For example, you may choose to go to the **First cell** in the table.

If you know the address of the cell to which you wish to move, select the **Go to cell** option. The address of the current cell will appear in the **Position** box. Simply overtype this cell address with the one to which you wish to move.

15.4 Entering information into a table

Information may be entered into the table in exactly the same way as in any other part of the document. As you type, text will be inserted into the cell and, if necessary, will wrap onto the next line. The height of the cell will be extended to accommodate extra text. The point at which the text wraps around onto the next line depends upon the width of the column. In the next section you will learn how to change the column width and control text wrap.

If you want to place text on a new line within the cell, press the Enter key. If you press the Enter key by mistake and so create an extra row in the table, simply press the Backspace key.

Creating an invoice for Creative Training

1 Create a new document.

2 Select the **Tables** option from the **Layout** menu or press Ctrl F9 . Select the **Create** option. The **Create table** dialog box will appear.

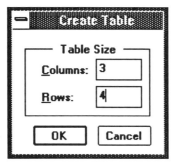

3 Type **3** as the number of columns. Press the Tab key to move the insertion point into the box containing the number of rows and type **4**.

4 Check the status bar at the bottom of the screen. The insertion point should now be in cell **A1**. Type **To:** and press the Enter key eight times to leave enough blank rows into which an address can be typed.

5 Click in cell **B1** and type **Invoice Number:**.

6 Click in cell **A2** and type **Introduction to WordPerfect for Windows** and press the Enter key twice.

7   Type the following information, pressing the $\boxed{\text{Enter}}$ key *twice* after every line of information.

> **2 days at:**
> **Expenses:**
> **Petrol:**
> **Hotel:**
> **Total Expenses:**
> **Invoice Total Excluding VAT:**
> **VAT at 17.5%:**

8   Click in cell **A3** and type **INVOICE TOTAL:**.

9   Click in cell **A4** and type **VAT Registration No: 414 8204 71**.

10 Save the document as **INVOICE**.

11 Select the **Print preview** option from the **File** menu. Click the **Full page** button on the button bar, if not already selected, and then the **Zm in** button to increase the viewing size by 25%. If, on a previous visit to Print preview, you have increased the viewing size by more than 25%, you may have to click the **Zm out** button at this point. Your document should resemble the following example.

To:	Invoice Number:	
Introduction to VordPerfect for Vindovs		
2 days at:		
Expenses:		
Petrol:		
Hotel:		
Total Expenses:		
Invoice Total Excluding VAT:		
VAT at 17.5%		
INVOICE TOTAL:		
VAT Registration No: 414 8204 71		

15.5   Formatting text in a table

Many of the usual formatting techniques can also be applied to text within tables. You can choose the appropriate formatting options from the menu just as you would for text in a standard document. Alternatively, you can position the insertion point in the cell, row or column to be formatted and then pull down the **Layout** menu, select the **Tables** option and then either the **Row**, **Cell** or **Column** option. Depending upon which option you have chosen, a dialog box will appear allowing you to choose appropriate formats.

For example, to enter bold text into the table you can select the **Bold** option from the **Font** menu or press ⌷Ctrl B⌷ before typing the text. To centre text in a table you can pull down the **Layout** menu and then choose the **Line** option followed by the **Centre** option or press ⌷Shift F7⌷. Alternatively, you can make text bold or centred by selecting appropriate options from the **Format cell**, or **Format column** dialog box.

Formatting text in a table

1   Using the document **INVOICE**, select and highlight the text in cell **A1**, access the **Font** menu and choose the **Bold** option.

2   Click the mouse in cell **B1** and pull down the **Layout** menu. Select the **Tables** option followed by the **Cell** option. Check the **Bold** option in the **Format cell** dialog box and click the **OK** button.

3   Click in cell **A3** and format the text in the cell to **Bold**.

4   Save the document.

Formatting text in a column

To format text for a whole column, position the insertion point in the column to be changed, pull down the **Layout** menu and choose the **Tables** option followed by the **Column** option. The **Format column** dialog box will appear.

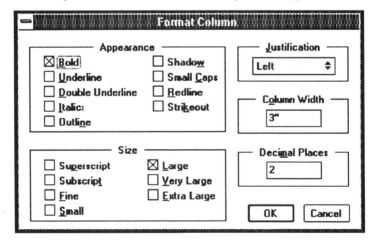

This can be used to change the column width and the appearance, size and justification of text within the current column(s).

Changing the format of text in a column

1   Make sure you have **INVOICE** open and make it the current document.

2 With the insertion point in cell **A1**, pull down the **Layout** menu and select the **Tables** option followed by the **Column** option.

3 Check the **Bold** option in the **Format column** dialog box and click the **OK** button. All of the text in column **A** should now be bold.

4 Save the document.

Formatting cells

The format options for individual cells are similar to those for the entire column. Position the insertion point in a cell, access the **Layout** menu, choose the **Tables** option followed by **Cell**. The **Format cell** dialog box will appear.

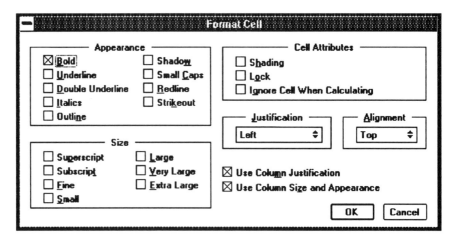

There are several options in this dialog box which combine to offer unique formatting for individual cells. Text may be positioned at the **Top**, **Bottom** or in the **Centre** of a cell by selecting the appropriate option from the **Alignment** pop-up menu and **Left**, **Full**, **Centre** or **Right** justified by selecting the appropriate option from the **Justification** pop-up menu. The **Mixed** option appears when cells of mixed alignment or justification have been selected. A cell or group of cells may be shaded by checking the **Shading** option in the **Cell attributes** box.

There are two special options available within the **Format cell** dialog box. Check the **Use column justification** option if you want the currently selected cells to take on the same justification as the rest of the column and check the **Use column size and appearance** option if you want the text in the currently selected cells to adopt the size and appearance of text in the rest of the column.

Formatting rows

If you position the cursor in a cell and access the **Layout** menu and choose the **Tables** option followed by **Row**, the **Format row** dialog box will appear.

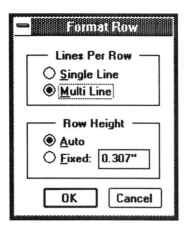

From within this dialog box you can specify that you want **Single** or **Multi** lines per row. If you select the **Single** option, only one line of text will be displayed in the cells in the row. Don't worry if you select this option by mistake, the text will still be there but will not be displayed until the **Multi** option is selected again. If you are typing text into a cell with the **Single** option selected, pressing the Enter key will enter remaining text into the next cell below.

The **Auto** and **Fixed** options control the height of the row. The default setting is **Auto** which means that WordPerfect will determine the height of the row according to the amount of text typed into the cell. If you select the **Fixed** option, you will need to type in a figure representing the height of the cell.

16   Editing tables

    Preparing for this chapter

In order to complete this chapter you need the following document:

Filename	File type	Chapter
INVOICE	Document	15

 If you have not created this document in the previous chapter you will need to refer back to the chapter number listed above and create the file.

 If you have purchased the disks that accompany this book you can copy the necessary files from the appropriate floppy disk. To do this complete the following instructions:

1. Make sure you have created a sub-directory on the hard disk called **C:\WPWIN\DATA** (*see* Creating a data directory, page xvi).

2. Load WordPerfect for Windows (see Loading WordPerfect for Windows, page xv).

3. Follow the instructions for Using the diskettes on page vii.

16.2   Changing table layout

When you first specify the number of columns within a table the columns will be of equal width. It is likely that at some point you will need to adjust the widths of each column or insert extra cells to improve the appearance of the text within the table. Before making changes to a table, it is important to select the cells you want to change first. Once you have selected the appropriate part of the table (individual cells, rows, columns or the entire table), you can then join and split cells, add borders and so on.

Selecting cells, rows and columns

The mouse I-Beam will change shape to an arrow as it approaches the edge of a cell. It will change to a left-pointing arrow if placed near the left edge of a cell, row or column, or an up-pointing arrow if placed near the top edge of a cell, row or column. To select a cell or a row, position the I-Beam at the left edge of a cell so that it changes shape to a left-pointing arrow. Click the mouse once to select the current cell.

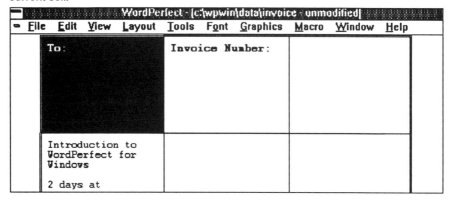

Double click the mouse to select the current row.

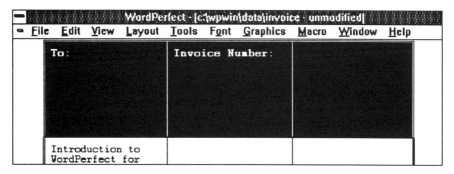

To include more rows in the selection, keep the mouse button held down and drag in the direction of the rows to be included.

To select a column or number of columns, position the I-Beam near to the top edge of a cell until it changes shape to an up-pointing arrow. Click once to select the current cell and twice to select the current column.

Triple click the mouse to select the entire table.

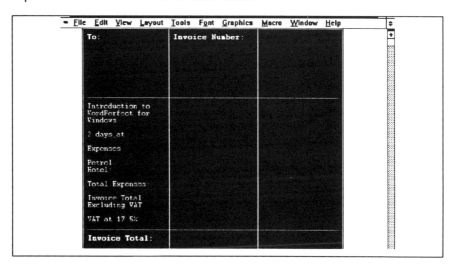

You may find it easier to use the keyboard to select cells. Select a single cell with the mouse and then hold down the | **Shift** | key whilst pressing the | ← |, | → |, | ↑ | or | ↓ | keys to extend the selection to the next cell in the depicted direction. To select a range of cells, click in the first cell to be selected, hold down the | **Shift** | key and click in the last cell to be selected. All cells in between the first and last cell will be included in the selection.

16.3   Changing column widths using the menu

Column widths may be adjusted using the ruler or by pulling down the **Layout** menu and selecting the **Tables** option followed by the **Column** option.

To change column widths accurately, access the **Layout** menu, select the **Tables** option then the **Column** option. The **Format column** dialog box will appear.

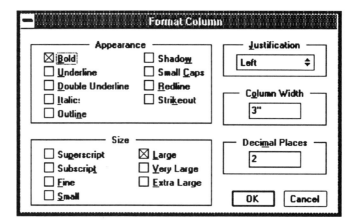

Type the desired column width into the **Column width** box.

1   Using **INVOICE**, position the insertion point in cell **A1**.

2   Access the **Layout** menu.

3   Select the **Tables** option followed by the **Column** option. Click the I-Beam in the **Column width** box and press the | **Delete** | key until all the current figures are deleted.

4   Type **3"** as the column width and click the **OK** button. Your document should resemble the following example.

To:	Invoice Number:	
Introduction to WordPerfect for Windows 2 days at: Expenses: Petrol: Hotel: Total Expenses: Invoice Total Excluding VAT:		

5   Save the document.

16.4   Changing column widths using the ruler

Although it may be more difficult to set column widths accurately using the ruler, the ruler provides the quickest and most visual method.

Select the **Ruler** option from the **View** menu. Triangles representing the start of each column will appear on the ruler. Drag a triangle to a new position on the ruler with the mouse. As you begin to drag the triangle to a new position the status bar will indicate the current position.

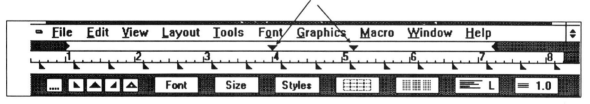

Changing column widths using the ruler

1   Still using **INVOICE**, make sure the ruler is in view. Click in cell **A1** and then locate the triangle for the start of column **B**.

2   Point the mouse into the triangle and drag it to 5.25 inches on the ruler and release the mouse.

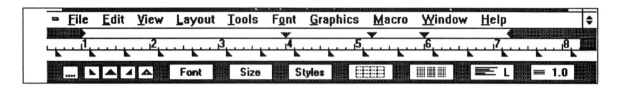

There should now be enough space in column **A** to allow all of the course information to be entered onto the invoice without the text wrapping around onto the next line. (Note that the width of column **B** has now been reduced; this will be adjusted in the next exercise.)

To:	Invoi ce Numbe r:	
Introduction to WordPerfect for Windows 2 days at: Expenses: Petrol: Hotel: Total Expenses:		

16.5   Joining and splitting cells

A group of cells may be joined together to form one single cell. Alternatively, single cells may be split into a number of columns or rows.

To join a group of cells, first select the cells to be joined. Pull down the **Layout** menu and select the **Tables** option followed by the **Join** option. If you join cells containing text, the text in the cells will now be separated by tabs.

To split a group of cells, select the cells to be split. Pull down the **Layout** menu and select the **Tables** option followed by the **Split** option. The **Split column/row** dialog box will appear.

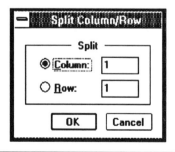

Click the **Column** or **Row** button and type in the number of columns or rows to split the cell into.

⊃ Splitting cells and applying text formats

1 Using the document called **INVOICE**, select cells **B1** and **C1**.

2 Pull down the **Layout** menu, select the **Tables** option followed by the **Join** option. Cells **B1** and **C1** will now be one cell.

3 With the insertion point in cell **B1**, pull down the **Layout** menu, select the **Tables** option and then the **Split** option.

4 In the **Split column/row** dialog box, check the **Row** option.

5 Type **2** as the number of rows into which the cell should be divided and click the **OK** button.

6 Click in cell **B2** and type **Invoice date:**

7 Select cells **B3** and **C3**.

8 Pull down the **Layout** menu and select the **Tables** option followed by the **Join** option.

9 Select cells **B4** and **C4** and join them together.

10 Select cells **A5**, **B5** and **C5** and join them together.

11 Save the document.

16.6 Changing table lines

Each cell of a newly created table will be displayed as a box with lines separating one cell from another. The format of table lines may be altered or lines may be removed from selected cells. Simply select the cells to change, pull down the **Layout** menu and select the **Tables** option followed by the **Lines** option.

The **Table lines** dialog box will appear. By selecting the arrow icons to the right of each box, you can choose the type of line to be displayed on the left, right, top or bottom of the selected cells. The **Outside** option affects the outside border of the selected cells.

⊃ Changing table lines

1 Using **INVOICE**, position the insertion point in cell **A1** and manoeuvre the mouse until it becomes a left-pointing arrow. Triple click the mouse button until the entire table becomes selected (highlighted).

2 Pull down the **Layout** menu and select the **Tables** option followed by **Lines**. Click and hold down the mouse in the **Outside** button and choose the **Thick** option.

3   Click the **OK** button. A thick line should now appear around the outside of the table.

4   Click in cell **A5**. Access the **Layout** menu and select the **Tables** option followed by the **Cell** option.

5   In the **Format cell** dialog box, check the **Shading** option in the **Cell attributes** box.

6   Click the **OK** button. The invoice should now resemble the example below.

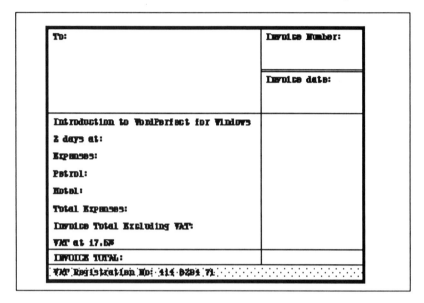

16.7 Inserting rows and columns

In addition to changing column widths, the structure of a table may be altered by adding and removing rows and columns. Additional rows will always be inserted above the current row (the row containing the insertion point) whilst additional columns will be inserted before the current column. The idea is to position the insertion point in a cell, pull down the **Layout** menu, choose the **Tables** option followed by **Insert**. You will be prompted to insert columns or rows and the number by choosing appropriate options in the **Insert columns/rows** dialog box.

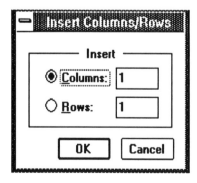

Alternatively, you can press **Alt Insert** for each row that you want to insert above the current row.

If you are inserting extra columns into a table which already extends the full width of the page, the current column will be divided to take account of the extra number of columns.

If you want to extend the table size beyond the current size, access the **Layout** menu, select the **Tables** option and then **Options**. In the **Table options** dialog box, enter the number of columns and rows required. The extra rows will be added to the bottom of the table whilst the columns will be added to the right.

16.8   Deleting rows and columns

Before starting to delete, it is important to make sure that the insertion point is in the correct row or column or that the correct rows or columns have been selected. To remove selected rows or columns, access the **Layout** menu, select the **Tables** option and then the **Delete** option. The **Delete columns/rows** dialog box will appear.

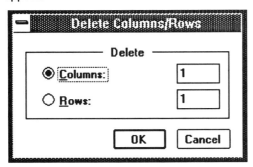

Click the **Columns** or **Rows** button and type the number of columns or rows to be deleted. Click the **OK** button to see the changes in the table. The keyboard shortcut to delete the current row is **Alt Delete**. Think carefully before deleting entire rows and columns. It may be that you simply want to remove the text from the selected cells and leave the structure of the table intact. If this is the case, select the relevant cells and press the **Delete** key. If you make a mistake and want to restore the table to its previous state, select the **Undo** option from the **Edit** menu.

 Inserting and deleting a row

1   Using **INVOICE**, position the insertion point in cell **A3**.

2   Pull down the **Layout** menu and select the **Tables** option followed by the **Insert** option. The **Insert columns/rows** dialog box will appear.

3   Select the **Rows** option and click the **OK** button to insert one extra row above cell **A3**.

4   Type **Course Information:**

5 With the insertion point in the new cell, access the **Layout** menu, select the **Tables** option followed by the **Delete** option. The **Delete columns/rows** dialog box will appear. Choose the **Rows** option and click the **OK** button to delete only the current row.

6 Save the document.

16.9 Deleting tables

It is possible to delete an entire table, delete the table but leave the text intact or delete the text and leave the structure of the table intact. To perform one of these operations, simply select all the cells in the table by positioning the insertion point somewhere within the table and triple clicking the mouse. Then press the Delete key. A dialog box will appear prompting you to make one of the above choices.

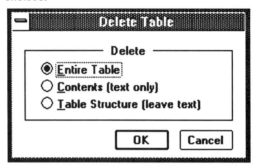

16.10 Consolidation exercise

Creating a training schedule for Creative Training

1 Close any existing files and select **New** from the **File** menu to create a new document.

2 Pull down the **Layout** menu and select the **Tables** option followed by **Create**. Type **4** as the number of columns, press the Tab key and type **15** as the number of rows in the **Create table** dialog box. Click the **OK** button.

3 Position the insertion point in cell **A1** and type **Creative Training Schedule 1993**.

4 Manoeuvre the mouse in cell **A1** until the left-pointing arrow appears. Double click the mouse to select the row and then access the **Layout** menu followed by the **Tables** and **Join** options.

5 With the insertion point still in cell **A1**, pull down the **Layout** menu and select the **Tables** option followed by the **Cell** option. Select the **Bold** , **Shadow** and **Double underline** options from the **Appearance** box in the **Format cell** dialog box, **Very large** from the **Size** box, **Centre** from the **Justification** pop-up menu and **Centre** from the **Alignment** pop-up menu. Click the **OK** button.

6   Select the range of cells **A2** through to **D2** by clicking the left mouse arrow in cell **A2**, holding the Shift key down and clicking again in cell **D2**. Pull down the **Layout** menu and select the **Tables** option followed by the **Lines** option. Click and hold the **Top** button and choose **None** as the option from the pop-up menu. Repeat this action to choose **None** for the **Inside** button.

7   Click in cell **B3** and type **Jan**. Click in cell **C3** and type **Feb**. Click in cell **D3** and type **Mar**. Select the row containing cells **B3** to **D3**, pull down the **Layout** menu, choose the **Tables** option and then the **Join** option.

8   With the insertion point still in cell **B3**, select the **Layout** menu and then the **Tables** option followed by the **Cell** option. In the **Format cell** dialog box, select the **Shading** option from the **Cell attributes** box and the **Bold** and **Small caps** options from the **Appearance** box.

9   Click in cell **A4**, hold down the Shift key and click in cell **A14**. Pull down the **Layout** menu and choose the **Tables** option followed by **Lines**. Choose **None** as the option for **Top** lines, **Bottom** lines and **Inside** lines.

10 Click in cell **A15** and set the **Top** line to **None**.

11 Click in cell **A4** and type **Courses**. Complete the rest of the information as follows:

    A5   **Spreadsheets**
    A6   **Lotus 1-2-3 for Windows**
    A7   **SmartWare II**
    A8   **Excel 4**
    A9   **Word Processing**
    A10 **WordPerfect for Windows**
    A11 **Word for Windows**
    A12 **Ami Pro**

12 Select the **Ruler** option from the **View** menu and drag the first column to the 4" mark on the ruler. Select cell **A4** and set the format for text in the cell to **Bold** and **Very large**.

13 Select cell **A5** and set the format for the text in the cell to **Bold, Italics** and **Large**.

14 Select cell **A9** and set the format for the text in the cell to **Bold, Italics** and **Large**.

15 Set the format to **Bold** and **Fine** text for all the cells containing the course titles.

16 Select cell **A9**, pull down the **Layout** menu and select the **Tables** option followed by **Insert**. Click the **Row** option and click **OK** to create an extra row of space above the current row.

17 Select cells **B9** through to **D9** and set the **Left** and **Inside** lines to **None**.

18 Select cells **A15** and **A16** and delete both rows. Select cells **B14** through to **D14** and set the **Inside** and **Left** lines to **None**.

19 Select cells **B4** to **D4** and set the **Left, Inside** and **Top** lines to **None**.

20 Save the document as **SCHEDULE.WP**. Complete the document until it resembles the following example.

Creative Training Schedule 1993			
	JAN	FEB	MAR
Courses			
Spreadsheet			
Lotus 1-2-3 for Windows			
SmartWare II			
Excel 4			
Word Processing			
WordPerfect for Windows			
Word for Windows			
Ami Pro			

16.11   Copying and moving table information

You can either copy or move the entire table, selected rows or columns or the text only. The idea is to select the cells to be copied or moved and then select the **Cut** (to move information) or **Copy** (to copy information) option from the **Edit** menu. The **Table cut/copy** dialog box will appear.

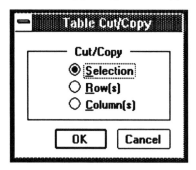

Choose the **Selection** button if you want to copy or move the text, the **Rows** button if you want to copy or move rows and the **Columns** button if you want to copy or move selected columns. Reposition the insertion point and select **Paste** from the **Edit** menu to complete the process.

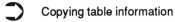 Copying table information

1 Create a new document.

2 Type **Booking Form for Personal Computer Training** and, using the **Font** dialog box, set the font to **New Century Schoolbook bold, 12 points**. Choose the **Outline** option from the **Appearance** box and **Very large** from the **Size** box. Press the ⎢**Enter**⎢key four times.

3 Pull down the **File** menu and select **SCHEDULE.WP** from the list of files at the bottom of the menu. If it does not appear in the list, open it.

4 Click in cell **A3**, hold down the ⎢**Shift**⎢key and click in cell **D14**. Select the **Copy** option from the **Edit** menu. The **Table cut/copy** dialog box will appear. Choose the **Selection** option.

5 Pull down the **Window** menu and select the new document from the list of files.

6 Click underneath the title and select the **Paste** option from the **Edit** menu.

7 Save the document as **BOOKING.WP**. Your document should be similar to the following example.

```
┌─────────────────────────────────────────────────────────────┐
│         Booking Form for Personal Computer Training           │
│                                                               │
│   ┌···························JAN·······FEB·······MAR·······┐   │
│   :                                                       :   │
│   Courses                                                     │
│   Spreadsheet          ┌─────────┬─────────┬─────────┐        │
│   Lotus 1-2-3 for Windows│       │         │         │        │
│   SmartWare II         ├─────────┼─────────┼─────────┤        │
│   Excel 4              ├─────────┼─────────┼─────────┤        │
│                        └─────────┴─────────┴─────────┘        │
│   Word Processing      ┌─────────┬─────────┬─────────┐        │
│   WordPerfect for Windows│       │         │         │        │
│   Word for Windows     ├─────────┼─────────┼─────────┤        │
│   Ami Pro              ├─────────┼─────────┼─────────┤        │
│                        └─────────┴─────────┴─────────┘        │
│ ont: New Century Schoolbook Outline              Pg 1 Ln 1.20"│
└─────────────────────────────────────────────────────────────┘
```

8 Click underneath the title and select the **Ruler** option from the **View** menu. Choose **Courier** from the **Font** button and **Left** alignment from the **Alignment** button. Press ⎢**Enter**⎢and complete the document so that it resembles the following example.

Booking Form for Personal Computer Training

Please complete the following information:

Contact Name:	Date:
Company Name:	Telephone Number:

Please indicate in the appropriate boxes the dates for the
courses you wish to attend and the number of delegates to be
trained. Where possible, please give two choices of dates.

	JAN	FEB	MAR

9   Save and close the document.

16.12   Table options

There are a number of options which can be applied to change the position or
structure of the table. Access the **Layout** menu and select the **Tables** option
followed by the **Options** option. The following dialog box will appear.

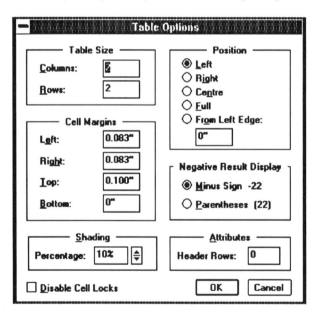

The size of the table (the number of columns and rows) may be adjusted as well as
the position of the table on the page, the margins between cells and the degree of
shading used within a table. For example, click the **Centre** button to centre the
table between the page margins. The **Header rows** option allows you to specify the

number of rows which will be repeated at the top of each page if a table extends over more than one page.

16.13 Drawing lines and boxes

There are several ways to improve a document. Lines and boxes may be added using the following features:

- line draw
- tables
- graphics

Although the line draw facility is somewhat limited, it enables you to draw boxes, graphs, and borders with a selection of ten preset line characters or any character from the WordPerfect character set. Using the arrow keys, you can draw in a new document window or around and over existing text.

There are several things to note about line draw:

- The screen will change to draft mode to enable the lines to appear correctly on the screen.

- WordPerfect will change to typeover mode. This means that if the insertion point is placed before or on text before beginning line draw, the lines will overwrite the text. To avoid complications, type the text first and leave enough space for the lines to go around the text.

- It is important to use a non-proportional font, such as Courier, and left justification.

To use line draw, position the insertion point where line draw is to begin and select **Line draw** from the **Tools** menu or press $\boxed{\textbf{Ctrl D}}$. The following dialog box will appear:

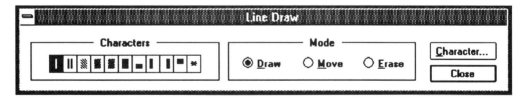

Select a character from the **Line draw** dialog box or click the **Character** button, delete the existing character and press $\boxed{\textbf{Ctrl W}}$ to select a character from one of the character sets listed. After selecting a character from the **WordPerfect characters** dialog box, click the **Insert and close** button. The character will appear in the **Line draw character** dialog box. Click the **OK** button to see it included as one of the characters in the **Line draw** dialog box. Having selected a character to draw with, select **Draw** as the **Mode**. Do not close the **Line draw** dialog box at this stage. Use the cursor movement keys to draw, and click the **Close** button to close the **Line draw** dialog box when finished. If any lines need to be erased, select the **Erase** option and use the arrow keys to indicate what is to be erased. If you need to move the insertion point without drawing, click the **Move** button.

Using line draw

1   Open **BOOKING.WP** and make it the current document.

2   Press [Ctrl End] to move to the end of the document and press [Enter] twice to create two blank lines. Press the [Spacebar] twice and type **Book early to avoid disappointment!**. Position the insertion point to the left of the text and one line above.

3   Press [Ctrl D] to open the **Line draw** dialog box. Select the second line character if not already selected and **Draw** as the **Mode**.

4   Click and hold the mouse in the title bar area of the **Line draw** dialog box and drag the box to a new position on the screen so that you have a clearer view of the work area.

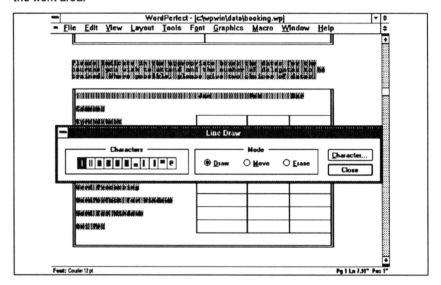

5   Press the [→] key until a line is drawn above and just past the text. Press the [↓] key twice and then press the [←] key until the line reaches the left margin.

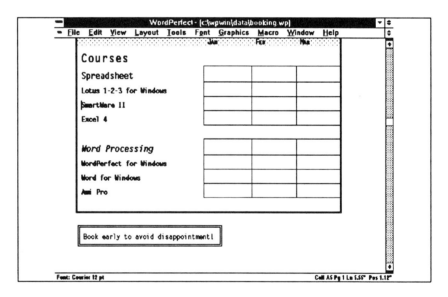

6 Finally, press the $\boxed{\uparrow}$ key until lines join to form a box.

7 Click the **Close** button.

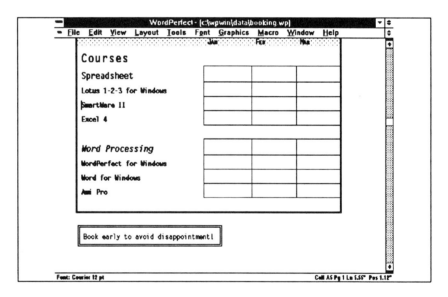

8 Save **BOOKING.WP**.

Quick draw keys

The following keys can be used to draw lines quickly from the insertion point to a margin. Position the insertion point where the line is to begin, press $\boxed{\text{Ctrl D}}$ to open the **Line draw** dialog box, select the character to be used for drawing and **Draw** as the **Mode**. Use the following keys in conjunction with the cursor movement keys to produce lines:

$\boxed{\text{Home}}$ extends to left margin

End	extends to right margin
Ctrl ↓	extends to bottom margin
Ctrl ↑	extends to top margin

 Preparing an organisational chart

1   Prepare a small organisational chart using the line draw facility. The chart should display the hierarchical structure of your group or department. Use the following example if you wish:

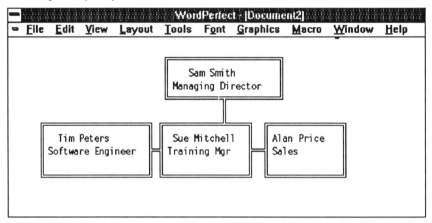

2   Save as **ORG.WP** and close.

16.14   Graphic lines

Graphic lines are commonly used to create lines between columns or to separate paragraphs etc. To be able to print graphic lines you will need to have a graphics printer.

Place the insertion point where you want the line to begin. Select the **Line** option from the **Graphics** menu followed by **Horizontal** or **Vertical** depending upon whether you want to create a horizontal or vertical line. A dialog box will appear as in the following example.

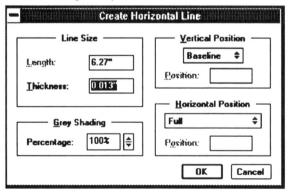

Specify the thickness of the line by typing a unit of measurement into the **Thickness** box and the shading of the line by entering a figure between 0 and 100. 0 represents white and 100 represents black.

Select the **Horizontal position** button and choose whether you want the line to be drawn from the insertion point to the **Left** margin or **Right** margin, to be **Centred** between the margins or to extend **Full** from one margin to the other.

Select the **Specify** option from the **Position** box to specify in inches the position at which the line should begin from the edge of the paper.

Select the **Vertical position** button if you want the line to be drawn from a position other than the current insertion point. Choosing the **Specify** option allows you to enter the position in inches from the top of the paper at which the line should begin. If you choose the **Baseline** option, a line will be drawn along the same line as the current insertion point.

 Using graphic lines

1 Open **ORG.WP** and make it current.

2 Position the cursor above the top box and press ⎡ **Enter** ⎤ four times. Type **Creative Training Organisational Chart** as the title at the top of the page.

3 **Centre** the title and make it **Bold** and **Very large**.

4 Position the insertion point two lines below the title.

5 Access the **Graphics** menu and select the **Line** option followed by the **Horizontal** option as in the following example:

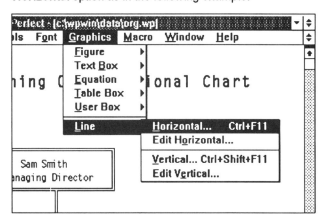

6 Select **Baseline** as the **Vertical** position and **Centre** as the **Horizontal** position in the **Create horizontal line** dialog box. Click the **OK** button.

7 Save the document.

17   Using the maths facilities

WordPerfect has an in-built maths facility enabling you to create formulae based upon values held in a table.

17.1   Preparing for this chapter

In order to complete this chapter you need the following document:

Filename	File type	Chapter
INVOICE	Document	15

 If you have not created this document in the previous chapters you will need to refer back to the chapter number listed above and create the file. Please note, this file has been modified in subsequent chapters.

 If you have purchased the disks that accompany this book you can copy the necessary files from the appropriate floppy disk. To do this complete the following instructions:

1 Make sure you have created a sub-directory on the hard disk called **C:\WPWIN\DATA** (*see* Creating a data directory, page xvi).

2 Load WordPerfect for Windows (*see* Loading WordPerfect for Windows, page xv).

3 Follow the instructions for Using the diskettes on page vii.

17.2   Creating formulae

As we have seen, each element of a table is referred to as a cell. Each cell can be identified by what is termed a cell address. This address is made up of the row and column co-ordinate. Rows are labelled by numbers 1, 2, 3 etc and columns by letters A, B, C etc. The first cell in a table is cell **A1**. The cell to its right is cell **B1** and the cell below is cell **A2**.

Formulae can be entered into any cell and may consist of numbers and cell addresses. For example, to add the figure in cell **A1** to the figure in cell **A2** and place the total in cell **A3**, you would position the insertion point in cell **A3**, pull down the **Layout** menu and select the **Tables** option followed by the **Formula** option. The **Tables formula** dialog box would then appear.

You would then enter the formula **A1 + A2** into the **Formula** box in the **Tables formula** dialog box. The **To cell** option in the **Copy formula** box will display the cell address of the cell where the result is to go (in this example, cell **A3**). Similarly, to multiply the figure in cell **D1** by 10% and place the result in cell **E1** you would move the insertion point into cell **E1**, access the **Layout** menu, select the **Tables** option followed by the **Formula** option and type the formula **D1 * 0.1** into the **Formula** box. When the formula is complete, you would need to click the **OK** button to place the result into the selected cell.

There are a number of mathematical operators which can be used in creating formulae:

+	addition
-	subtraction
/	division
*	multiplication

In addition to the usual operators listed above, parentheses (brackets) can be placed around any part of the formula to force WordPerfect to perform a particular part of the formula first. For example, let us suppose that you have created a table containing the following cells and figures:

A1	20
A2	10
A3	3

To calculate the contents of cell **A1** minus cell **A2**, multiplied by cell **A3** and place the results in cell **A4** you would position the insertion point in cell A4 and type **A1-A2*A3** into the **Tables formula** dialog box. WordPerfect would calculate this as 20-10 which equals 10 and then multiply 10 by 3 to give a result of 30 in cell A4. However, if you were to place parentheses around the latter part of the formula so that it read **A1-(A2*A3)**, WordPerfect would calculate the latter part of the formula first, resulting in a very different calculation. Using the figures in the previous example, WordPerfect would multiply 10 by 3 which results in 30 and then take 30 from 20, resulting in minus 10.

 In this exercise you will practise using the maths facility with **INVOICE**. This exercise will also consolidate topics covered in earlier sections, namely splitting cells, deleting rows and changing table lines.

1   Open **INVOICE** if it is not already open and make it the current document. Click in cells **A3** and **B3**, pull down the **Layout** menu and select the **Tables** option followed by the **Split** option. The **Split column/row** dialog box will appear. Select the **Row** option and type **16** as the number of rows. Click the **OK** button.

2   Click in cell **A4**, hold down the Shift key and click in cell **A18**. Select the **Layout** menu followed by the **Tables** and then **Lines** options. Set the **Left** lines to **Thick**, the **Top**, **Inside**, **Right** and **Bottom** lines to **None** and the **Outside** should be **Mixed**. If you make a mistake, select the **Undo** option from the **Edit** menu.

3   Select cells **B4** through to **B10**. Set the **Left** lines to **Single**, the **Top**, **Bottom** and **Inside** lines to **None**.

4   Click in cell **A4**, access the **Layout** menu and select the **Tables** option followed by **Delete**. Select to delete **Rows** and click the **OK** button.

5   Delete all blank rows.

6   Edit cell **A4** to read **2 days at: £300**.

7   Type **£600** in cell **B4**, **£50** in cell **B6** and **£100** in cell **B7**.

8   Move the insertion point into cell **B8**. Access the **Layout** menu followed by the **Tables** and **Formula** options. Type the formula **B6+B7** into the **Tables formula** dialog box.

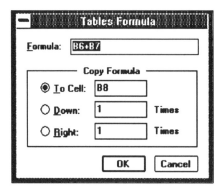

9   Click the **OK** button. The result of the formula (150.00) will appear in the table whilst the formula will be displayed in the status bar. Type a **£** sign in front of the first character of the result.

10 Save the document.

There are special formulas known as *functions* available for calculating sub-totals, totals and grand totals quickly and efficiently. The procedure outlined above still applies. Position the insertion point in the cell to contain the result, access the **Layout** menu and select the **Tables** option and then the **Formula** option. To calculate a sub-total, type a plus symbol (+) in the **Tables formula** dialog box. WordPerfect will add together the figures in the preceding cells.

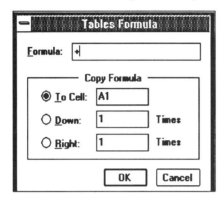

To produce a total, type an equal symbol (=) in the **Tables formula** dialog box. WordPerfect will add together all cells above the current cell which contain sub-totals until it reaches a cell containing another function.

To produce an overall total, type an asterisk (*). WordPerfect will add together all totals to make a grand total.

It is wise to check your calculations manually at first to make sure that you are creating an accurate formula. For example, if you are using the sub-total function all cells above the current cell are going to be taken to be part of the sub-total and it may be that you do not want include all cells in the calculation. WordPerfect will also include numbers from cells containing dates, invoice numbers, references etc if those cells are referenced in formulae.

 Further maths using **INVOICE**.

1   Open **INVOICE** if it is not already open and make it the current document.

2   Click in cell **B9**, pull down the **Layout** menu and select the **Tables** option followed by the **Formula** option. Type **B4+B8** as the **Formula** and click the **OK** button. Type a £ symbol before the first character of the number.

3   Click in cell **B10** and enter the formula **B9*17.5/100** to calculate the VAT payable. The result should be **131.25**. Type a £ symbol before the first character.

4   Click in cell **B11** and enter the formula **B9-B10**. The result should be **615.75**. Again, enter a £ symbol in the appropriate place.

5   Save the document.

6   To calculate the expenses using the special sub-total function you would need to instruct WordPerfect to ignore cell **B4** when calculating. Click in cell **B4**, access the **Layout** menu and select the **Tables** option followed by the **Cell** option. Check the **Ignore cell when calculating** option in the **Cell attributes** box and click the **OK** button.

7   Select the figure in cell **B8** and press the ⎾ **Delete** ⏌key to delete it. Enter a **+** symbol as the new formula in the **Tables formula** dialog box.

8   Do not save the document.

17.4   Re-calculating formulae

Formulae can be re-calculated if the figures in the cells change. Move the cursor into the table, access the **Layout** menu and select the **Tables** option followed by the **Calculate** option. The cells containing formulae should then update to take account of any changes.

 Re-calculating formulae

1   Using **INVOICE**, position the insertion point within the table.

2   Access the **Layout** menu and select the **Tables** option followed by the **Calculate** option. You should find that the some cells now contain two question marks (**??**). This is because cell **B4** is referenced in formulae and yet you have instructed WordPerfect to ignore that cell when calculating. This means that using the sub-total function did not provide the most efficient method for adding the expenses on this particular invoice.

3   Close the document without saving the changes.

17.5   Deleting formulae

A formula may be edited or deleted by moving the insertion point into the cell containing the formula, accessing the **Layout** menu and selecting the **Tables** option followed by the **Formula** option. The formula will appear in the **Tables formula** dialog box. Edit the formula using the usual editing keys or delete it using the delete keys. You may need to select the **Calculate** option to re-calculate the formulae in the table (*see* previous section).

17.6   Copying formulae

A formula is simply an instruction to WordPerfect to take the contents of a cell or group of cells and perform some kind of calculation with them. WordPerfect takes note of the logic of a formula and will copy the logic of the formula to adjacent rows or columns if required. This means that the cell addresses referenced by the formula will adjust to reflect the rows or columns to which they are being copied. A formula in cell **A3** which multiplies **A1** by **A2** would multiply **B1** by **B2** when copied to the next column to the right, ie into cell **B3**.

In the following example a form has been prepared for ordering stationery and the quantity of items ordered per month are noted. Cell **B8** contains a sub-total function (a **+** symbol) which adds up all the cells above which contain figures. The number of decimal places has been set to zero (**0**) for the cell containing the sub-total by positioning the insertion point in the cell, accessing the **Layout** menu and selecting the **Tables** option followed by the **Column** option. The **Format column** dialog box contains a box in which the number of decimal places can be specified.

Stationery Order Form

	JAN	FEB	MAR	APRIL	MAY	JUNE
Number of Items						
Envelopes (boxes)	24	19	0	36	8	12
A4 Paper (reams)	18	81	0	19	4	4
Paper Clips (boxes)	12	19	12	14	0	12
Toners	4	6	4	0	0	2
Total	58					

Instead of creating a separate formula to sub-total the number of items requested each month, the formula in cell **B8** in the above example could be copied to the adjacent columns. The first step would be to ensure that the insertion point was in cell **B8**, pull down the **Layout** menu and then select the **Tables** option followed by the **Formula** option. Selecting the **Right** option and typing in the number of cells to the right of the current cell to which the formula should be copied would result in a sub-total being produced for each specified column to the right.

Continuing with the example above, **Right** has been specified as the direction in which to copy the formula and **5** as the number of columns to copy the formula to.

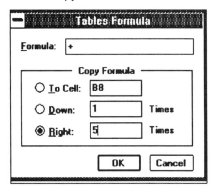

WordPerfect has adjusted the formula so that each column now contains a sub-total of each item for the appropriate month.

Stationery Order Form						
	JAN	FEB	MAR	APRIL	MAY	JUNE
Number of Items						
Envelopes (boxes)	24	19	0	36	8	12
A4 Paper (reams)	18	81	0	19	4	4
Paper Clips (boxes)	12	19	12	14	0	12
Toners	4	6	4	0	0	2
Total	58	125	16	69	12	30

If you want a formula to be copied to a number of rows below the current row, select the **Down** option from the **Tables formula** dialog box and type in the number of rows to which the formula should be copied. If you want an *exact copy* of the formula placed in another cell, select the **To cell** option and type the address of the cell to which the formula should be copied.

To re-cap then, if a cell reference has been typed in the **To cell** box, the formula will be copied as it currently stands. If either the **Down** or **Right** option has been selected, the formula will adjust and become relevant to the row or column to which it is copied.

 Re-calculating and copying formulae

1   Create the following table and save it as **ORDER**.

Stationery Order Form						
	JAN	FEB	MAR	APRIL	MAY	JUNE
Number of Items						
Envelopes (boxes)	24	19	0	36	8	12
A4 Paper (reams)	18	81	0	19	4	4
Paper Clips (boxes)	12	19	12	14	0	12
Toners	4	6	4	0	0	2
Total	58					

2   Change several figures in the table and re-calculate the results.

3   Copy the formula for Jan across to all months through to June.

4   Create an extra column after June, give it the title **6-monthly total**. Adjust
    column widths if necessary and make any necessary formatting changes.

5   Calculate the total number of envelopes ordered.

6   Copy the formula down so that totals are produced for each item ordered.

7   Save the document with the changes.

Importing spreadsheet information

Spreadsheet information can be brought in from the following software applications:

- Lotus 1-2-3

- Microsoft Excel

- Quattro

- Quattro Pro

- PlanPerfect

The information may be *linked* to a WordPerfect document which means that as the information in the spreadsheet file changes, the information in the WordPerfect document will be updated whenever the document is opened. Otherwise information may simply be *imported*. This means that the information in the WordPerfect document will not be updated if the spreadsheet changes. It is also important to note that formulas are not brought into the WordPerfect document with the imported spreadsheet file, only the result of the formulas. Therefore, you cannot update the figures in WordPerfect using the calculate feature.

Before starting to import the spreadsheet, position the insertion point where the information from the spreadsheet is to be imported or linked. Select **Spreadsheet** from the **Tools** menu and select **Create link** to link the spreadsheet or **Import** to simply import it. If you choose to create a link with the spreadsheet, the **Create spreadsheet link** dialog box will appear.

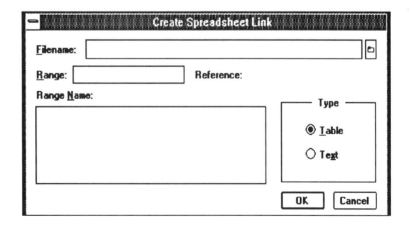

If you choose to import the spreadsheet, the **Import spreadsheet** dialog box will appear.

```
┌─────────────────────────────────────────────────────────────────┐
│ ▬              Import Spreadsheet                                 │
├─────────────────────────────────────────────────────────────────┤
│                                                                   │
│  Filename:  ┌──────────────────────────────────────────┐ ┌─┐     │
│             └──────────────────────────────────────────┘ └─┘     │
│                                                                   │
│  Range:  ┌────────────────────┐    Reference:                    │
│          └────────────────────┘                                  │
│  Range Name:                       ┌──── Type ──────┐             │
│  ┌──────────────────────────────┐  │                │            │
│  │                              │  │  ● Table        │            │
│  │                              │  │                 │            │
│  │                              │  │  ○ Text         │            │
│  │                              │  │                 │            │
│  └──────────────────────────────┘  │  ┌────┐ ┌──────┐│            │
│                                     │  │ OK │ │Cancel││           │
│                                     └──┴────┴─┴──────┴─┘           │
└─────────────────────────────────────────────────────────────────┘
```

In either case, type in the path, filename and extension of the file you wish to import or select the file icon to the right of the filename and locate the file and its path using the **Select file** dialog box. It is important to know beforehand where the spreadsheet files are located as they may be stored on a different disk or in a different sub-directory from the WordPerfect files.

If you want to import a particular range of cells from the spreadsheet file, select the **Range** box. The size of the spreadsheet will be displayed. For example, if information is entered into cells **A1** through to **B20** in the spreadsheet, **A1:B20** would appear in the **Range** box. Edit the range to include only those cells to be imported or type in new cell references. If range names have been created in the spreadsheet program a list of names will appear in the **Range name** box. Select the required range from the **Range name** box.

Select the **Table** option if you want to import the information into a table which WordPerfect will create for you or the **Text** option if you want the information to be placed as text separated by tab positions. Click the **OK** button.

If the spreadsheet has been linked to a WordPerfect document, the document may be updated to incorporate subsequent changes made to the spreadsheet by taking the following steps. Move the insertion point into the imported information and select the **Spreadsheet** option from the **Tools** menu. Select the **Link options** option and, in the **Link options** dialog box, select the **Update on retrieve** option if you want the spreadsheet information to be updated each time the WordPerfect document is opened. Select the **Show link codes** if you want the name and range of the spreadsheet to which the document is linked to appear in the document. These link codes will not print.

If at some time in the future you need to change the link information, access the **Tools** menu and select the **Spreadsheet** option followed by the **Edit link** option. Change the path, filename and range as required.

Importing spreadsheet information - this exercise can only be completed if you have purchased the disks

1   With a clean document window on screen import the spreadsheet **STAFF.WK3** from the **C:\WPWIN\DATA** directory, into the current document.

2   Specify that the information should be linked and the links should be updated each time the document is opened.

3   Select the **Preferences, Display** options from the **File** menu and display horizontal scroll bars. Save the document as **LINK.WP**.

19 Graphics

19.1 Preparing for this chapter

In order to complete this chapter you need the following document:

Filename	File type	Chapter
CONFINFO.WP	Document	12

 If you have not created this document in the previous chapters you will need to refer back to the chapter number listed above and create the file.

 If you have purchased the disks that accompany this book you can copy the necessary files from the appropriate floppy disk. To do this complete the following instructions:

1 Make sure you have created a sub-directory on the hard disk called **C:\WPWIN\DATA** (*see* Creating a data directory, page xvi).

2 Load WordPerfect for Windows (*see* Loading WordPerfect for Windows, page xv).

3 Follow the instructions for Using the diskettes on page vii.

19.2 Using graphic images

Graphic images can be inserted into a document to improve presentation and layout. The idea is to create an empty graphic box, position it in the document and then fill it with an image. There are five types of boxes available: **figure**, **text**, **table**, **user** and **equation**, each offering a particular style of border, caption and shading. Although the names of the boxes give the impression that each type of box should hold different information, this is not the case. Each kind of box can contain a picture, table, figure or text. You choose a box for the *style* which it represents. The style for each type of box is outlined below.

- A **figure box** is a box with a single border, no shading and a caption underneath.

- A **text box** is a shaded box with no border, a thick line above and below and a caption underneath.

- A **table box** has no border or shading. It has a thick line above and below and a caption at the top.

- A **user box** has no border, shading or caption. It simply leaves a set amount of space in the document where the information can be placed.

- An **equation box** is used with the **Equation editor**.

WordPerfect can automatically number each type of box in sequence. For example, table boxes may be numbered Table 1, Table 2, Table 3 and so on. If you want to use the automatic numbering feature, it is important to place similar types of information in similar boxes.

19.3   Creating a graphics box

To create a box, position the insertion point where the box is to be inserted and access the **Graphics** menu. Select the type of box which will offer the border, shading and caption you require and click the **Create** button.

If you choose to create a figure box you will be presented with the **Figure editor** screen. This will allow you to select a graphic and apply a variety of options to display the graphic within the box.

If you choose to create a text box, a **Text box editor** screen will appear into which you can type the text to be displayed within the box. You can also use the **Text box editor** to control the appearance and position of the text.

If you select an equation box, the **Equation editor** will appear, displaying menu options relevant to mathematical or scientific equations.

If you choose to create a table box or user box the **Select editor** dialog box will prompt you to choose the type of editor to work with.

19.4   Incorporating text

The most appropriate box to use for incorporating text is the text box. Once in the **Text box editor**, you can use the menu options to apply all the usual formatting features to text that you type. To change the position of the box, select the **Box position** button. The following dialog box will appear.

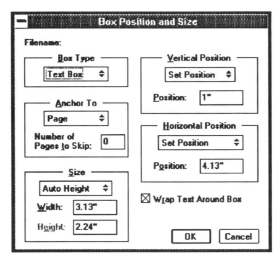

The **Box position and size** dialog box gives, amongst other things, a greater degree of control over the size and position of the box. Some of the options are described below.

Changing box type

Select the **Box type** button to place the text in a different type of box. For example, select **User box** from the pop-up menu to display the text in an area with no border or shading.

Anchoring boxes

Select the **Anchor to** button and choose to attach the graphic to the **Paragraph**, **Page** or **Character**. If a graphic is anchored to a paragraph, it will move with the paragraph as text is added to or deleted from the page. If a graphic is anchored to the page, it will remain in a set position on the page irrespective of what other information is added to the page. If a graphic is anchored to a character, it will stay with the character. This last option might prove useful if you want to anchor a logo in a header.

Sizing a box

To have WordPerfect determine the size of a box, select the **Auto height** option from the **Size** box. Choose **Set both** if you wish to enter your own dimensions for the box. Once the box has been created, it may be re-sized using the mouse. Position the mouse in the box and click. A set of square handles will appear around the box indicating that it has been selected. Position the mouse near to a handle and it should change shape to a double-headed arrow. Hold the mouse button down and drag the arrow in or out to increase or decrease the size of the box.

Positioning a box

Click in the **Vertical position** box to position the graphic accurately between the top and bottom of the page. Choose one of the options from the pop-up menu. The default option is **Set position**. This allows you to enter the exact position in inches from the top of the page. The **Top** option positions the box in line with the top margin whilst the **Centre** option centres the box accurately between the top and bottom margins. The **Bottom** option aligns the box with the bottom margin.

Similar options are available to position the box horizontally. Click in the **Horizontal position** box and choose one of the following options from the pop-up menu. Select the **Margin, left** option if you want to align the left edge of the box with the left margin of the page or the **Margin, right** option if you want to align the right edge of the box with the right margin of the page. Select the **Margin, centre** option if you want to align the box accurately between the left and right margins and the **Margin, full** option to expand the box to fill the space between the left and right margins.

If you have multiple columns set up in the document there are several options which control the positioning of boxes across columns. Select the required column option from the group described below and then type in the number of the column to which the positioning should relate. For example, type **2** if the positioning of the box should relate to column 2. Type **2-4** if it should extend across columns 2 to 4.

The **Column, left** option aligns the box with the left edge of the specified column(s). The **Column, right** option aligns the right edge of the box to the right edge of the specified columns. The **Column, centre** option centres the box within the specified column(s) and the **Column, full** option extends the box to fill the specified columns.

Alternatively, you can select the **Set position** option and type in the exact horizontal location for the box. Having created the box, you can move it to a new location in the document using the mouse. Select the box with the mouse until it displays a set of handles. The mouse should change shape to a four-headed arrow. Hold the mouse button down and drag the box to a new position.

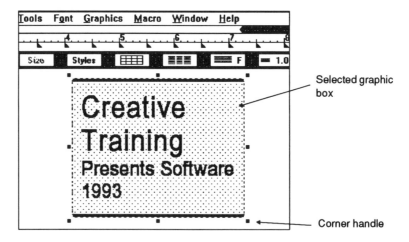

Selected graphic box

Corner handle

 Creating a text box

1   Create a new file.

2   Access the **Graphics** menu and select the **Text box** option followed by **Create**. The **Text box editor** screen will appear.

3   Type the following information:
    Creative Training
    Presents
    Software 1993

4 Select the first line of the heading and change the font to **Helvetica**, **Bold**, **24 points** and the second and third lines to the same font but only **18 points** in size.

5 Centre all three lines.

6 Click the **Box position** button. The **Box position and size** dialog box should appear. Select **Top** as the **Vertical position** and **Margin, centre** as the **Horizontal position**. Click the **OK** button. Click the **Close** button and the text box should resemble the following example.

19.5   Incorporating graphics

Create a figure box or user box to be filled with a graphic. WordPerfect provides 36 graphics files which can be used to improve the presentation of a document. In addition, graphics can be imported from other programs. If you select **Figure box** you will be taken into the **Figure editor** screen, an example of which can be seen below.

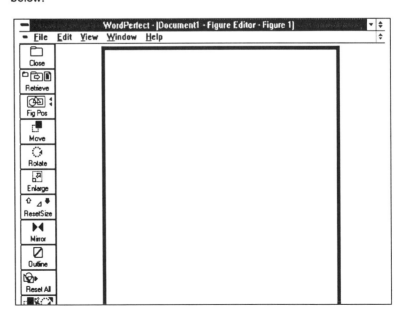

If you select **User box**, the **Select editor** dialog box will prompt you to choose to enter the **Figure editor**, **Text editor** or **Equation editor**.

The buttons in the **Figure editor** offer various graphics options. To bring a graphic into a box, click the **Retrieve** button. A list of WordPerfect graphics files will be displayed. Unless you have changed the default directory for these files, they will usually be located in **C:\WPWIN\GRAPHICS** and take an extension of **.WPG**. If necessary, change the directory to access other graphics files; otherwise, select a file from the list.

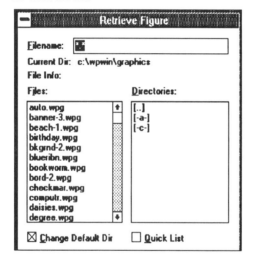

If you are unsure how the graphic file will look, select the file from the list and click the **View** button. In the following example, **BIRTHDAY.WPG** is displayed in the **View** screen. To close the **View** screen, select the document menu by clicking in the hyphen symbol and select the **Close** option.

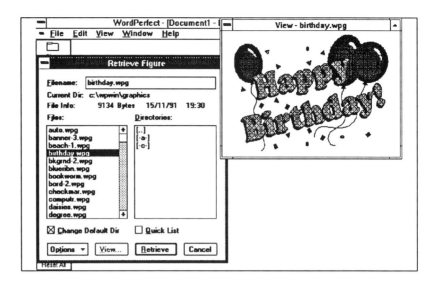

⊃ Creating a user box

1 Access the **Graphics** menu. Select the **User box** option followed by **Create**. Select **Figure editor** from the **Select editor** dialog box. The **Figure editor** screen will appear.

2 Click the **Retrieve** button and select **COMPUTR.WPG** from the list of WordPerfect graphics files. Click the **Retrieve** button.

3 Click the **Fig pos** button and choose **Top** as the **Vertical position** and **Margin, left** as the **Horizontal position**. Click the **OK** button.

4 Click the **Close** button.

5 Select the box with the mouse and pull the box down until it is in line with the heading.

6 Create a new user box and select **Figure editor** from the **Select editor** dialog box.

7 Retrieve **BOOKWORM.WPG** into the box.

8 Select **Top** as the **Vertical position** and **Margin, right** as the **Horizontal position**.

9 Click the **Close** button.

10 Pull the bookworm graphic in line with the computer graphic.

11 Save the document as **CONFMAT.WP**.

19.6   Changing box appearance

To change the appearance of a box, click the mouse button on the box you would like to change. The type and number of the box will appear in the status bar along with an instruction to press the right mouse button to access the graphics menu.

Having pressed the right mouse button, you will be prompted to choose to edit the box caption, edit the box itself or change box position. The options are explained below.

The **Edit caption** option allows you to edit the current caption or type a caption for the box if one does not already exist. The **Edit box** option takes you through to the appropriate box editor and provides the means to change the text, graphic or equation in the box. You can also double click the left mouse button in the graphics box to access the appropriate box editor. The **Position** option is a direct link to the **Box position and size** dialog box. As a shortcut, hold down the Shift key and double click the graphics box.

19.7 Placing tables in boxes

Tables can be placed within graphics boxes in much the same way that ordinary text can.

 Creating a table box

1 Using **CONFMAT.WP**, press Enter several times until the insertion point is below the title.

2 Select **Times roman** as the font and **12 points** as the size. Type the following text.

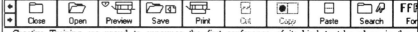

Creative Training are proud to announce the first conference of its kind to take place in the north of England. Representatives from all the major software houses will be present to introduce the latest in computer software and answer all your questions. To help you make decisions about the type of software available on the market, we have included information on each of the major categories of software and an itinerary of events.

Spreadsheets
A spreadsheet is used primarily to perform financial calculations. The computer screen represents a piece of paper divided into columns and rows into which text and numbers can be entered. The major advantage of using a spreadsheet is that figures can be calculated easily and information quickly updated.

Word Processors
A word processor is a computer program which replaces the typewriter. Information can be quickly entered at the keyboard and changes can be made efficiently. Many have special formatting features which improve the quality of printed material.

Databases
A database is a collection of information. Common examples of databases include telephone directories, library cards and address books. The advantage of using an electronic database is that information can be quickly recorded, changed and extracted.

3 Set the font of the subheadings to **Times roman**, **Bold**, **14 points** and **Large**.

4 Save the document with these changes.

5 Move to the end of the document and access the **Graphics** menu. Select the **Table box** option followed by **Create**. When prompted, select **Text editor** and click the **OK** button.

6 In the **Text editor** screen, click the **Box position** button. Choose **Bottom** as the **Vertical position** and **Margin, centre** as the **Horizontal position**.

7 Set the **Size** option to **Set both** and type **5.93** as the width and **3** as the height. Click the **OK** button.

8 Select the **Ruler** option from the **View** menu.

9 Set a centre tab at **3"** and a right tab at **5"** and drag all other tabs off the ruler. Create the following table.

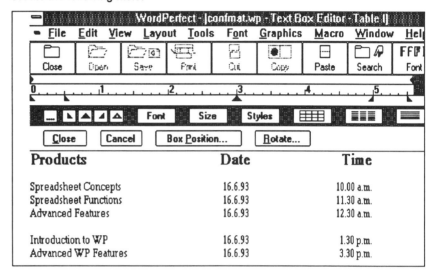

Products	Date	Time
Spreadsheet Concepts	16.6.93	10.00 a.m.
Spreadsheet Functions	16.6.93	11.30 a.m.
Advanced Features	16.6.93	12.30 a.m.
Introduction to WP	16.6.93	1.30 p.m.
Advanced WP Features	16.6.93	3.30 p.m.

10 Select the table headings and change their font to **Times roman, Bold, 14 points** and **Large**. Select the rest of the table and set the font to **Times roman, 12 points**.

11 Click the **Close** button. The table should appear in the document. Save the document with changes.

19.8 Adding captions

A caption can be added to any of the boxes and will appear in the format determined by the type of box selected. To add a caption to a table box, for example, select the table box by clicking the right mouse button in it. From the pop-up graphics menu, select the **Edit caption** option. The **Caption editor** screen will appear displaying a number for the table. Type in the required caption and use any formatting features available from the menu. Select the **Close** option to leave the screen and view the caption in the document.

Adding a caption to a table box

1 Using **CONFMAT.WP**, select the table box displaying the training programme.

2 Click the right button and choose **Edit Caption** from the pop-up menu.

3 In the **Caption editor** screen, leave a space after "Table 1" and select **Times roman** , **Bold** and **8 points** from the menu. Type **Training Programme**.

4 Select **Close**. Your screen should now resemble the following example.

Table I Training Programme		
Products	**Date**	**Time**
Spreadsheet Concepts	16.6.93	10.00 a.m.
Spreadsheet Functions	16.6.93	11.30 a.m.
Advanced Features	16.6.93	12.30 a.m.
Introduction to WP	16.6.93	1.30 p.m.
Advanced WP Features	16.6.93	3.30 p.m.
Database Concepts	17.6.93	10.00 a.m.

19.9 Numbering graphic boxes

The caption numbering style may be set for all boxes of a particular type. Move the insertion point before the code for the first box to be changed or at the top of the document if you have not yet produced any graphic boxes, and access the **Graphics** menu. Select the type of box to be changed and then select the **Options** option. The appropriate **Options** dialog box will appear.

Click the **First level** button in the **Caption numbering** box and select **Off**, **Numbers**, **Letters** or **Roman numerals** as the type of numbering. If you choose **Numbers** as the option then sequential numbers will be inserted in the caption for the type of box selected. Choose an appropriate option for second level numbering from the **Second level** pop-up list. For example, if you choose **Numbers** as the type of numbering for the second level then the caption for the first box of its type will be preceded by **1.1**.

You can change the style of the numbering by clicking the arrow to the right of the **Style** box and choosing one of the available options: **Bold, Italics, Underline** or **Small caps**. A style code will then be placed in the **Style** box. If you want text to be printed for each caption, type the text in the middle of the style code. It is important to note that this text should also include a second level number if you want one to be displayed. For example, if you want each graphic box to be consecutively numbered with both first and second level numbering and display the word "Graphic", type **Graphic 1.2** in the Style box between the style codes.

19.10   Positioning captions

Options are also available in the **Options** box to control the position of each caption. Click the **Caption position** button and choose a position from the pop-up list.

It is important to note that whenever you use the **Options** dialog box to change graphic settings, a code will be inserted in the document at the current insertion point. This code will determine the settings for all graphic boxes of a particular type from the insertion point forwards until a new **[Opt]** code is located. Make sure that new option settings are inserted to the right of any previous option settings, otherwise the previous code will override the new code.

19.11   Re-numbering boxes

To re-number all boxes of a particular type from the insertion point forwards, access the **Graphics** menu and choose the type of box to be re-numbered. Then choose the **New number** option. When prompted, type the number which is to be the first number and click the **OK** button. For example, type **3** if you want the next box to start with the number **3**. There is no need to specify a new start number for second level numbering, WordPerfect will adjust the numbering automatically. All boxes and captions of the selected type will then be re-numbered. If you insert a graphic box into a document, WordPerfect will automatically re-number all boxes below.

19.12   Editing graphics

Having created a graphic box, the information inside the box may be changed at any time. To edit the graphic, select the type of box from the **Graphics** menu and click the **Edit** option. Type the number of the box to be edited. The appropriate editor screen will be displayed. As a shortcut you can also double click the mouse in the box.

A set of buttons are displayed in the **Figure editor** screen which offer a degree of control over the display of a graphic image. Some of the options are described below.

- **Retrieve** will retrieve a different WordPerfect graphic into the box.

- **Fig pos** will access the **Box position and size** dialog box.

- **Move** will allow the graphic to be repositioned in the document. After selecting the **Move** button, hold down the left mouse button until a four-headed arrow appears. Drag the arrow in the desired direction, keeping an eye on the status bar at the bottom of the screen. The **X** position indicates the amount the graphic is being moved horizontally in relation to its original position. A negative number means that you are moving the graphic to the left of its original position, and a positive number to the right. The **Y** position relates to the vertical position of the graphic.

- **Rotate** allows the graphic to be rotated within its box. The following example shows **BOOKWORM.WPG** in an upright position.

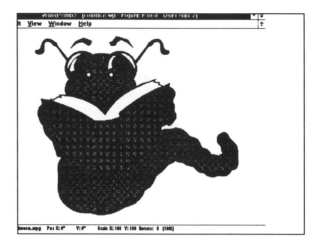

When you select the **Rotate** option a rotation angle appears. Point the mouse to the top, left or right handle and drag in any direction to rotate the graphic. The rotation angle can be seen in the following illustration.

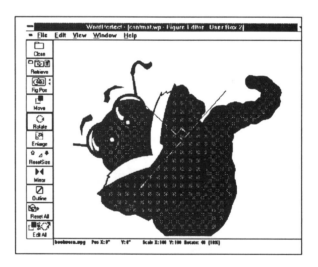

- **Enlarge** allows a portion of the graphic to be enlarged. If this button is selected, a set of cross hairs will be displayed. The idea is to drag a rectangle around the area of the graphic to be enlarged. In the following example, a rectangle has been dragged around the top of the bookworm.

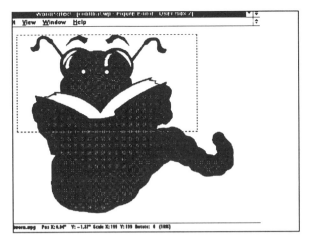

When the mouse is released, the portion of the graphic within the rectangle will be enlarged as in the following example.

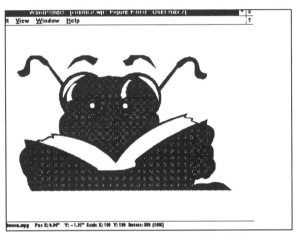

- **Re-set size** returns the graphic to its original size.

- **Mirror** flips the graphic to display a mirror image. A graphic normally drawn from left to right will be re-drawn from right to left, as can be seen in the following example.

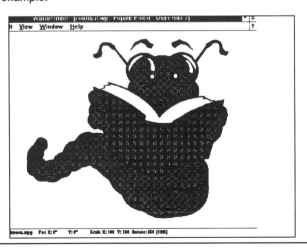

- **Outline** produces the graphic as an outline with no shading or colours.

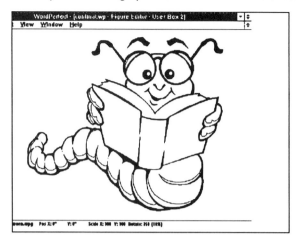

Although the buttons provide a quick method for accessing the options described above, all of the options plus others are available through the menu. For example, if you want to invert a graphic so that black becomes white and vice versa, you can select the **Invert** option from the **Edit** menu. If you want to restore the graphic to its original settings, select the **Reset all** option from the **Edit** menu.

 Changing a graphic

1   Using **CONFMAT.WP**, select the bookworm graphic and double click the left mouse button to access the **Figure editor**.

2   Click the **Rotate** button and rotate the graphic approximately 45% to the right.

3   Click the **Enlarge** button and drag a rectangle around the top half of the graphic.

4   Click the **Outline** button to turn the graphic into a line drawing instead of a solid object.

5   Select the **Reset all** option from the **Edit** menu to return the graphic to its original settings. Click the **Close** button.

6   Click the right mouse button in the table at the bottom of the document. Select **Edit caption** from the pop-up menu. The caption should read Table I. Click the **Close** button and save the document.

19.13 Working with borders

You can change the frame around a particular group of graphic boxes by positioning the insertion point before the first box of its kind in the document and accessing the **Graphics** menu. From the **Graphics** menu select the type of box to be changed and then choose the **Options** option. From the **Figure options** dialog box, select the appropriate **Border styles** for the **Top**, **Left**, **Bottom** and **Right** edge of each box.

You also have the option to specify the amount of space to be left between each side of a graphic and its frame. This is the **Inside** border space. Enter a measurement for the **Outside** border space if you want a set distance between the edges of a graphic and surrounding text.

Click the **Percent** button in the **Gray shading** box if you want the background of a graphic to be shaded. Type the percentage of grey or click the arrow buttons to increase or decrease the percentage, ie make the shading darker or lighter.

19.14 Text wrapping

If you want document text to wrap around a graphic frame check the **Wrap text around box** option in the **Box position and size** dialog box. This option is checked as a default. If you un-check the option, text will run over the top of the graphic.

19.15 Deleting graphic boxes

If you no longer require a graphic box, select the box by clicking on it with the mouse. Handles will appear around the outside of the box indicating that it has been selected. Press the Delete key.

19.16 Creating a template document

A template is a document containing information and formatting features to be used as a standard for other documents. For example, the company title and graphics boxes in **CONFMAT.WP** could be used as a starting point for many other standard letters.

To create a template document, simply remove all unwanted features from an existing document and save the document with a new name.

 Creating a template document

1   Using **CONFMAT.WP**, reveal the codes and move the insertion point to the first character of the document after the codes for the graphic boxes at the top of the document.

2   Press Alt F3 to hide the codes and delete all remaining text and boxes.

3   Reveal the codes again and delete any remaining formatting codes just leaving the boxes and some hard returns below for blank lines. Switch the codes off.

4   Save the document as **TEMPLATE.WP**.

This document can now be used as a basis for many other documents. You can either open this document, type in new information and save with a new name (so preserving the original template) or open this document and merge information from an existing file.

To incorporate information from an existing file, position the insertion point where the information is to be inserted, select the **Retrieve** option from the **File** menu and choose the file to be retrieved. A dialog box will display the message **"Insert file into current document?"**. Select the **Yes** option.

⤴   Using a template

1   Open **TEMPLATE.WP** if it is not already open.

2   Position the insertion point below the graphics boxes.

3   Select the **Retrieve** option from the **File** menu.

4   Select **CONFINFO.WP** as the file to be retrieved and click the **Yes** button.

5   Save the document as **INFO2.WP** and close. It should resemble the following example.

Edit   View   Layout   Tools   Font   Graphics   Macro   Window   Help

Creative Training
Presents
Software 1993

Product Information

Please find enclosed some general information on the range of software products available.

Spreadsheets

A spreadsheet is primarily used to perform financial calculations.   The computer screen represents a piece of paper divided into columns and rows into which text and numbers can be entered. The intersection of each column and row is known as a cell and each cell has a unique address. For example,

r 12pt (10cpi)   Pg 1 Ln 3.17"

20 Macros

A WordPerfect macro is a program that records a sequence of keystrokes or menu options so that they can be replayed over and over again. You would create a macro for a repetitive task.

20.1 Preparing for this chapter

In order to complete this chapter you need the following document:

Filename	File type	Chapter
NEWLETT.WP	Document	2

 If you have not created this document in the previous chapters you will need to refer back to the chapter number listed above and create the file. Please note, this file has been modified in subsequent chapters.

 If you have purchased the disks that accompany this book you can copy the necessary files from the appropriate floppy disk. To do this complete the following instructions:

1   Make sure you have created a sub-directory on the hard disk called **C:\WPWIN\DATA** (*see* Creating a data directory, page xvi).

2   Load WordPerfect for Windows (*see* Loading WordPerfect for Windows, page xv).

3   Follow the instructions for Using the diskettes on page vii.

20.2 Creating macros

Macros are best understood by example. Generally the following steps must be followed:

Access the **Macro** menu. Select the **Record** option (alternatively, press Ctrl F10). A **Record macro** dialog box will appear. Type in a new filename. All macros are saved as separate files on disk with the extension ***.WCM**. For example, a macro named **PRINT** would be saved to disk as **PRINT.WCM**.

Once you have named the macro you will be prompted to give the macro a description. This is optional. You can either leave the description blank, or type up to 69 characters. There is also the option to type in an abstract giving instructions on how to use the macro or notes on what the macro can do.

The words "Recording Macro" will appear in the status bar. From this point on, everything you type and every command you access will be recorded. Type or press the keystrokes to be recorded and then select the **Stop** option from the **Macro** menu (alternatively press Ctrl Shift F10 to stop recording the macro). To cancel a macro whilst recording, select the **Stop** option from the **Macro** menu.

20.3   Running macros

To run a macro, first position the cursor where you want the macro to start, then select the **Play** option from the **Macro** menu. Type the name of the macro or select the macro name from the list. Depending on how WordPerfect has been installed, you may be presented with a large list of available macros. Apart from the macros you have created, there are a number of other macros that are supplied with the product. Select the **Play** option to run the chosen macro. If you need to stop the macro running press Esc . The keyboard shortcut to run a macro is Alt F10 .

 Creating a macro to set up a draft document

1   Assuming that you produce many draft documents, you could create a macro that automatically sets up double spacing, automatic page numbering, a header containing the text "Draft Only" and a footer containing the system date. Close the current document and select the **Record** option from the **Macro** menu.

2   Type **DRAFT** as the macro name.

3   Type **Defines page settings for a standard draft document** as the macro description.

4   Click on the **Record** button to start recording the macro. The mouse pointer will change to a circle with a diagonal line across.

5   Access the **Layout** menu and select the **Line** and **Spacing** options. Use the up arrow to the right of the spacing box to change the line spacing to **2**. Click the **OK** button to complete.

6   Access the **Layout** menu and select **Page** and **Numbering** options. Use the **Position** box to change page numbering to **Top right**. Click in the **Accompanying text** box before the ^B. Type **Page** and press the Spacebar . Click on the **OK** button to complete.

7   Access the **Layout** menu and select the **Page** and **Headers** options. Click on **Header A** and then click on the **Create** button. Type **Draft Only** and press Enter to leave a blank line. Click on the **Close** button to complete.

8   Access the **Layout** menu and select the **Page** and **Footers** option. Click on **Footer A** followed by **Create**. Press Enter to leave a blank line and select the **Date** and **Code** options from the **Tools** menu. Centre the date and click on the **Close** button to complete.

9   Select the **Stop** option from the **Macro** menu to stop recording.

10 Close the document window without saving.

11 Select the **Play** option from the **Macro** menu. Double click on the macro **DRAFT.WCM** from the list (use the scroll bars to move up and down the list).

12 Reveal codes to check that the codes for spacing, page numbering, headers and footers have been entered. Position the insertion point at the end of the codes and hide the codes again.

13 Type the following text:

Dear Sally

You must get to grips with WordPerfect's macro feature! I've created a macro to set double line spacing, page numbering and headers and footers. It has saved me an enormous amount of time so far because I can use the macro every time I want to create a draft document with these settings.

14 Save the document as **DRAFT.WP**.

 Creating a macro to enter a signature block

In this exercise you will create a macro that enters text which is known as a *signature block*.

1   Close the current document and select the **Record** option from the **Macro** menu.

2   Type **SIG** as the macro name and **Standard signature block** as the description.

3   Click on the **Record** button. Type **Yours Sincerely** and press the Enter key five times.

4   Type your name and press Enter. Type **Senior Executive**.

5   Select the **Stop** option from the **Macro** menu.

6   Close the document window without saving the changes. Open **NEWLETT.WP** and move the insertion point to the end of the letter. Press Enter to create a new line.

7   Access the **Macro** menu and select the **Play** option. Find **SIG.WCM** in the list and double click to run the macro. The signature block should appear at the bottom of the letter.

8   Save the document.

20.4   Attaching and removing macros from menu

Up to nine macros can be assigned to the **Macro** menu and listed whenever the **Macro** menu is accessed. To add a macro to the menu select the **Assign to menu** option from the **Macro** menu and click on the **Insert** button. Type the name of the macro to be added or click on the button to the right of the **Macro name** box to select from a list. Click on the **Menu text** box or press the ⌜Tab⌟ key. The default menu text is the filename. This can be deleted and you can type up to 30 characters to identify the function of the macro. Click the **OK** button to complete.

This procedure can be used to insert, edit or delete macro names on the menu. Each macro will be assigned a number and after accessing the **Macro** menu, simply press the number corresponding to the macro you want to run.

 Adding macros to the menu

1 Select the **Assign to menu** option from the **Macro** menu and click the **Insert** button.

2 Type **SIG** as the macro name. Click in the **Menu text** box, delete the filename and type **Add signature block** as the menu prompt. Click the **OK** button.

4 Repeat the above steps to add **DRAFT.WCM** to the menu. Type **DRAFT** as the macro name and **Setup for draft document** as the menu prompt.

5 Access the **Macro** menu. The two macros should appear in the list.

20.5 Assigning macros to the button bar

As you have already seen, the button bar displays a group of time-saving icons that can be invoked by clicking on the relevant button with the mouse. An icon representing a macro can be added to the button bar in the following way. Access the **View** menu and select the **Button bar setup** option. Select the **Edit** option followed by the **Assign macro to button** option. Choose the name of the macro from the list and select **Assign**. Click the **OK** button to add the macro to the button bar. An icon displaying a cassette and the name of the macro will be produced for each macro added to the button bar.

20.6 Customising the button bar

The WordPerfect standard button bar provides easy access to some of the most frequently used WordPerfect commands or macros. You can however, create button bars which are customised to your own needs.

To create a button bar access the **View** menu and select the **Button bar setup** option followed by **New**. The **Edit button bar** dialog box will be displayed. The instructions in the dialog box are quite clear. To add a button, choose a menu item in the normal fashion. For example, select the **Print preview** option from the **File** menu to add a print preview button; select the **New** option from the **File** menu to add a button to create a new document.

Buttons will be arranged in order of selection. To rearrange the order in which are they are displayed, drag a button to a new location on the button bar. If you no longer need a button simply drag it off the button bar. Add as many buttons as necessary. If there are more buttons than can be displayed on the screen, scroll arrows will appear to allow you to access all buttons.

Click the **OK** button to save the button bar and type a name in the **Save button bar** dialog box. Click the **Save** button to carry out the save. WordPerfect will add a .WWB extension. You can create as many button bars as necessary.

20.7   Using a button bar

Access the **View** menu and choose the **Button bar setup** option followed by the **Select** option. Select the name of the button bar from the list and click the **Select** button. The default WordPerfect button bar, (WP{WP}.WWB), can also be edited if necessary. The selected button bar will remain current until a new button bar is chosen, even if you exit the WordPerfect program.

20.8   Editing a button bar

Having selected a button bar (*see* the previous section), you may edit or customise the bar. Access the **View** menu and choose the **Button bar setup** option followed by the **Edit** option. Follow the instructions in the dialog box to customise the bar and click the **OK** button to close the dialog box.

20.9   Button bar options

Button bar options give you the opportunity to re-position the bar to the **Left, Right, Top** or **Bottom** of the screen and alter it to display **Text only, Picture only** or both **Picture and text**. To set these options, choose the **Button bar setup** option from the **View** menu and then the **Options** option. The options set remain in effect for all new button bars created until the settings are changed again.

    Customising a button bar

1   Add three new buttons to the default button bar; one to access **Print preview** , one to access a **New** file and one to **Retrieve** a file.

2   Create a new file by clicking on the appropriate button in the button bar.

3   Retrieve **NEWLETT.WP** into the document and preview it using the **Print preview** button.

4   Close the document without saving the changes.

21   Consolidation

This last chapter in Part 2 is designed to reinforce a number of the topics covered so far. It is strongly recommended that you complete this exercise before moving on to Part 3. For those working without the disks, it should be noted that **NEWS.WP** will be referred to later in the book.

21.1   Preparing for this chapter

In order to complete this chapter you need the following document:

Filename	File type	Chapter
NEWS.WP	Document	11

 If you have not created this document in the previous chapters you will need to refer back to the chapter number listed above and create the file.

 If you have purchased the disks that accompany this book you can copy the necessary files from the appropriate floppy disk. To do this complete the following instructions:

1   Make sure you have created a sub-directory on the hard disk called **C:\WPWIN\DATA** (*see* Creating a data directory, page xvi).

2   Load WordPerfect for Windows (*see* Loading WordPerfect for Windows, page xv).

3   Follow the instructions for Using the diskettes on page vii.

21.2   Exercises

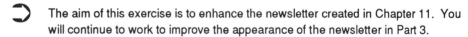
The aim of this exercise is to enhance the newsletter created in Chapter 11. You will continue to work to improve the appearance of the newsletter in Part 3.

1   Open **NEWS.WP** and make it the current file.

2   Select the **Margins** option from the **Layout** menu and set **0.5"** margins all around the document.

3   Choose the **Print** button from the button bar and set a **Binding offset** of **0.5"**. Click the **Close** button.

4   Access the **Layout** menu and select the **Page** option followed by **Headers**. Select the **Header A** button and then the **Create** option.

5   Type **Issue 1**, select the text and choose the **Font** option from the **Font** menu. Choose **New Century Schoolbook, 10 points** and **Bold** as the font settings and click the **OK** button.

6   Click the **Placement** button and choose the **Every page** button in the **Place on** box. Click the **Close** button.

7   Create a **Header B**. Type **Newsletter** as the header text and set the font to **New Century Schoolbook, 10 points** and **Bold**. Select the text and access the **Layout** menu. Choose the **Line** option and then the **Flush right** option.

8   Click the **Placement** button and place **Header B** on **Every page**. Click the **Close** button.

9   Print preview the document. You should see both headers on every page of the document.

10 Create a new document and save it as **CLIENTS**. This will become a secondary merge file. Select the **Merge** option from the **Tools** menu and then **Merge codes**. Move through the list of codes and highlight the **{FIELD NAMES}name1~....nameN~~** option. Click on the **Insert** button.

11 Type **TITLE** into the **Field name** box and click on the **Add** button to add the field.

12 Click at the beginning of the field name "Title" in the **Field name** box. The field name will appear in reverse video. Type **FIRSTNAME** as the second field name. The field number will change from **1** to **2**. Click on the **Add** button.

13 Repeat the above steps to include the following fields:

SURNAME
ADDRESS
TOWN
POSTCODE

14 When all the fields have been added, click the **OK** button to return to the **Insert merge codes** dialog box. Click on the **Close** button.

15 Press ⃞ **Enter** at the end of each of the field names displayed across the top of the screen. Press ⃞ **Ctrl End** to move the cursor below the page break. The status bar indicates that the "Title" field needs to be entered. Type **Ms.** and press ⃞ **Alt Enter** to add the end of field code. Type the remaining information as shown in the following list:

Joan{END FIELD}
Pritt{END FIELD}
14 North Street{END FIELD}
Southampton{END FIELD}
SO4 2PT

Press Alt Shift Enter to complete the record.

16 Enter the following two records:

Mr.
Sam
Davies
25 The Embankment
Luton
LU4 8ZY

Mrs.
Theresa
Thirkettle
57 Armitage Road
Bromley
BR1 6TU

17 Enter **4** more records of your own making and save the document as **CLIENTS**.

18 Create a primary file for mailing labels with a paper definition for a set of **A4** mailing labels in **2** columns and **8** rows. Enter appropriate merge fields into the primary file and set the information to print in the centre of each label. Save the document as **CLI_LABS**.

19 Create a new document and merge **CLIENTS** with **CLI_LABS** to produce a set of mailing labels. Close the merged document without saving the changes.

20 Make **NEWS.WP** the active document and edit the table at the bottom of the document to resemble the following example. Save the document with the changes.

Training Personnel

NAME	POSITION	TEL NUMBER
Timothy Reardon	Training Manager	453671 ext.284
Trudy Lilley	Training Co-ordinator	453671 ext.298
Sally Thomas	Administrative Officer	453671 ext.819
Ashley Boves	Support Manager	453671 ext.440
Peter Blick	Technical Support	453822 ext.882
Carol Aimes	Trainer	453911 ext.911

21 Position the insertion point after the title "Creative Training" and access the **Graphics** menu. Select the **Figure** option followed by **Create**. In the **Figure editor** window click the **Retrieve** button. The **Retrieve figure** dialog box will

appear. Select **C:\WPWIN\GRAPHICS** in the **Directories** box. From the list of **Files**, select **MBA.WPG** and click on the **Retrieve** button.

22 Click the **Outline** button and then the **Mirror** button. Then click the **Close** button.

23 Click on the graphic. A set of handles should appear around the outside. Position and hold the mouse on the bottom left-hand corner handle until a double-headed arrow appears. Drag the mouse diagonally up and to the right to make the graphic frame smaller. Click in the graphic, hold the mouse down until a four-headed arrow appears and drag the graphic frame in line with the paragraph "Happy New Year". See the following example.

Happy New Year!

Creative Training would like to thank all customers for their help and support throughout 1994 and wish you all a successful and prosperous 1995.

<u>Staff</u>

Two new members of staff have recently joined the team. Brenda Dickinson has taken up the post of Sales and Marketing Director and comes to us with a wealth of experience in these fields. Brenda has spent the last 15 years as the European Marketing Director for Wattles

24 Delete the subheading "Awards" and press Enter several times to create space. Access the **Graphics** menu and select the **Text box** option followed by **Create**. Set the font to **Courier, 12 points, Bold** and **Very large**. Type **Awards**. Click the **Box position** button. De-select or un-check the **Wrap text around box** option. Click the **OK** button. Click the **Close** button.

25 Click the right mouse button on the text box and select the **Select box** option from the pop-up menu. Click and hold the mouse on the bottom right-hand handle and drag the box in to decrease its size. Move the box into the space which was originally occupied by the "Awards" subheading. Note, do not make the height of the box too small, otherwise the word "Awards" will not be displayed.

26 Position the insertion point on the line below the text box, access the **Graphics** menu and select the **User box** option followed by **Create**. Select the **Figure editor** option from the **Select editor** dialog box.

27 Click the **Retrieve** button and select **BLUERIBN.WPG** from the list of **Files**. Click the **Rotate** button and rotate the figure slightly to the left. Click the **Outline** button. Click the **Fig pos** button and de-select the **Wrap text around box** option. Click the **OK** button and then the **Close** button.

28 Move the **User box** graphic next to the **Text box** and make it smaller, as in the following example.

Technology department of our parent company, Efficient Office. She is
looking forward to the challenge of her new position.

Awards

We were very pleased to be given the SPECO award for Outstanding
Customer Service. We are always striving to improve the services on
offer to our clients and in the next quarter we will be asking for
your help in completing a questionnaire.

Schedule

Last year we published a training schedule for the first quarter of
1994. This proved to be very popular and a schedule will now be
produced quarterly throughout the year.

29 Create a **Table box** and retrieve **BOOKWORM.WPG** into the box. Size and
position the box on the screen until it resembles the following example.

In addition to the graphics
products which we have recently
added to our training schedule,
we are now able to offer
training on all Windows
products. We are also in the
process of developing a range of
general courses.

The following courses will be
available from March 1st:

Recruitment Skills

Leadership

Time Management

30 Print preview the document and save. The first page of the document should
resemble the following example (*see* next page).

31 The second page should look like the example below.

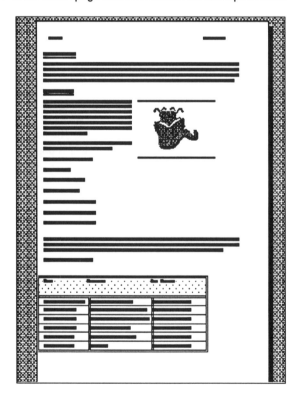

Part 3

Advanced level

WordPerfect has the facility to display text in columns. Although two or three column layouts are most commonly used, you can use a greater number of columns if required. WordPerfect provides three styles of columns:

- **Newspaper** - newspaper columns (or snake columns) start at the top of the first column, continue to the bottom of the page, *snake* to the top of the second column, and so on.

- **Parallel** - instead of snaking from column to column in a continuous flow, parallel columns put related blocks of text side by side in a *tabular* format. (With earlier versions of WordPerfect, parallel columns were used to produce tables. However, WordPerfect for Windows has an in-built table feature which is much simpler to use - *see* Chapter 15.)

- **Parallel with block protect** - a block protect option is available with parallel columns to prevent the text for a column being split across a page.

22.1   Preparing for this chapter

In order to complete this chapter you need the following documents:

Filename	File type	Chapter
CONFINFO.WP	Document	12
TEMPLATE.WP	Document	19

If you have not created these documents in the previous chapters you will need to refer back to the chapter numbers listed above and create the files. Please note, CONFINFO.DOC has been modified in subsequent chapters.

If you have purchased the disks that accompany this book you can copy the necessary files from the appropriate floppy disk. To do this complete the following instructions:

1   Make sure you have created a sub-directory on the hard disk called **C:\WPWIN\DATA** (*see* Creating a data directory, page xvi).

2   Load WordPerfect for Windows (*see* Loading WordPerfect for Windows, page xv).

3   Follow the instructions for Using the diskettes on page vii.

Columns can be defined before or after text has been typed. If the text has already been entered, position the insertion point at the beginning of the text that is to be put into columns, or select the text, before creating columns. If you position the insertion point before creating the columns, all text after the insertion point will be placed in columns. If you have selected the text first, then only the selected text will be placed in columns.

The easiest way to create columns is to use the ruler. However, if you require more than five columns or need to define column widths accurately, then you will need to create columns through the **Layout** menu. Up to 24 columns can be defined in the **Layout** menu.

Using the ruler

Position the insertion point at the point in the document from where the columns are to take effect. Point and hold the mouse on the **Columns** icon on the ruler and from the **Columns** menu, select the number of columns required.

If you set column definitions before typing text, WordPerfect will move the insertion point into the second column as you reach the bottom of the first column. If you want to end a column of text and begin typing in the next column, press
| **Ctrl Enter** | to create a page break. The insertion point will then move into the next column. If you insert extra text into an existing column (before the page break), text from the existing column will flow into the next column. If you delete text from a column, text from the next column along will be drawn back into the current column.

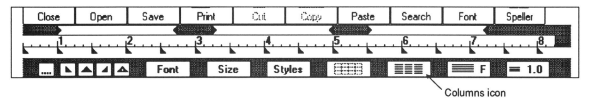

Columns icon

All text below the current cursor position will flow into the number of specified columns. If you want text below a certain point to return to normal layout, move the insertion point to the beginning of text to be returned to normal layout and select the **Columns off** option from the **Columns** icon menu.

Using the menu

As an alternative to using the ruler you can select the **Columns** option from the **Layout** menu and then select the **Define** option. The **Define columns** dialog box will appear. Type the number of columns required, the type of column, the width of each column as indicated by the left and right margin settings and the distance between columns. If you require columns of an even width and the same space apart, leave the default settings as they stand.

As with all WordPerfect formatting, the changes in column layout are embedded within the document as codes. The following illustration shows the codes for a two-column newspaper style format.

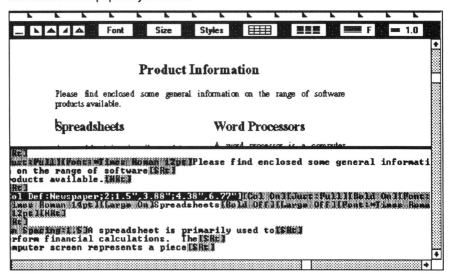

These codes can be deleted in the usual way. If you want to delete columns from a document, reveal codes and delete the **[Col def:]** code. All the settings which accompany the columns will also be deleted. If you only want to delete one set of columns, locate the **[Col on]** or **[Col off]** code for the particular column and delete it.

Newspaper style columns

1   Close all open documents. Open the document **TEMPLATE.WP**. Select **Save as** from the **File** menu and type **COLUMNS.WP** to save the file with a new name.

2   Access the **View** menu and select the **Ruler** option if it is not already displayed.

3   Position the insertion point at several lines below the title, access the **File** menu and select the **Retrieve** option to retrieve another file into the current document. Select **CONFINFO.WP** from the list of files and click the **Retrieve** button. At the prompt "Insert file into current document?", select the **Yes** option.

4   Position the insertion point at the beginning of the subtitle "Spreadsheets". This is where the columns are to start.

5   Select the **Column** icon on the ruler, hold the mouse button down and choose **2** as the number of columns from the **Columns** menu. The document should be displayed in two-column format.

6   Preview the document. It should look similar to the following illustration.

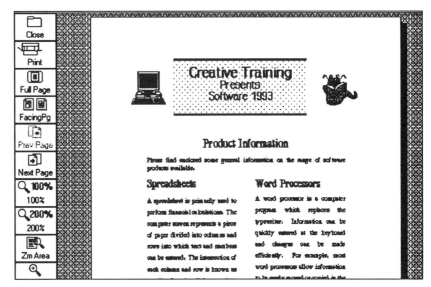

7   Back at the edit screen, reveal the codes for the column definition. Delete the code for the column definition, **[Col def:Newspaper;2...]**. You may also need to delete any page breaks which WordPerfect inserted when you were working with columns. The text will return to single-column layout.

8   Position the insertion point at the start of the subtitle "Spreadsheets" and place the text in three newspaper style columns.

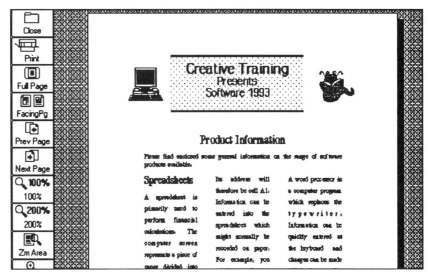

9   Delete the format codes for the three-column newspaper layout.

22.4   Using a combination of column layouts

In the two examples we have already seen, the entire text is displayed in multi-column format. This need not be the case. Column formatting can be turned on and off as required.

1 Open **COLUMNS.WP** and make it the current document.

2 Position the cursor at the beginning of the subtitle "Word processors". Select the **Column** icon from the ruler and choose **2** as the number of columns.

3 Preview the document. The text in the first paragraph is in single-column format and the remaining text is displayed in two columns.

4 Move your cursor to the start of the subtitle "Databases" and select the **Columns** icon on the ruler and then the **Columns off** option. This will turn the column settings off for the remaining text. Preview the document and save the changes.

22.5   Moving between columns

There will be times when you need to edit text in different columns. With the mouse, simply click where the text needs to be changed and use the standard editing keys. To move between columns using the menu, select the **Go to** option from the **Edit** menu, click the **Position** button and select a position from the pop-up list.

22.6   Changing column widths

Column widths can be easily adjusted using the ruler. Position the insertion point at the point where you want the column widths to change. The ruler should display column markers indicating the number and width of the columns set. Drag the column markers to a new position on the ruler and the corresponding text will be adjusted.

22.7   Creating parallel columns

If you want to format text in a short document into columns it may be better to choose parallel columns rather than newspaper style columns. With newspaper style columns text will flow to the bottom of the first column before flowing into the top of the second column. If the document is only short, the right-hand side of the page may appear empty. With parallel columns you have the option to force text into the next column across the page by pressing the page break code, `Ctrl Enter`.

Columns can be displayed side by side on the screen as they will when printed or on separate pages. The advantage of displaying the columns on separate pages is that WordPerfect can re-format the text in the columns quickly. They will still be printed side by side and you can see this if you print preview the document. To display side by side columns on the screen, select the **Display columns side by side** option in the **Display settings** dialog box. This can be accessed by choosing **Preferences** from the **File** menu and then **Display**.

 Parallel columns

1   Open **COLUMNS.WP** and remove any previous column formatting codes so that the document returns to a single-column format.

2   Position the insertion point before the subtitle "Spreadsheets". Access the **Layout** menu and select the **Columns** option followed by **Define**. Type **2** as the number of columns.

3   Select the **Type** option. There are two parallel layout options. The options are similar, the only difference being that the **Parallel block** option will prevent a block being split across a page. Select the **Parallel** option and click the **OK** button.

4   Select the **Columns on** option. At the moment the text looks just the same as with newspaper columns. Move your cursor before the subtitle "Word processors" and press | **Ctrl Enter** | to force a page break. Remove any unnecessary spaces at the beginning of the paragraph.

5   Click before the subtitle "Databases". Select **Columns** and then **Columns off** options from the **Layout** menu to return all text below this point to single-column format.

6   Preview the document.

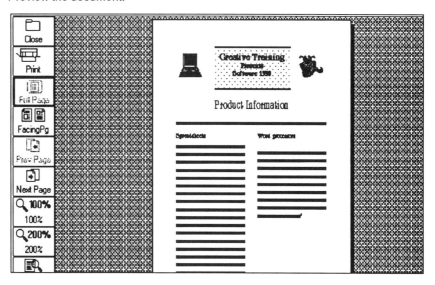

7   Save and print the document then close the window.

23 Defining styles

Throughout this book you have used a variety of text attributes and formatting features to enhance the appearance of your documents. As you know, individual formatting codes can be inserted into documents to control the appearance of selected text. If you regularly use the same formatting features for sections of text within a document or for an entire document, it would be more appropriate to combine the formatting codes into a *style* and apply the style as required. For example, suppose you regularly produce a newsletter in which you centre and embolden the title, set the title font to Helvetica, 36 points and the title size to very large. Instead of entering the same codes each time you format a newsletter title, you could create and apply a style called "Title" (or some other appropriate name) containing all the relevant codes. Whenever you edit a style, WordPerfect will automatically re-format any text which has had the style applied.

23.1 Preparing for this chapter

In order to complete this chapter you need the following documents:

Filename	File type	Chapter
NEWS.WP	Document	11
CONFINFO.WP	Document	12
TEMPLATE.WP	Document	19

 If you have not created these documents in the previous chapters you will need to refer back to the chapter numbers listed above and create the files. Please note, these files have been modified in subsequent chapters.

 If you have purchased the disks that accompany this book you can copy the necessary files from the appropriate floppy disk. To do this complete the following instructions:

1 Make sure you have created a sub-directory on the hard disk called **C:\WPWIN\DATA** (*see* Creating a data directory, page xvi).

2 Load WordPerfect for Windows (*see* Loading WordPerfect for Windows, page xv).

3 Follow the instructions for Using the diskettes on page vii.

There are two types of style available, **Paired** styles and **Open** styles. A paired style produces two sets of codes in a document. The first code, **[Style on]**, switches the style on and the second code, **[Style off]**, switches it off. A paired style is useful for formatting short blocks of text such as headlines, notes, captions and body text. Open styles affect text from the insertion point to the end of the document and cannot be switched off. They are useful for setting styles which affect the entire document. For example, an open style might set the margins, line spacing, tabs and paper size for the entire document.

23.3   Creating styles

To create a style, access the **Layout menu** and select the **Style** option or press Alt F8 . Select the **Create** option and the **Style properties** dialog box will appear.

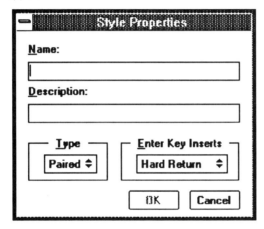

Type a style name (up to 20 characters) in the **Name** box and an optional description of the style in the **Description** box. Click the **Type** button and choose **Paired** or **Open** from the pop-up list. If you choose to create a paired style you can change the function of the Enter key. The Enter key can function as a hard return (its normal function) or it can turn a style off if you choose the **Style off** option or turn a style off and then on again if you choose the **Style off/on** option. This last option is useful if you are applying a specific style for bulleted or indented text. In this case, pressing the Enter key at the end of a paragraph will turn the style off for that paragraph and turn it on again for the start of the next paragraph. When you have made all your choices, click the **OK** button. The **Style editor** window will appear.

If you have chosen the **Open** style type, the following **Style editor** window will appear.

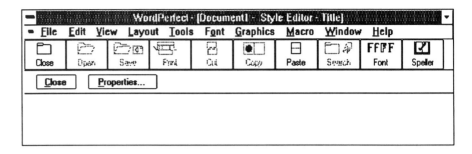

If you have chosen the **Paired** style type, the **Style editor** window will be slightly different as in the following example.

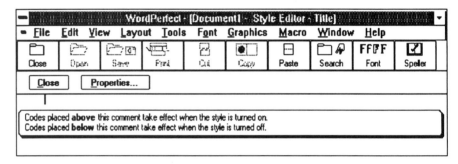

The **Style editor** for paired styles is divided into two sections with a comment area in between. Click the insertion point in the area above the comment to insert formatting features which should be applied to text when the style is switched on. Apart from a few special formatting features (mainly options relating to page formatting) these features will no longer take effect when the style is switched off. Click in the area below the comment and insert formatting features to take effect when the style is switched off.

These formatting features should be different to those inserted before the comment area because formatting features inserted before the comment area are automatically switched off when the style is switched off. It should be noted, however, that formatting features selected whilst in the document will override the effects of applying a style.

To include formatting features as part of a style, select the appropriate menu options or use appropriate keyboard shortcuts. The codes for the selected features will appear in the reveal codes section of the window.

Standard text can also be inserted with the style and will appear each time the style is activated. Type the text in the window.

Click the **Close** button to see the style added to the list in the **Styles** dialog box. Select a style from the list and click the **On** button to switch the style on immediately, or click the **Close** button to close the **Styles** dialog box.

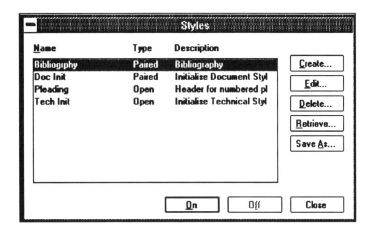

To turn a style on at any time, select the **Styles** option from the **Layout** menu and click the **On** button. To turn a style off, select the **Styles** option from the **Layout** menu and click the **Off** button.

Styles are created and saved with a document. To use a style with more than one document, you will need to save your styles in a *library*. This will be covered in section 23.5.

Creating styles

1   Open **TEMPLATE.WP** and retrieve **CONFINFO.WP** into it underneath the title.

2   Select the **Styles** option from the **Layout** menu. Click the **Create** button in the **Styles** dialog box. The **Style properties** dialog box will appear. Type **Title** in the **Name** box and **Title for newsletters** in the **Description** box. Select **Paired** as the style **Type** and click the **OK** button.

3   Make sure the insertion point is above the comment line in the **Style editor** window.

4   Select the **Font** option from the **Font** menu. Select **Helvetica bold**, **36 points** and **Shadow** as the options and click the **OK** button. Access the **Layout** menu and select the **Line** option followed by the **Centre** option. Click the **Close** button.

5   Click the **Create** button in the **Styles** dialog box. Type **Subtitle** in the **Name** box. Press the Tab key and type **Subtitles in newsletters** in the description box. Select **Paired** as the style **Type**. Click the **OK** button.

6   Make sure the insertion point is above the comment line, access the **Font** menu and select the **Font** option. Choose **Helvetica bold**, **18 points** and **Underline** from the **Font** dialog box and click the **OK** button. Click the **Close** button.

7   Click the **Create** button in the **Styles** dialog box and type **Body text** as the **Name** for the style and **Main body of text** as the **Description**. Select **Paired** as the style **Type**. Access the **Layout** menu and choose the **Paragraph** option followed by **Indent**. Set the font to **Times roman**, **12 points** and click the **OK**

button. Select the **Justification** option from the **Layout** menu and choose **Left** as the type of justification. Set all margins to **0"**. Click the **Close** button.

8 Create an **Open** style called **Page** and type **Page format** as the description. Set **0.5"** margins around the page. Select the **Layout** menu and select the **Columns** option followed by **Define**. Enter **3** as the number of columns and **Newspaper** as the type. Click the **OK** button and close the **Style editor** and then the **Style** dialog boxes.

9 Save the document as **STYLES.WP**.

23.4   Applying styles

Styles may be switched on before typing text or applied to selected text. To switch on a style before typing, select the **Styles** option from the **Layout** menu. Select the style from the list in the **Styles** dialog box and click the **On** button. Alternatively, select the **Styles** icon on the ruler.

To return to normal typing, press the right cursor arrow to move the cursor past the **[Style off]** code or select the **Styles** option from the **Layout** menu and click the **Off** button.

To apply an **Open** style to existing text, place the insertion point at the point in the document from which the style should take effect or at the beginning of the document if you want it to affect the entire document. Follow the steps outlined above to switch the style on. If you want to apply a **Paired** style, select the text before switching the style on.

Applying styles

1 Open **STYLES.WP** and make it the current document.

2 Position the insertion point before the first character of the first paragraph. Access the **Layout** menu and select the **Styles** option. Select the **Page** styl and click the **On** button. Also select the **Body text** style and click the **On** button.

3 Select the document title and apply the **Title** style to it.

4 Save the document with the changes.

23.5   Creating a style library

Although styles are saved when you save a document, they are only available for use with the current document. However, you can save styles into a style library which can then be used with any document. To build a style library, select the **Styles** option from the **Layout** menu. Select the **Save as** option and enter a name for the library entry in the **Save as** box in the **Save styles** dialog box.

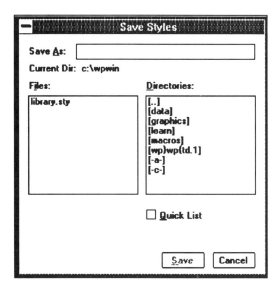

WordPerfect will add a **.STY** extension to the filename and save the library entry in the directory specified. To set a default directory for styles, select the **Preferences** option from the **File** menu and then choose the **Location of files** option. Type the directory in the **Style** box. If no directory is specified, the library will be stored in the directory from which WordPerfect was installed.

It is a good idea to give the style library an appropriate name. For example, save newsletter styles in a file called **NEWS**. WordPerfect will add **.STY** to the filename to make it **NEWS.STY**. Whenever you make changes to a style, make sure that you update the style library entry by re-saving it.

23.6   Using a style library

To use the library with a new document, access the **Layout** menu and select the **Styles** option followed by **Retrieve**. Choose the library name from the list of files in the **Retrieve styles** dialog box.

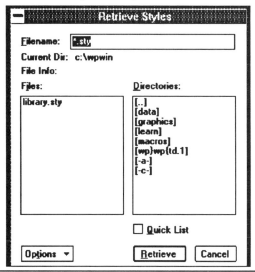

If the current document contains any styles with the same names as styles in the library being retrieved, you will be prompted to replace the current document styles with those in the style library. Select **No** if you wish to retain the current styles.

⊃ Saving and retrieving a style library

1   Open the document called **STYLES.WP**.

2   Access the **Layout** menu and choose the **Styles** option. Click the **Save as** button in the **Styles** dialog box.

3   Save all styles into a style library called **STYLES.STY**.

4   Open the document called **NEWS.WP**. Access the **Layout** menu and choose the **Styles** option. Click the **Retrieve** button and choose **STYLES.STY** from the list of styles. Click the **Retrieve** button again. These should now appear in the list of available styles for **NEWS.WP**.

5   Save the document.

24 Paragraph numbering

24.1 Numbering overview

Automatic numbering and styles may be applied to paragraphs. You may choose to have paragraphs numbered or lettered sequentially or you may define different levels of numbering or lettering so that paragraphs may be formatted in a hierarchical fashion. If you want paragraphs to be displayed hierarchically in order of importance, you can define different numbering styles for each level of paragraph.

A main paragraph would normally be preceded by a level 1 style number, a sub-paragraph relating to the main paragraph would normally be preceded by a level 2 style number and so on. Paragraphs with level 1 style numbers normally align with the left margin, paragraphs with level 2 style numbers are normally indented to the first tab position in the ruler, paragraphs with level 3 style numbers are normally indented to the second tab position and so on. You can alter the position of the paragraphs by adjusting the tab settings in the ruler.

To number a paragraph, move the insertion point to the position where the paragraph number is to be inserted and access the **Tools** menu. Select the **Outline** option followed by the **Paragraph number** option. The **Paragraph numbering** dialog box will be displayed.

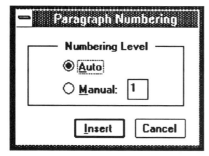

You have two choices. Select the **Auto** option if you want WordPerfect to judge the level of numbering required or **Manual** if *you* want to determine the numbering level to be used. WordPerfect will judge the level of numbering required from the position of the insertion point. If the insertion point is at the beginning of a paragraph then the next sequential number or letter for level 1 will be used. If you have pressed the Tab key then the next number for level 2 will be inserted. If the wrong level of numbering has been entered, position the insertion point before the number and press Tab to insert the next level of numbering or Shift Tab to insert the previous level of numbering. With each successive press of the Tab key, the text will be indented to the next level of numbering. Press Shift Enter to move down a line without creating a new paragraph.

As you enter additional paragraph numbers, WordPerfect will automatically adjust any existing paragraph numbers to compensate.

A **[Par num:]** code will be inserted into the document at the insertion point. Delete this code in **Reveal codes** if you make a mistake and want to start again.

 1 Create a new document and type the following text.

Office Safety Procedures

Fire Precautions

A fire extinguisher should be available in each office
Regular fire drills should be carried out (weekly)
Fire alarms should be serviced monthly
Fire exits should be kept clear at all times
Fire exits should be clearly marked

First Aid

A first aid kit should be placed in every office
One person from each office should be qualified in first aid
An accident record book should be kept. The employee responsible should keep a note
of the date and time of the accident, the type of accident and the action taken.

---

2 Save the document as **HEALTH.WP**.

3 Position the insertion point before the paragraph "A fire extinguisher should ...", access the **Tools** menu and select the **Outline** option followed by the **Paragraph number** option. Select the **Auto** option if it is not already selected and click the **Insert** button. WordPerfect will insert the first number for level 1 numbering.

4 Position the insertion point before the first character in the paragraph "Regular fire drills.." and press ⌨ **Alt F5** . Choose the **Auto** option and click the **Insert** button.

5 Insert paragraph numbers for each of the following paragraphs. Your screen should resemble the following example. However, the type of numbering which appears is dependent upon choices made in the **Define paragraph numbering** dialog box.

Office Safety Procedures

Fire Precautions

1.A fire extinguisher should be available in each office
2.Regular fire drills should be carried out (weekly)
3.Fire alarms should be serviced monthly
4.Fire exits should be kept clear at all times
5.Fire exits should be clearly marked

First Aid

6.A first aid kit should be placed in every office
7.One person from each office should be qualified in first aid
8.An accident record book should be kept. The employee responsible should keep a note

---

6 Click the insertion point before the first character in paragraph 2 ("Regular fire drills ..") and press the ⎡Tab⎤ key. The paragraph number format will change. Its appearance will depend upon settings in the **Define paragraph numbering** dialog box.

7 Repeat the above steps for the next two paragraphs. Your screen should be similar to the following example.

```
Office Safety Procedures

Fire Precautions

1.A fire extinguisher should be available in each office
        a.Regular fire drills should be carried out (weekly)
        b.Fire alarms should be serviced monthly
        c.Fire exits should be kept clear at all times
2.Fire exits should be clearly marked

First Aid

3.A first aid kit should be placed in every office
4.One person from each office should be qualified in first aid
5.An accident record book should be kept. The employee responsible should keep a note
```

8 Position the insertion point before paragraph 2 and press the ⎡Tab⎤ key again. This paragraph will now adopt the style defined for numbering level 3.

```
Office Safety Procedures

Fire Precautions

1.A fire extinguisher should be available in each office
                i.Regular fire drills should be carried out (weekly)
        a.Fire alarms should be serviced monthly
        b.Fire exits should be kept clear at all times
2.Fire exits should be clearly marked

First Aid

3.A first aid kit should be placed in every office
4.One person from each office should be qualified in first aid
5.An accident record book should be kept. The employee responsible should keep a note
6.of the date and time of the accident, the type of accident and the action taken.
```

9 Position the insertion point before the first character in paragraph 2 again and press ⎡Shift Tab⎤ to return the number format to the style for level 2.

10 Save the document.

24.2 Defining a numbering style

WordPerfect contains a number of predefined formats for numbering which can be selected from the **Define paragraph numbering** dialog box. To access this box, pull down the **Tools** menu and choose the **Outline** option followed by **Define** or press ⎡Alt Shift F5⎤.

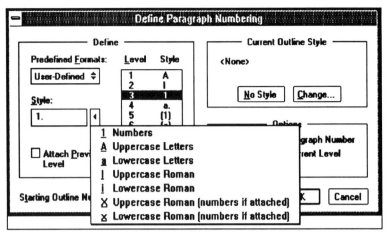

Assuming that you want to have paragraphs structured hierarchically, you can choose eight different levels of numbering, each level having its own style. Click the **Predefined formats** button and choose a predefined format from the pop-up menu. Look at the styles defined for each level in the **Level** and **Style** boxes.

If you want to define your own number format, select the **User-defined** option from the **Predefined formats** pop-up menu. Click the level number that you want to define and choose a style from the **Style** pop-up menu. In the example above, level 3 has been selected from the **Level** box and the user can choose a new style for level 3 from the **Style** pop-up list.

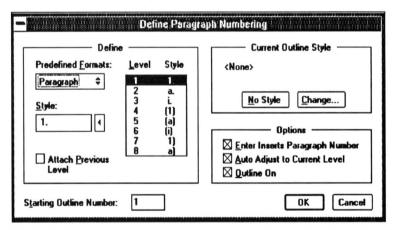

Check the **Attach previous level** box if you want the previous level of numbering to appear before the current number. For example, suppose you have a main paragraph and two sub-paragraphs below. To number the main paragraph you would choose the **Outline** and **Paragraph number** options from the **Tools** menu and **Numbering level 1**. To number the two sub-paragraphs you would choose **Numbering level 2** from the **Paragraph numbering** dialog box. Depending on the style defined for each level of numbering the paragraphs may be numbered as follows:

1. This is the main paragraph containing the main body of text.

    a. This is the first point relating to the main paragraph.

b. This is the second point relating to the main paragraph.

If you check the **Attach previous level** button, however, the paragraph numbers will appear as follows:

1. This is the main paragraph containing the main body of text.

    1.a. This is the first point relating to the main paragraph.

    1.b. This is the second point relating to the main paragraph.

You can also enter a new **Starting outline number** to begin paragraph numbering with a number other than 1 or lettering other than A.

When you define a numbering style, WordPerfect will insert a **[Par num def:]** code at the current insertion point which will affect all paragraph numbering from this point on. Each time you define a numbering style in a document, the numbering will start again from 1. If you are confused, reveal codes and delete all **[Par num:]** and **[Par num def:]** codes and begin again.

If the **Auto adjust to current level** option is selected in the **Define paragraph numbering** dialog box, the next paragraph will automatically take the next number in the sequence.

24.3 Using the outline feature

The **Outline** feature provides a convenient way of organising information. Similar to the paragraph numbering feature described above, numbers or letters precede each level of paragraph and different formatting can be applied to each level. Look at the following example of an outline.

The main difference between using the outline feature and paragraph numbering is that, with outlining, the next number or letter in a sequence is automatically inserted when you press the $\boxed{\text{Enter}}$ key. Sections can also be moved around within an outline and, if necessary, the entire outline can be copied to another document.

The standard definition for each level of outline numbering is set in the **Define paragraph numbering** dialog box. To look at the definition, pull down the **Tools** menu and select the **Outline** option followed by **Define**. Select the **Outline** option from the **Predefined formats**. However, you can choose one of the other predefined number formats or create a user-defined format - *see* section 24.2.

Having chosen the numbering style all that remains is to switch the outline feature on.

Move the insertion point to the point in the document from which the outline is to take effect and pull down the **Tools** menu. Select the **Outline** option followed by **Outline on**. A message will appear in the status bar indicating that the outline feature has been activated.

Press the $\boxed{\text{Enter}}$ key to begin a new line and the first number for level 1 will appear. Select the **Paragraph** and then the **Indent** option from the **Layout** menu or press $\boxed{\text{F7}}$ to indent the paragraph. Alternatively, press the $\boxed{\text{Spacebar}}$ to put a space after the number. Type the first paragraph. At the end of each paragraph, press the $\boxed{\text{Enter}}$ key and WordPerfect will insert the next number in the sequence for level 1. Press $\boxed{\text{Enter}}$ again if you want to leave an extra space before typing the paragraph text.

When you want to type a second level paragraph, press the $\boxed{\text{Tab}}$ key. The first number for level 2 will appear. Press the $\boxed{\text{Spacebar}}$ to insert a space or $\boxed{\text{F7}}$ to indent the text.

With each successive press of the $\boxed{\text{Tab}}$ key the paragraph numbering will be formatted to the next level. For example, to format the paragraph to level 3 numbering, press the $\boxed{\text{Tab}}$ key twice. To return to a previous level of formatting, press $\boxed{\text{Shift Tab}}$ the required number of times.

When you have finished using the outline, access the **Tools** menu and select the **Outline** option followed by **Outline off**.

 Organising information using an outline

1   Create a new document and type **Creative Training Annual Report** as the title. Set the font to **Helvetica bold** and **24 points** in size. Press the $\boxed{\text{Enter}}$ key twice.

2   Type the following text: **Please find enclosed a copy of the Annual Report. Creative Training are pleased to announce record profits for 1993 and we intend to improve our overall performance for 1994.** Press the $\boxed{\text{Enter}}$ key twice.

3   Access the **Tools** menu and select the **Outline** option followed by **Outline on**. Press the $\boxed{\text{Enter}}$ key and the first outline number will appear. Press $\boxed{\text{F7}}$ to indent the text to the first tab position and type: **Achievements in 1993**

4   Press the Enter key once and then the Tab key to insert the second level of outline numbering. Press F7 and type the following text: **We are now registered for BS 5750.**

5   Press the Enter key and WordPerfect will insert the second level 2 number. Press F7 and type the following text: **We have been awarded the SPECO award for Outstanding Customer Service. We are always striving to improve the services on offer to our clients and this year we will be introducing two new services:**

6   Press the Enter key and then the Tab key again. WordPerfect will insert the first level 3 number. Press F7 and type **Technical support** and press the Enter key. Press F7 and type **Free seminars on the latest software innovations.** Press the Enter key again.

7   To move back to first level numbering, press Shift Tab twice and type **Staff.**

8   Press the Enter key and then the Tab key. Press F7 and type **Two new members of staff have recently joined the company.**

9   Press the Enter key and then the Tab key. Press F7 and type **Brenda Dickinson has taken up the post of Sales and Marketing Director.**

10 Press the Enter key followed by F7 and type **Trudy Lilley is our new Training Co-ordinator.**

11 Press the Enter key. Press Shift Tab twice to move back to the first level of numbering and type **Training.**

12 Complete the outline as follows:

     A.   **A training schedule will be produced quarterly.**

     B.   **The training team will be relocated to our Barnet office.**

13 Save the document as **OUTLINE.WP.**

24.4   Copying, moving and deleting an outline family

Each section of an outline consisting of a main paragraph and its sub-paragraphs is known as a *family*. You can select a family group and make an exact copy, move the family to another position within the outline, delete the family or change the numbering level.

To select a family, position the insertion point in the first line of the main paragraph, access the **Tools** menu and select **Outline** followed by **Move family**, **Copy family** or **Delete family**. The family group will become highlighted and you will then be prompted to use cursor arrow keys to move or change the outline structure.

Select the **Copy family** option if you want to make a copy of the family structure which you can then replace with new information. A highlighted copy of the family will be placed in the document. Press the Enter key to place the copy. Position the insertion point before the first character to be changed and press the Insert key. Begin typing new text. Alternatively you can leave the outline numbers, delete the copy of the text and type new information.

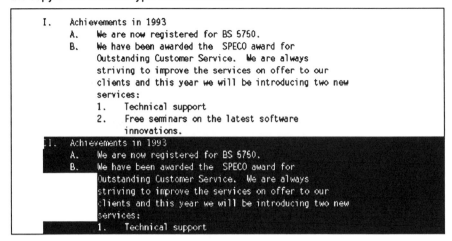

To move a family, select the **Move family** option and, when the family is highlighted, press the ↑ or ↓ cursor arrow keys as many times as required until the family is in its new position within the outline. Press the Enter key to secure its position. WordPerfect will automatically re-number the outline to take account of any changes.

If you want to change the numbering levels for the family, select the **Move family** option and, whilst highlighted, press the → or ← key to indent or outdent the family one level. See the following example.

```
Please find enclosed a copy of the Annual Report.  Creative
training are pleased to announce record profits for 1993 and
we intend to improve our overall performance for 1994.
        A.      Achievements in 1993
                1.      We are now registered for BS 5750.
                2.      We have been awarded the  SPECO award for
                        Outstanding Customer Service.  We are always
                        striving to improve the services on offer to
                        our clients and this year we will be
                        introducing two new services:
                        a.      Technical support
                        b.      Free seminars on the latest software
                                innovations.
I.      Staff
        A.      Two new members of staff have recently joined the
                company.
                1       Brenda Dickinson has taken up the post of Sales
```

To delete a family, choose the **Delete family** option and respond with **Yes** when
you are prompted to delete the highlighted family.

1   Open **OUTLINE.WP**. Position the insertion point in the first line of the second
    main paragraph (the paragraph on Training).

2   Access the **Tools** menu, select **Outline** and choose the **Move family** option.
    Press the ⌴↑⌴ once so that this family becomes the first family in the outline.

3   Save and close the document.

25   Generating an index

An index is a list of terms or key words which have been used throughout a document. This list is usually generated in alphabetical order at the end of a document and provides a quick reference to the topics which can be found in the document.

25.1   Preparing for this chapter

In order to complete this chapter you need the following document:

Filename	File type	Chapter
CONFINFO.WP	Document	12

 If you have not created this document in the previous chapters you will need to refer back to the chapter number listed above and create the file. Please note, this file has been modified in subsequent chapters.

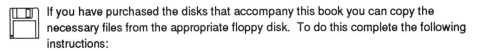 If you have purchased the disks that accompany this book you can copy the necessary files from the appropriate floppy disk. To do this complete the following instructions:

1   Make sure you have created a sub-directory on the hard disk called **C:\WPWIN\DATA** (*see* Creating a data directory, page xvi).

2   Load WordPerfect for Windows (*see* Loading WordPerfect for Windows, page xv).

3   Follow the instructions for Using the diskettes on page vii.

25.2   Creating index entries

There are two ways to create index entries. The first is to create a separate file, known as a *concordance file*, containing the words to be used in the index. WordPerfect will search the document for the words in the concordance file and display the words and their corresponding page numbers in the index. The second method is to mark each entry in the document.

Using a concordance file

To create a concordance file, choose the **New** option from the **File** menu and enter each index word on a line of its own. Save the file with an appropriate name. As WordPerfect can generate the index more efficiently if the concordance file lists the words in alphabetical order, position the insertion point at the start of the document and select the **Sort** option from the **Tools** menu. In the **Sort** dialog box, select the **Line** option as the **Record type** and **Ascending** as the **Sort order**. Leave the **Key definitions** with their default settings. Click the **OK** button to begin the sort. See the following example of a concordance file.

```
35mm slides
Calculation
Cell
Charts
Computer
Database
Desktop publishing
Drawings
Financial
Formatting features
Keyboard
OHPs
Presentation software
Product
```

It may be useful to have both the concordance file and the document to be indexed open at the same time. You can then select the **Tile** option from the **Window** menu and view both documents on the screen. You should be able to see at a glance which words should be included in the index.

 Creating a concordance file

1   Open **CONFINFO.WP**.

2   Create a new document.

3   Select the **Tile** option from the **Window** menu.

4   Type the following index entries into the new document window.

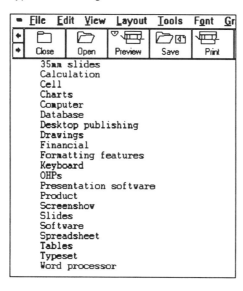

5   Save the document as **CONCORD.WP**.

25.3   Marking index entries

An index can display two levels of words, either headings or subheadings. If you decide to mark each entry in a document instead of creating a concordance file, you will need to indicate whether the entry is to be a heading or a subheading. Concordance file entries will automatically be displayed in the index as headings unless you mark entries to appear as subheadings.

To mark an index entry, select the text in the document or concordance file, access the **Tools** menu and choose the **Mark text** option followed by the **Index** option. The text will appear in the **Mark index** dialog box as a heading and can be edited if necessary. To mark the text as a heading, simply click the **OK** button. To mark the text as a subheading, type an entry in the **Heading** box and then click in the **Subheading** box. The index entry will appear in the **Subheading** box. Click the **OK** button to complete the process.

An index entry may appear as both a heading and a subheading. Select the text and follow the steps outlined above to mark the text as a heading. With the text still selected, type a heading in the **Mark index** dialog box under which the selected text is to appear in the index and click in the **Subheading** box to enter the selected text as a subheading. Click the **OK** button to complete the process.

If you decide to mark index entries in the document, you must follow the steps above and mark every piece of text to be included in the index.

 Marking entries

1   Make **CONCORD.WP** the current document. Double click the word "Financial" to select it. Access the **Tools** menu and select the **Mark text** option followed by the **Index** option. The **Mark text** dialog box will appear.

2   Type **Spreadsheet** into the **Heading** box. Press the ⌷Tab⌷ key to move the insertion point into the **Subheading** box. WordPerfect will automatically enter the word "Financial" (the selected text from the document) in the **Subheading** box. Click the **OK** button.

3   Select the entry "Formatting features". Access the **Tools** menu and select the **Mark text** option followed by **Index**. Type **Word processor** in the **Heading** box and press the ⌷Tab⌷ key to move the insertion point into the **Subheading** box. WordPerfect will enter the words "Formatting features" in the **Subheading** box. Click the **OK** button to complete the entry.

4   Mark the entries "Screenshow", "slides" and "35mm slides" as **Subheadings** of "Presentation software".

5   Mark "Typeset" as a **Subheading** of "Desktop publishing".

6   Save the document.

The next step is to define the index. To do this, access the **Tools** menu and select
the **Define** option followed by the **Index** option. The **Define index** dialog box will be
displayed.

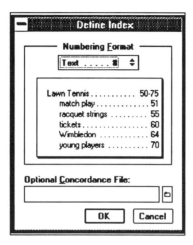

Select a **Numbering format** from the pop-up menu. The following numbering
formats are available in the **Define index** dialog box:

**No
numbering**   an option to have no page numbers

Text #   the index entry will be followed by a space and then the page number

Text (#)   the index entry will be followed by a space and then the page number
in brackets

Text #   the index entry will be followed by page numbers which are right
aligned

Text....#   same as above but with leader dots preceding page numbers

As you choose a numbering format WordPerfect will display a sample in the dialog
box. If you are generating the index using a concordance file, type the full path and
filename in the optional **Concordance file** box or click the disk icon to the right of
the box and choose the file and its directory from the list.

WordPerfect will insert a **[Def mark:index]** code in the document, defining the index
at the insertion point. An example of the code can be see in the following illustration.

```
$R
slides, charts and drawings.  Slides can then be printed, plotted, put onto
35mm slides or presented in a screenshow                                 .

[Def Mark:Index.FlRgtDotLdr;c:\wpwin\data\concord.]
```

Defining an index

1   Make **CONFINFO.WP** the current document.

2   Press ⌈ **Ctrl End** ⌋ to move the insertion point to the end of the document and
    ⌈ **Ctrl Enter** ⌋ to insert a page break. Make sure the insertion point is below the
    page break.

3   Access the **Tools** menu and select the **Define** option followed by **Index**. The
    Define index dialog box will be displayed.

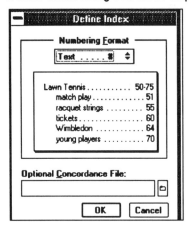

4   Select the type of **Numbering format** that you require.

5   Type **C:\WPWIN\DATA\CONCORD** in the **Concordance file** box or click the
    disk icon and select the file from the list. When you have completed the
    definition, click the **OK** button.

25.5   Generating an index

To generate the index, access the **Tools** menu and select the **Generate** option or
press ⌈ **Alt F12** ⌋. The **Generate** dialog box will be displayed prompting you to
choose the **Yes** option if you want all lists, indexes, table of contents etc to be
updated.

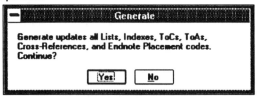

If you choose to continue, WordPerfect will search the document for words which
match each marked index entry or words which match those in the concordance file.
It will generate an index of those words and their corresponding page numbers
where it finds the code defining the index.

Although it searches for an exact match, the search is not case sensitive. For
example, if "computer" is a word in the concordance file, it will not find "computers"
but it will find "COMPUTER" or "Computer".

Generating an index

1   Using **CONFINFO.WP,** access the **Tools** menu and select the **Generate** option. The **Generate** dialog box will appear.

2   Select the **Yes** option to update the index. The index should be generated and resemble the following example.

Desktop publishing . . . . -II-
    Typeset . . . . -II-
Drawings . . . . -III-
Keyboard . . . . -I-
OHPs . . . . -III-
Presentation software . . . . -II-
    35mm slides . . . . -III-
    Screenshow . . . . -III-
    Slides . . . . -III-
Product . . . . -I-, -II-
Software . . . . -I-, -II-
Spreadsheet . . . . -I-
    Financial . . . . -I-
Tables . . . . -III-
Word processor . . . . -I-

26   Table of contents

A table of contents provides a list of topics contained within a document. You would normally find one at the beginning of reports, books or manuals.

26.1   Preparing for this chapter

In order to complete this chapter you need the following document:

Filename	File type	Chapter
OUTLINE.WP	Document	24

 If you have not created this document in the previous chapters you will need to refer back to the chapter number listed above and create the file.

 If you have purchased the disks that accompany this book you can copy the necessary files from the appropriate floppy disk. To do this complete the following instructions:

1   Make sure you have created a sub-directory on the hard disk called **C:\WPWIN\DATA** (*see* Creating a data directory, page xvi).

2   Load WordPerfect for Windows (*see* Loading WordPerfect for Windows page xv).

3   Follow the instructions for Using the diskettes on page vii.

26.2   Marking table of contents entries

Before creating a long document it is a good idea to decide upon the topics to be covered in advance. Once you have produced an outline of topics, enter a list of subheadings below each main heading. You might like to use the outline feature to simplify this task. Each level of heading can then be included in the table of contents and made distinctive with its own format. A table of contents can display five levels of heading, each with its own numbering format.

The first step is to select the text to be included in the table of contents. Then access the **Tools** menu and select the **Mark text** option followed by the **Table of contents** option. The **Mark table of contents** dialog box will be displayed.

Select the level that you wish the text to take (from 1 to 5) and then click the **OK** button. Repeat this procedure for all text to be included in the table of contents. WordPerfect will place a **[Mark:ToC]** code at the beginning and **[End mark:ToC]** at the end of each piece of text marked in this way.

 Marking entries for a table of contents

1 Open **OUTLINE.WP**. Move the insertion point to the end of the first section of the outline, before the paragraph "I. Achievements in 1993". Press Ctrl Enter to create a page break. Place a second page break before the paragraph "III. Training". If any unwanted outline numbers appear, press Backspace to delete them.

2 Select "Achievements in 1993". Access the **Tools** menu and select the **Mark text** option followed by **Table of contents**. Select **Level 1** in the **Mark table of contents** dialog box and click the **OK** button.

3 Select the **Reveal codes** option from the **View** menu to see the table of contents codes around the selected text.

4 Switch reveal codes off. Select "BS 5750" and access the **Tools** menu. Select the **Mark text** option followed by **Table of contents**. Select **Level 2** in the **Mark table of contents** dialog box and click the **OK** button.

5 Select "SPECO award" and mark this as **Level 2** in the **Mark table of contents** dialog box.

6 Select "Technical support" and mark this as **Level 3** and "Seminars" also as **Level 3**.

7 Select important text from each of the other two sections of the outline and mark the text as **Level 1** or **2**.

8 Save the document with the changes.

26.3   Defining a table of contents

The next step is to insert the table of contents in the document and set the correct page numbering. Move to the position where the table of contents is to be inserted (usually at the beginning of a document). The table would normally be placed on a page of its own so press Ctrl Enter to create a page break. It is important to set correct page numbering for the document otherwise the pages of the table of contents will be included in the page numbering scheme. Move to the first page of the document after the table of contents and access the **Layout** menu. Select the

Page option followed by the **Numbering** option and then **New page number**. Set this first page to page number **1**.

Move the insertion point to the start of the page to contain the table of contents. Access the **Tools** menu and select the **Define** option followed by the **Table of contents** option.

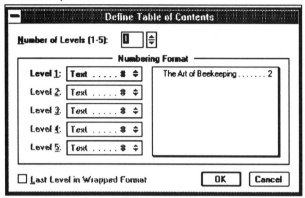

In the **Define table of contents** dialog box select the number of levels of text to be incorporated in the **Number of levels [1-5]:** pop-up menu. Click each button for the number of levels chosen and select a **Numbering format** for each level. The formats are identical to those described in the section on indexing and samples of each format selected will be displayed. If there is more than one line of text, click the **Last level in wrapped format** box if you want the last level wrapped around at the left margin instead of indented.

Although there are five options governing number formats, they control only the position and display of the page numbers, and not the type of numbering. If you want to change the type of numbering, select the **Page** option from the **Layout** menu and then the **Numbering** option. Choose an alternative type of numbering from the **Numbering type** pop-up list.

 Creating a table of contents

1   Open **OUTLINE.WP** if it is not already open. Press Ctrl Home Home to move to the top of the document and press Ctrl Enter to create a page break.

2   With the insertion point in the first page of the document containing the outline, access the **Layout** menu. Select the **Page** option followed by the **Numbering** option. Click the **Position** button and select **Bottom centre** from the pop-up list. Select **1,2,3,4** as the **Numbering type**. Click in the **New page number** box and set this first page to page number **1**. Click the **OK** button.

3   Move the insertion point to the start of the page to contain the table of contents. Type **Table of contents** and choose the following format options: **Times roman**, **36 points** and **Shadow**.

4   Press the Enter key several times to move the insertion point down the page. Access the **Tools** menu and select the **Define** option followed by **Table of contents**.

5   In the **Define table of contents** dialog box select **3** as the number of levels of text to be incorporated and choose **Text.....#** as the format for **Level 1, Text.....#** as the format for **Level 2** and **Text   #** as the format for **Level 3**. Click the **OK** button and save the document.

Generating lists

All lists can be generated at the same time. Once the steps to identify the text to be included in a table of contents, index or some other list have been identified, all that remains is to generate the list. To do this, access the **Tools** menu and select the **Generate** option. Select the **Yes** option to complete the generation of all lists. The lists will be generated at the point where the table of contents or index were defined.

  Generating a table of contents

1   Open **OUTLINE.WP**. If you have followed the steps outlined above to define the table of contents all that remains is for you to generate the table of contents.

2   Access the **Tools** menu and select the **Generate** option.

3   At the prompt to generate all lists, choose the **Yes** option. The table of contents should resemble the example below.

Table of Contents

```
Staff.  .  .  .  .  .  .  .  .  .  .  .  .  .  .  .  .  .  .  .  .  .  .  .  .  1
        Marketing Director.  .  .  .  .  .  .  .  .  .  .  .  .  .  .  .  1
        Training Co-ordinator  .  .  .  .  .  .  .  .  .  .  .  .  .  .  1

Achievements in 1993 .  .  .  .  .  .  .  .  .  .  .  .  .  .  .  .  .  .  2
        BS 5750 .  .  .  .  .  .  .  .  .  .  .  .  .  .  .  .  .  .  .  .  2
        SPECO .  .  .  .  .  .  .  .  .  .  .  .  .  .  .  .  .  .  .  .  .  2
                Technical support  .  .  .  .  .  .  .  .  .  .  .  .  2
                Seminars  .  .  .  .  .  .  .  .  .  .  .  .  .  .  .  .  2

Training .  .  .  .  .  .  .  .  .  .  .  .  .  .  .  .  .  .  .  .  .  .  .  3
        Training schedule .  .  .  .  .  .  .  .  .  .  .  .  .  .  .  .  3
        Training team .  .  .  .  .  .  .  .  .  .  .  .  .  .  .  .  .  .  3
```

Creative Training Annual Report

If you change any of the text in the document at some future point, you may need to follow the steps above to regenerate the list. It will not be automatically updated.

Creating a master document

Large documents are often memory intensive and slow down many of WordPerfect's processes such as searching, spell checking and calculating. It is often more productive to divide a large document into several smaller documents and have each document linked by a *master file*. This feature is particularly useful if you are creating large reports, books or manuals.

27.1 Preparing for this chapter

In order to complete this chapter you need the following documents:

File name	File type	Chapter
CONFER.WP	Document	8
NEWS.WP	Document	11
CONFINFO.WP	Document	12
INVOICE	Document	15
SCHEDULE.WP	Document	16
BOOKING.WP	Document	16

If you have not created these documents in the previous chapters you will need to refer back to the chapter numbers listed above and create the files. Please note, these files have been modified in subsequent chapters.

If you have purchased the disks that accompany this book you can copy the necessary files from the appropriate floppy disk. To do this complete the following instructions:

1   Make sure you have created a sub-directory on the hard disk called **C:\WPWIN\DATA** (*see* Creating a data directory, page xvi).

2   Load WordPerfect for Windows (*see* Loading WordPerfect for Windows, page xv).

3   Follow the instructions for Using the diskettes on page vii.

27.2 Creating a master document

A master document is a normal WordPerfect document. You type information into the document and, at the point where you would like to incorporate information from another document (known as a *subdocument*), you insert a special code. Once the master file is created, you can then apply standard formatting features to all of the documents referred to by the master document as well as having pages, paragraphs and graphic boxes sequentially numbered across all files. It is important, however, that subdocuments do not contain conflicting numbering or formatting codes if these are to be sequential or standard across all documents.

To create a master document, type any required text and then, at the point that you want to create a link with another document, select the **Master document** option from the **Tools** menu followed by **Subdocument**. The **Include subdocument** dialog box will be displayed.

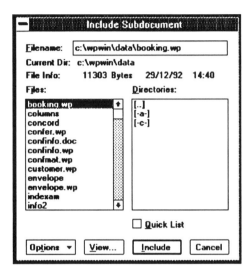

Type the name of the file and click the **Include** button. View each file in turn if you are unsure which files to include in the master document. When you have included a file, a **[Subdoc:]** code will appear on the screen. Press Ctrl Enter if you want to create a page break between this subdocument and the following subdocument.

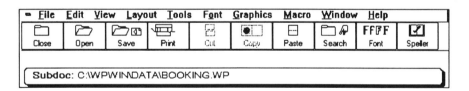

Repeat the above steps for each subdocument to be included and your document should resemble the following example (*see* next page).

Close	Open	Save	Print	Cut	Copy	Paste	Search	Font	Speller

Subdoc: C:\WPWIN\DATA\CONFER.WP

Subdoc: C:\WPWIN\DATA\CONFINFO.WP

Subdoc: C:\WPWIN\DATA\INVOICE

Subdoc: C:\WPWIN\DATA\NEWS.WP

⊃ Creating a master file

1 Create a new document and type the following text: **Please find enclosed samples of the marketing material used by Creative Training. If you require further information to support our application, please do not hesitate to call.**

2 Press the ⌐Enter⌐ key twice. Access the **Tools** menu and select the **Master document** option followed by the **Subdocument** option. Select **BOOKING.WP** from the **Include subdocument** dialog box and click the **Include** button. Press ⌐**Ctrl Enter**⌐ to create a page break.

3 Repeat the above steps to include the following subdocuments in the master document:
CONFER.WP
CONFINFO.WP

4 Save the document as **MARKET.WP**.

27.3 Expanding a master document

Before you can print or make editing changes to any of the subdocuments, you must expand the master document to display all of the subdocuments on the screen. To expand the master document, access the **Tools** menu and select the **Master document** option followed by **Expand master**.

Each subdocument will be retrieved into the master document and displayed within **[Subdoc start]** and **[Subdoc end]** codes. If you make any changes above or below those codes, the changes will be saved as part of the master document only. If you make changes within the start and end codes, the changes will be saved as part of the subdocument. Any codes inserted in the master document will take effect until a competing code is encountered.

Expanding a master document

1 Open **MARKET.WP** if it is not already open.

2 Select the **Master document** option from the **Tools** menu followed by **Expand master**. All subdocuments should be retrieved into the master document.

3 Preview the document.

4 Position the insertion point at the top of the master document, before any codes for the subdocuments. Set the left margin to **1.5"**.

5 Position the insertion point at the top of **BOOKING.WP** (after the subdocument start code) and set the left margin to **2.5"**.

27.4 Condensing a master document

Before you close a master document you should *condense* it so that only the subdocument links are displayed on the screen. To condense a file, access the **Tools** menu and select the **Master document** option followed by **Condense master**. The **Condense master document** dialog box will prompt you to save all subdocuments. You can choose therefore to abandon any changes to subdocuments or continue to save. If you select the **Yes** option, WordPerfect will prompt you to replace existing subdocument files.

 Condensing a master file

1 With **MARKET.WP** open and current on the screen, select the **Master document** option from the **Tools** menu and choose the **Condense master** option.

2 Select **Yes** to save changes to all subdocuments and replace each document as necessary. Close all documents.

27.5 Generating lists

Indexes, tables of contents and other lists can be generated as part of a master document. Mark text entries in each of the subdocuments as normal and then position the insertion point where the list should be generated in the master document. Define the index or table of contents following the steps outlined in sections 25.4 and 26.3 and then complete the generation process.

27.6 Printing

A master document can be printed using the usual steps for printing. However, make sure that the master document is expanded first, otherwise only the condensed version will be printed.

28 File management

When you have been using WordPerfect for a while you will find that you need to tidy up your data sub-directory. There will be files that you no longer need that can be removed from disk. More immediately, you will need to *backup* important documents onto floppy diskettes. Backing up is a precaution. By having a copy of an important document on a floppy diskette you are prepared if there should be some unforeseen problem with your hard disk.

This chapter will provide an overview of the *File Manager*. If you need to work extensively with the File Manager it is recommended that you refer to the reference material which accompanies the application.

28.1 Preparing for this chapter

In order to complete this chapter you need the following documents:

File name	File type	Chapter
NEWLETT.WP	Document	2
NEWS.WP	Document	11

 If you have not created these documents in the previous chapter you will need to refer back to the chapter numbers listed above and create the files. Please note, these files have been modified in subsequent chapters.

 If you have purchased the disks that accompany this book you can copy the necessary files from the appropriate floppy disk. To do this complete the following instructions:

1   Make sure you have created a sub-directory on the hard disk called **C:\WPWIN\DATA** (*see* Creating a data directory, page xvi).

2   Load WordPerfect for Windows (*see* Loading WordPerfect for Windows, page xv)

3   Follow the instructions for Using the diskettes on page vii.

The WordPerfect for Windows File Manager is a powerful application that enables you to search easily through drives and directories. There are several options available including deleting and copying files.

To use the File Manager, access the **File** menu and select the **File manager** option. The following screen is displayed:

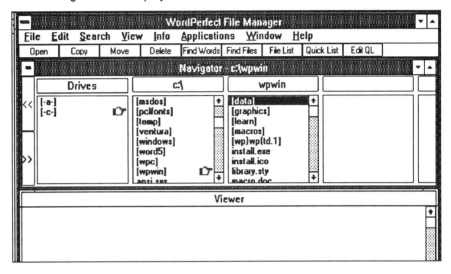

The File Manager workspace can comprise four different types of File Manager windows:

- A file list window - containing a list of files in a given directory and information about those files.

- A navigator window - containing lists of filenames. This window can be used for easy browsing through directories and files.

- A file viewer window - displaying the contents of the file currently selected in the file list or navigator window.

- A quick list window - containing the current quick list settings.

These windows can be manipulated in the same way as other windows.

1   Access the File Manager and practice minimising, maximising and re-sizing the available windows.

2   Select the **Layouts** option from the **View** menu. Select a predefined arrangement for the windows.

3   Access the **View** menu again and select the **Layouts**, **Setup** options. Create your own custom layout.

28.3　The navigator window

If there is no navigator window visible, select the **Navigator** option from the **View** menu or press $\boxed{\textbf{Ctrl N}}$. There are several panels across the screen which enable you to select files from floppy or hard disk and then select the appropriate option from the menu. The options include opening, copying, moving and deleting files. Follow the steps outlined below to use the File Manager effectively. From the left panel, select the drive where the files can be located. Select **A** for floppy disk and **C** for hard disk. The next panel to the right will now display a list of files and sub-directories for the selected drive. Select a sub-directory or file from the list. A pointing hand will indicate the current selection. The next panel to the right will display a list of sub-directories and files in the current sub-directory.

In the previous screen example, drive C has been selected. The next panel to the right displays a list of directories and files in the root of C. The sub-directory **C:\WPWIN** is then selected. The third panel displays all the sub-directories and files within **C:\WPWIN**. Work through the directory structure until the desired file is located, select it and then select a menu option.

1 Activate the navigator window if not already displayed.

2 Display the contents of the sub-directory **C:\WPWIN\DATA** (or the sub-directory containing your data files).

28.4　The file list window

To display the file list window select the **File list** option from the **View** menu or press $\boxed{\textbf{Ctrl F}}$. Alternatively, click on the buttons on the top of any navigator column. The file list window can display the following information:

- size in bytes

- creation date

- creation time

- DOS file attributes

- full path to the file

- descriptive name, extracted from the file's document summary

- descriptive type, taken from the summary

Normally only the filename, size, date and time are displayed. The other columns can easily be added by clicking and holding the mouse in the empty portion of the column-heading row. A pop-up menu will be displayed. Select the column to be added from the menu. The order in which the files are displayed can be changed by selecting the options from the **View options** dialog box (access the **View** menu and select the **Options** option). Select the option to list by and then select **Ascending** or **Descending** to define the sort order.

1   Add a new column to the file list window to show a descriptive name for the file.

2   Sort the list by **Date** in **Descending** order.

28.5   Quick list window

To make a quick list window visible select the **Quick list** option from the **View** menu or press Ctrl Q .

The quick list window shows all directories currently in the quick list window. If you double click on any line, a file list window will appear for that directory. To edit or create new quick list entries select the **Edit quick list** option from the **View** menu. There are options to **Add** or **Delete** entries from the list.

1   Add the sub-directory **C:\WPWIN\DATA** (or your data directory) to the quick list window. Note, you can print the contents of the navigator, file list or quick list windows by selecting the **Print window** option from the **File** menu.

28.6   Using the File Manager

The file manager can be used to manipulate one or more files in the current navigator or file list window. To select a file, click on it. To select a group of files, click on the first file and drag the mouse to select all the required files. To select all the files select the **Select all** option from the **Edit** menu or press Ctrl S .

To deselect all the selected files, select the **Deselect all** option from the **Edit** menu or press Ctrl E .

When the required file or files are selected you can then manipulate those files. For example, you may want to delete the files, copy the files to a floppy disk or open the file(s). Some of the available file operations are outlined below.

Deleting files

When you have used WordPerfect for a while you will find that your data directory is becoming cluttered with documents that you no longer want. It is good practice to delete these files on a regular basis. In the file list or navigator window select the file(s) that you want to delete, select the **Delete** option from the **File** menu, or use one of the shortcuts to delete (press the Delete key, click on the **Delete** button or press Ctrl D).

If you have selected a single file to delete, you will be prompted to confirm by clicking on the **Delete** button. If you have selected a number of files, you will have the option to **Delete all**, thereby deleting all the selected files. Alternatively, you can delete some of the selected files by selecting **Skip** if you do not want to delete the displayed file or **Delete** to delete it.

Copying files

Use the copy facility to make a duplicate of a file or a selection of files. Select the file(s) you want to copy from the navigator or file list window and then select the **Copy** option from the **File** menu or press `Ctrl C`.

A dialog box will appear listing the file(s) to be copied. The **To directory** box can be used to specify where you want to copy the file(s) to. Either type the destination or use the button at the end of the box to quickly choose the directory. If you have chosen to copy more than one file you have similar options to those for deleting; you can copy all the files or select to skip some files.

Moving or renaming files

Documents can be moved to another directory or drive or can be given new names by the following method. Select the file(s) to be moved or renamed from the navigator or file list window and then select the **Move/rename** option from the **File** menu or press `Ctrl R`.

If you have selected a single file you can type the new name for the file or the directory the file is to be moved to (similar process to copying). With a selection of files you can move or rename all the files or you can use the **Skip** option as before.

Printing a file from the File Manager

This is a useful facility if you want to print a number of files. Select the file(s) to be printed from the navigator or file list window. Select the **Print** option from the **File** menu or press `Ctrl P`.

Finding files

If you are saving files to a number of different sub-directories you may forget where a certain file is located. The find feature will help you locate the file quickly. Make sure the navigator or file list window is displaying the sub-directory at the starting point for your search - the root if you want to search the whole drive. Select the **Find file** option from the **Search** menu and type the name of the file you are looking for in the **File pattern** box. If you don't know the whole name use the standard DOS wildcards, * for a number of characters and ? for a single character. For example *.WP would find all files with the .WP extension; **MEMO?.DOC** would find all files with the filename MEMO followed by one other character, ie MEMO1, MEMO2 etc.

If you are searching only the current directory check the **Directory** option. To search the whole drive check the **Drive** option. Click on the **Find** button.

As a result of the search, all the files matching your search pattern will be displayed in the window.

Creating a new sub-directory

You may decide that you want to save all your letters in one sub-directory and create another sub-directory to hold all your memos. Or, if you create documents for more than one person, you may want to have separate sub-directories for each person. To create a new sub-directory, select the **Create directory** option from the **File** menu or press Ctrl T .

A dialog box will appear. Type the name and path of the new directory in the **New directory** box and click on the **Create** button.

1   Create a new directory **C:\WPWIN\MEMOS.**

2   Move the document **NEWLETT.WP** to the new sub-directory.

3   Rename the document **NEWLETT.WP** to **MEMO.WP.**

4   Copy the document **MEMO.WP** to **MEMO2.WP** and **MEMO3.WP.**

5   Display the **C:\WPWIN** sub-directory in the file list window. From this point, search for all numbered memo files by using the search pattern **MEMO?.WP.**

6   Display the **C:\WPWIN\MEMOS** sub-directory in the navigator window.

7   Delete the documents **MEMO2.WP** and **MEMO3.WP.**

8   If you have a floppy disk to hand, find and copy the document **NEWS.WP** to the floppy disk.

29 Consolidation

This last chapter in Part 3 is designed to reinforce a number of topics covered throughout the book.

29.1 Preparing for this chapter

In order to complete this chapter you need the following document:

Filename	File type	Chapter
NEWS.WP	Document	11

 If you have not created this document in the previous chapters you will need to refer back to the chapter number listed above and create the file. Please note, this file has been modified in subsequent chapters.

 If you have purchased the disks that accompany this book you can copy the necessary files from the appropriate floppy disk. To do this complete the following instructions:

1 Make sure you have created a sub-directory on the hard disk called **C:\WPWIN\DATA** (*see* Creating a data directory, page xvi).

2 Load WordPerfect for Windows (*see* Loading WordPerfect for Windows, page xv).

3 Follow the instructions for Using the diskettes on page vii.

29.2 Exercise

1 Open **NEWS.WP**.

2 Enhance the document until it resembles the following illustrations (*see* next page).

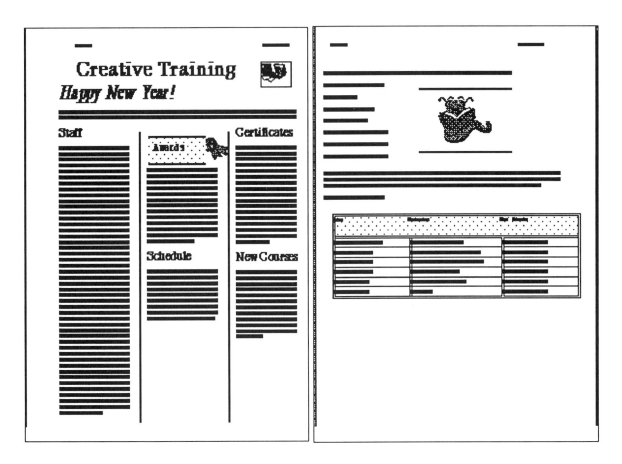

This illustration is designed to show the position of text and graphics. For textual content, refer to Chapter 11.

Appendix A - Menus

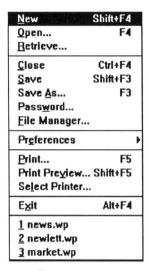

New Shift+F4
O̲pen... F4
R̲etrieve...
C̲lose Ctrl+F4
S̲ave Shift+F3
Save A̲s... F3
Password...
F̲ile Manager...
P̲references ▶
Print... F5
Print Pre̲view... Shift+F5
Select Printer...
Exit Alt+F4
1̲ news.wp
2̲ newlett.wp
3̲ market.wp

File menu

U̲ndo Alt+Bksp
U̲ndelete... Alt+Shift+Bksp
Cu̲t Shift+Del
C̲opy Ctrl+Ins
Paste Shift+Ins
Append
Link ▶
Se̲lect ▶
Co̲nvert Case ▶
Search... F2
Search Next Shift+F2
Search Pre̲vious Alt+F2
Replace... Ctrl+F2
Go To... Ctrl+G

Edit menu

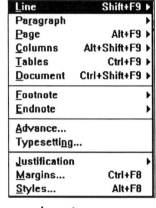

Line Shift+F9 ▶
Pa̲ragraph ▶
Page Alt+F9 ▶
C̲olumns Alt+Shift+F9 ▶
T̲ables Ctrl+F9 ▶
D̲ocument Ctrl+Shift+F9 ▶
F̲ootnote ▶
E̲ndnote ▶
Advance...
Typesettin̲g...
J̲ustification ▶
Margins... Ctrl+F8
Styles... Alt+F8

Layout menu

Speller... Ctrl+F1
T̲hesaurus... Alt+F1
W̲ord Count...
L̲anguage...
D̲ate ▶
O̲utline ▶
Sort... Ctrl+Shift+F12
Merge Ctrl+F12 ▶
Mark Text F12 ▶
De̲fine Shift+F12 ▶
Generate... Alt+F12
Docu̲ment Compare ▶
M̲aster Document ▶
Spr̲eadsheet ▶
Commen̲t ▶
L̲ine Draw... Ctrl+D

Tools menu

F̲ont... F9
C̲olour...
✓**N̲ormal** Ctrl+N
B̲old Ctrl+B
I̲talics Ctrl+I
U̲nderline Ctrl+U
D̲ouble Underline
R̲edline
Stri̲keout
Subscrip̲t
Sup̲erscript
S̲ize Ctrl+S ▶
O̲verstrike
WP Characters... Ctrl+W

Font menu

F̲igure ▶
Text B̲ox ▶
E̲quation ▶
T̲able Box ▶
U̲ser Box ▶
L̲ine ▶

Graphics menu

Play... Alt+F10
R̲ecord... Ctrl+F10
Stop Ctrl+Shift+F10
Pause
A̲ssign to Menu...
1̲ Add signature block
2̲ merge.wcm

Macro menu

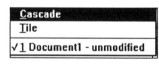

Cascade
T̲ile
✓**1̲ Document1 - unmodified**

Windows menu

Index...
Keyboard...
How Do I...
Glossary...
Using Help...
W̲hat Is...
About WordPerfect...

Help menu

Appendix B - Keyboard shortcuts

Moving around a document

→	Right a letter
←	Left a letter
↑	Up a line
↓	Down a line
Home	Beginning of line
End	End of line
Ctrl →	Right a word
Ctrl ←	Left a word
Page Dn	Next screen
Page Up	Previous screen
Alt Page Dn	Top of next page
Alt Page Dn	Top of preceding page
Ctrl End	Bottom of document
Ctrl Home	Top of document
Ctrl ↑	Up one paragraph
Ctrl ↓	Down one paragraph

Deleting text

Backspace	Character to left of cursor
Delete	Character at cursor position
Ctrl Backspace	Word at cursor position
Home **Backspace**	From cursor to the beginning of word
Ctrl Del	From cursor to the end of line

Function keys

		Ctrl	**Shift**	**Alt**
F1	Help	Speller	What is?	Thesaurus
F2	Search		Search next	Search previous
F3	Save as	Screen	Save	Reveal codes
F4	Open	Close doc.	New	Close app.
F5	Print	Date text	Print preview	Para. number
F6	Previous pane	Next doc.	Next pane	Next window
F7	Indent	Hanging indent	Centre	Flush right
F8	Select	Margins	Select cell	Styles
F9	Font	Tables	Line layout	Page layout
F10	Menu	Macro record		Macro play
F11	Retrieve figure	Horiz. line	Edit figure	Text box
F12	Mark text	Merge	Define	Generate

Useful keys

Ctrl Enter	Hard page break
Alt Enter	End of field
Alt Shift Enter	End of record
Ctrl B	Bold
Ctrl C	Copy
Ctrl F	Full justification
Ctrl G	Go to dialog box
Ctrl I	Italics
Ctrl J	Centre justification
Ctrl L	Left justification
Ctrl N	Normal text
Ctrl R	Right justification
Ctrl S	Font size menu
Ctrl U	Underline
Ctrl X	Cut
Ctrl V	Paste
Ctrl Z	Undo

Index

Accessing the file manager 220
Advance 94
Application control menu 4
Applying styles 194
Arithmetic operators 145
Assigning macros to the button bar 175
Attaching a macro 174
Auto code placement 49
Binding offset 100
Blank lines 113
Borders 168
Boxes 139
    Adding captions 163
    Anchoring 157
    Captions 165
    Changing appearance 161
    Changing type 157
    Check 9
    Deleting 169
    Dialog 8
    Drawing 139
    Figure box 155
    List 8
    Numbering 164
    Placing tables 162
    Point size 43
    Positioning 157
    Renumbering 165
    Sizing 157
    Text 8, 155
Bullet points 56
Button 4
    Maximise 4
    Minimise 4
    Restore 5
Button bar 11
    Assigning macros 175
    Customising 175
    Editing 176
    Options 9, 176
Calculating totals 147
Cancelling
    Menu 7
    Print job 103
Centring a line of text 51
Changing
    Appearance of text 41
    Box 161
    Column width 129, 188
    Document 21
    Graphic 168
    Layout 126
    Print order 103
    Table lines 131
    Tabs 55
Check box 9
Click viii
Closing a document window 40

Codes 46
    Attributes 47
    Auto code placement 49
    Initial 49
    Merge 70
    Removing 69
    Reveal 46
Columns 184
    Changing widths 188
    Combination layout 187
    Codes 186
    Creating 188
    Moving between 188
    Newspaper style 185
    Parallel 188
Commands 3
    Copy 24, 33
    Cut 33
    Delete 24
    Exit 19
    Exit Windows 19
    File 36
    Find 25
    If 114
    Install xii
    Move 25
    Options 24
    Paste 33
    Print 18
    Rename 25
    Reset 37
    Save 17
    Save as 17
    Search 67
    View 23, 36, 40
    WIN xv
    Zoom 37
Condensing a master document 219
Copy 24
    Files 224
    Formulas 148
    Outline 203
    Table information 136
    Text 32
Creating
    Formulae 144
    New sub-directory 225
    Parallel columns 188
    Style library 194
    Styles 191
    Template document 169
Customising the button bar 175
Data directory xvi
Dates 59
Defining
    Index 209
    Numbering style 199
Delete 24

Block of text 31
Endnote 90
Footnote 90
Outline 203
Deleting and inserting text 27
Deleting
    Fields 111
    Formulas 148
    Graphics boxes 169
    Rows and columns 133
    Tables 134
Desktop x
Dialog box 8
    Advance 94
    Box position and size 157
    Create spreadsheet link 152
    Format
        Cell 124
        Column 123
        Row 124
    Go to 120
    Import spreadsheet 153
    Line draw 139
    Open options 23
    Record macro 172
    Table cut/copy 136
    Table options 138
    Tables formula 145
Diskettes vii
Document 15
    Appearance 51
    Binding offset 100
    Centring 51
    Changing 21
    Changing appearance of text 41
    Condensing a master document 219
    Control menu 3
    Copying text 32
    Creating 15
        Master document 216
        Template 169
        Window 39
    Deleting text 27, 31
    Double-sided 99
    Endnotes 87
    Expanding a master document 218
    Footnotes 87
    Headers and footers 85
    Incorporating graphics 159
    Indenting text 58
    Initial codes 49
    Inserting
        Dates 59
        Text 27
    Justification 51
    Large 80
    Line spacing 53
    Moving around 26
    Moving text 32
    Multiple 39
    Opening a window 21
    Page break 60
    Paper size 80
    Print multiple copies 100
    Printing 18

    Double sides 99
    From disk 99
        Master document 219
    Restoring text 32
    Saving 16
    Searching 66
    Search and replace 68
    Setting margins 80
    Spell checking 62
    Tabs 54
    Thesaurus 65
    Typeover 28
Double indent 58
Drag ix
Drawing lines and boxes 139
Editing 62
    Button bar 176
    Graphics 165
Eliminating blank lines and fields 113
Endnotes 87
Entering information into a table 121
Envelopes 106
Expanding a master document 218
Figure box 155
File list window 222
File manager 220
    Accessing 220
    Creating a sub-directory 225
Find 25
Finding files 224
Fonts 42
    Initial 46
    Point size 43
Footnotes and endnotes 87
    Changing position 90
    Deleting 90
    Options 89
Formatting text in a table 122
Generating
    Index 206, 210
    Lists 215, 219
Graphics 155
    Adding captions to boxes 163
    Anchoring boxes 157
    Borders 168
    Captions 165
    Changing box 157, 161
    Creating a graphics box 156
    Deleting boxes 169
    Editing 165
    Graphic images 155
    Incorporating into a document 159
    Incorporating text 156
    Lines 142
    Numbering boxes 164
    Placing tables in boxes 162
    Positioning a box 157
    Renumbering boxes 165
    Sizing a box 157
    Template 169
    Text wrapping 169
Hanging indent 58
Hardware requirements xi
Headers and footers 85
Help 11

Highlight ix
Icons vi
Importing spreadsheet information 152
Incorporating
    Graphics 159
    Text 156
Indenting text 58
Index 206
    Creating entries 206
    Defining 209
    Generation 206, 210
    Marking entries 208
Initial fonts 46
Inserting
    Dates 59
    Text 27
Installing WordPerfect xi
    Options xiii
    Printer selector xiv
Italic text 44
Joining and splitting cells 130
Justification 51, 52
Keyboard ix, 229
Labels 96
    Mail merge 107
    Mailing 98
    Positioning text 98
Large documents 80
Leaving WordPerfect for Windows 19
Line draw 139
Line spacing 53
Lines and boxes 139
List box 8
Loading WordPerfect xv
Macros 172
    Assigning to the button bar 175
    Attaching 174
    Creating 172
    Removing 174
    Running 173
Mail merge 70, 104
    Adding
        Fields 111
        Records 109
    Deleting fields 111
    Eliminating blank lines and fields 113
    Envelopes 106
    Labels 107
    Merging primary and secondary files 74
    Overview 104
    Primary file 70
    Secondary file 72
    Selecting records 115
Mailing labels 98
Margin release 58
Margins 80
Marking
    Index entries 208
    Table of contents entries 212
Master document 216
    Condensing 219
    Expanding 218
    Generating lists 219
    Printing 219
Mathematics 144

Calculating totals 147
Copying formulas 148
Creating formulae 144
Deleting formulas 148
Operators 145
Recalculating formulae 148
Maximise button 4
Menus 228
    Fonts 42
    Layout 122
    Macro 172
    Pages 38
    Tab 55
    Tools 107
Menu bar 3
Merging primary and secondary files 74
Microsoft Windows viii
Minimise button 4
Mouse techniques viii, 3
    Click vii
    Drag ix
    Highlight ix
    Selecting a block of text 30
Move 25
    Around a document 26
    Around a table 120
    Between columns 188
    Between document windows 40
    Files 224
    Outline 203
    Table information 136
    Text 32
Multiple
    Documents 39
    Page printing 99
Navigator window 222
Notes 90
Numbering 197
    Graphics boxes 164
Open dialog box 23
Opening a document window 21
Option buttons 9
    Button bar 176
    Table 138
    Copying 203
    Deleting 203
    Moving 203
Outline feature 201
Page break 60
Pages menu 38
Paper
    Location 93
    Orientation 93
Paper size 80, 92
    Editing 94
    Envelopes 95
    Labels 97
Paper type 93
Paragraph numbering 197
Placing tables in boxes 162
Point size 43
Positioning box captions 165
Primary mail merge file 70
Print 219
    Advance 94

Binding offset 100
Document 18
Driver 91
File 224
From disk 99
Hints and tips 91
Labels 96
Manager 101
Multiple copies 100
Multiple pages 99
Options 36, 94, 98
Paper size 92
Preview 35
Status 101
Task list 102
Pull-down menus 7
Quick draw keys 141
Quick list window 223
Recalculating formulae 148
Record 109
Eliminating fields 113
Fields 111
Selecting for mail merge 115
Removing
Codes 69
Macro 174
Text attributes 47
Rename 25, 224
Renumbering boxes 165
Replace 68
Restore button 5
Restoring text 32
Ruler 10, 118
Running macros 173
Saving a document 16
Scroll arrow lists 9
Scroll bar 5
Search and replace 68
Searching a document 66
Secondary merge file 72
Selecting records for mail merge 115
Sort 110
Spell checking 62
Status bar 6
Stopping and starting a print job 103
Styles 190
Applying 194
Creating 191
Editor 192
Library 194
Numbering 199
Types 191
Table of contents 212
Defining 213
Generating lists 215
Marking entries 212
Tables 118
Changing
Column width 128
Layout 126
Lines 131
Copying information 136
Deleting 133, 134
Editing 126
Entering information 121

Formating 122-124
In boxes 162
Joining and splitting cells 130
Menu 119
Moving around 120
Moving information 136
Options 138
Tabs 54
Bullet points 56
Changing 55
Menu 55
Ruler 54
Text 2
Blocks 30
Bold 44
Centring a line 51
Changing appearance 41
Deleting 27, 31
Indenting 58
Inserting 27, 59
Italics 44
Justification 51
Line spacing 53
Normal 44
Page break 60
Positioning text on labels 98
Removing attributes 47
Restoring 32
Search and replace 68
Searching 66
Size 44
Tabs 54
Thesaurus 65
Typeover 28
Underline 44
Wrapping 169
Text box 8, 155
Thesaurus 65
Tile 106
Title bar 2
Tools menu 107
Typeover 28
Types of style 191
Underline text 44
Using a style library 195
View 23
Windows viii
Closing a document window 40
File list 222
Moving between document windows 40
Navigator 222
Program manager xvi
Quick list 223
WordPerfect vi
Codes 46
File manager xvii
Importing information 152
Installing xi
Leaving 19
Loading xv
Menu system 6
Screen 2
Zooming 37

ORDER FORM

I wish to purchase the following book(s) and /or disks in the From Start to Finish *Series:*

Qty	ISBN	Title	Price
__	0 273 03816 8	**dBASE IV 1.1**	£12.99
__	0 273 03881 8	**dBASE IV 1.1** Disk pack*	£12.99 + VAT
__	0 273 03814 1	**Microsoft Word 2.0 for Windows**	£12.99
__	0 273 03883 4	**Microsoft Word 2.0 for Windows** Disk pack*	£12.99 + VAT
__	0 273 60182 2	**PageMaker 5.0 for Windows**	£12.99
__	0 273 60186 5	**PageMaker 5.0 for Windows** Disk pack*	£12.99 + VAT
__	0 273 60402 3	**PageMaker 5.0 for the Mac** Disk pack**	£12.99 + VAT
__	0 273 60183 0	**QuarkXPpress 3.1 for Windows**	£12.99
__	0 273 60187 3	**QuarkXPress 3.1 for Windows** Disk pack*	£12.99 + VAT
__	0 273 60396 5	**QuarkXPress 3.1 for the Mac** Disk pack**	£12.99 + VAT
__	0 273 03815 X	**WordPerfect 5.1 for Windows**	£12.99
__	0 273 03885 0	**WordPerfect 5.1 for Windows** Disk pack*	£12.99 + VAT

* containing three 3.5"disks and three 5.25" disks
** containing three 3.5"disks

NB Please add £2.35 to your order for Postage & Packing in the UK.
Payment should be made in £ Sterling.

I enclose a cheque (payable to **Pitman Publishing**)
for £ _____

Alternatively, please debit my credit card:

□ □ □ □

Please supply cardholder's address below if paying by credit card.

Card No:

☐☐☐☐☐☐☐☐☐☐☐☐☐☐☐☐

Expiry Date _____

Signature _____

PLEASE USE CAPITALS
Mr/Mrs/Miss/Ms
Initials   Surname _____

My job title is _____

Institute _____

Address _____

_____

Town _____

County _____ Postcode _____

Return this form with your remittance to
Customer Services Dept, Pitman Publishing
Southport Book Distributors, 12-14 Slaidburn Crescent
Southport PR9 9YF

OR Tel: 0704 26881   OR Fax: 0704 231970

Prices and availability are subject to change without notice.
Pitman Publishing, part of the Longman Group UK Limited Registered office: 5 Bentinck Street, London W1M 5RN